Library of
Davidson College

RANULF OF CHESTER

RANULF OF CHESTER
A RELIC OF THE CONQUEST

JAMES W. ALEXANDER

THE UNIVERSITY OF GEORGIA PRESS
ATHENS

Copyright © 1983 by the University of Georgia Press
Athens, Georgia 30602
All rights reserved
Set in 10 on 13 Trump Medieval
Printed in the United States of America

The paper in this book meets the guidelines for permanence and durability of the Committee on Production Guidelines for Book Longevity of the Council on Library Resources.

Library of Congress Cataloging in Publication Data

Alexander, James W.
Ranulf of Chester, a relic of the conquest.

Bibliography: p.
Includes index.
1. Ranulf, de Blundevill, Earl of Chester,
ca. 1172–1232.
2. Great Britain—History—Plantagenets,
1154–1399.
3. Great Britain—Court and courtiers—Biography.
I. Title.
DA209.R36A77 1983   942.03′092′4 [B]   83-3459
ISBN 0-8203-0673-8

In Memoriam
James W. Alexander (1869–1962)

CONTENTS

PREFACE ix

I. THE YOUNG EARL 1

II. LOYALIST BARON 18

III. A PINCHPENNY PATRON 37

IV. FEUDAL LORD AND EARL OF CHESTER 52

V. "GREATEST BARON OF THE REALM" 69

VI. PRUD'HOMME 92

ABBREVIATIONS 103

APPENDIX 105

NOTES 117

BIBLIOGRAPHY 163

INDEX 189

PREFACE

Ranulf III, earl of Chester, was for much of his adult life the most important and powerful magnate of England, categorized by Bishop William Stubbs (*The Constitutional History of England*, 2:47) as "almost the last relic of the great feudal aristocracy of the Conquest." He has long deserved a biography, and I am grateful to the late Professor Sidney Painter for suggesting that I write the book which has now taken shape. Ranulf's dominating position at a time of rapid and stormy historical change in England is justification enough for writing his life history; I hope that this study will not only illuminate the life of a great man, but also give some understanding of the society of his time, although I make no claim that this monograph revolutionizes our understanding of English history at the turn of the thirteenth century. Nor have I attempted to write a general history of Ranulf's age—such works already exist (for example, W. L. Warren's *Henry II*, John Gillingham's *Richard the Lionheart*, Painter's and Warren's studies of the reign of King John, Powicke's *Henry III and the Lord Edward*). Alas, there can be no psychohistory here: the evidence is simply insufficient to enable a historian to undertake serious analysis of Ranulf's personality, nor can one necessarily judge a man's motives and feelings by his actions, except on a gross level.

It has been gratifying and humbling to have had the advice and help of so many friends and colleagues in the years during which I have been at work on this study. My first debt, an old one, is to my grandfather; a man of great learning and of wide reading, he was of enormous influence in my being nurtured with an appreciation of literature, of scholarship, and of the humanities in general. This book is for him. I have received grants-in-aid of research from the Penrose Fund of the American Philosophical Society and from the Universities of Saskatchewan and of Georgia. The Public Record Office supplied me with photographs of the Chester and Bolingbroke charters from the Great Cowcher Book of the Duchy of Lancaster, and Professor Fred A. Cazel of the University of Connecticut kindly shared both his hospitality and his transcripts of the unpublished Fine Rolls of the early thirteenth century. The splendid library collections of Princeton University, Johns Hopkins University, the University of California at Santa Barbara, and the Peabody Institute were opened to me with gracious generosity.

Help with various specific questions was very kindly given me, often at expense of considerable amounts of their time, by Professor Robert Benson of the University of the South, Professor Cazel, Dr. Brian Harris, general editor of the *Victoria History of the County of Cheshire*, Professor Bennett Hill of the University of Illinois, Professor C. Warren Hollister of the University of California at Santa Barbara, Professor Thomas K. Keefe of Appalachian State University, Dr. Edmund King of Sheffield University, Professor Ralph V. Turner of the Florida State University, Professor Charles R. Young of Duke University, and Professor Charles T. Wood of Dartmouth College. I am indebted as well to my former students who as research assistants contributed vitally to this book: Dr. Victoria Chandler of Georgia College; Michael Horsey; Dr. Jane K. Laurent, University of North Carolina at Charlotte; Robert M. McPherson; Pamela Morris Saussy; and Roxane Murray, Madison, Wisconsin.

My most important obligation is, of course, to my lady Betsye, for reasons bearing no relation to historical scholarship.

I.
THE YOUNG EARL

Biographical figures have a way of luring their authors into traps laid by romanticism and by a tendency to exaggerate their subject's importance. Foote Gower in his history of Cheshire published in 1800, rhapsodized, "This Monarch, Randal [Ranulf] the Third, surnamed Blundeville . . . was as celebrated in his time as any of the Seven Champions of Christendom. And what is more, the famed story of his Atchievements is as much founded in Truth as that of others in Fable."[1] Nor is mythmaking confined to early antiquarians; although all we know of Ranulf's physical appearance is that he was small,[2] a modern popular history of England in the High Middle Ages describes him as "spare, graceless, black-a-vised."[3] Perhaps the ballads of which he is generally assumed to have been the hero have their modern semifictional counterparts, but I believe he was not in fact the hero of the ballad to which William Langland refers in *Piers Plowman*.[4]

Ranulf III nevertheless remains an impressive figure when the legends surrounding him have been discarded. He not only was a distinguished man and public figure in the England and Normandy of his time, he was also a man of distinguished family connections. The last but one of the Norman line of the earls of Chester descending from Hugh of Avranches, Ranulf was also allied through blood to some of the most important figures of Norman and early Angevin

England. Like Richard Lionheart, he was a descendant of King Henry I; Ranulf, however, descended from Robert of Gloucester. Bertrada de Montfort, Ranulf's mother, brought to her son the kinship which made him a first cousin of Henry III's bane, Earl Simon de Montfort of Leicester, as well as of that Simon who dominated the first phases of the Albigensian Crusade. His grandfather was a half brother of William de Roumare, earl of Lincoln, and brother to Adeliza, wife of Richard fitzGilbert de Clare, earl of Hereford.[5] Ranulf's grandfather, Ranulf II, de Gernons, was the first earl of Chester clearly to exhibit ambitions of cutting a large figure on the national scene; his importance in English politics anticipated that of his more famous grandson.

Ranulf was born in about 1170;[6] despite modern tradition, the allegations are late (and therefore suspect) that he was born in Oswestry and that he was surnamed de Blundeville.[7] The earl's sister Matilda married David, earl of Huntingdon, brother of William, king of Scots, in August of 1190;[8] their son, John the Scot, became the eldest coheir of Ranulf III and succeeded him in the earldom. Ranulf's sister Agnes wed William de Ferrers, earl of Derby, in 1192; since Thomas of London was slain in 1170, Matthew Paris errs in saying that Becket celebrated this marriage.[9] His two other sisters' marriages pose problems of dating. Mabel married William III d'Aubigny, earl of Arundel; the union must have taken place before 1200, since their son William was born in that year. They also had another son, Hugh, who succeeded his brother as earl in 1234, and six daughters.[10] The last of Ranulf's sisters, Hawise, married Robert, son of Saher de Quency, earl of Winchester; the marriage can have been neither earlier than 1198 nor later than 1202. Margaret, their daughter and heiress, married John de Lacy, constable of Chester, who succeeded Ranulf III as earl of Lincoln.[11] Ranulf's sisters, then, were wedded to important figures; although no evidence exists that these marriages were arranged by Ranulf

III, they enhanced his own status among the English baronage and placed in his hands further instruments through which his own power and influence could be made effective. Ranulf had a brother, Roger, who appeared as a witness to two of his charters; I can find no information about this Roger, who did not attest Ranulf's charters after the mid 1190s.[12] Ranulf also had an illegitimate half sister Amicia, the wife of Ralph Mainwaring, justiciar of Chester, who died in 1202.[13] Further circumstantial evidence of her illegitimacy is that Ranulf gave her no marriage portion; that she was not a coheiress proves nothing, since she may have predeceased Ranulf. Her marriage to Ralph Mainwaring, however, argues against her enjoying equal standing with her other sisters, since her husband was an important Cheshireman but certainly not a man comparable in degree or position to the older brothers-in-law of Earl Ranulf. I can find no evidence of a sister of Ranulf's, unnamed, who was said to have married Llewelyn of Wales.[14]

Little personal information exists concerning Ranulf while he was yet a minor. As a boy, during his father Earl Hugh's lifetime, he had been tutored by the earl's chief forester, Alexander Sylvester. Since Ranulf was about eleven when his father died on June 30, 1181, we may assume that he had been schooled in basic literacy by this time.[15] During the earl's minority (1181–87), Cheshire was administered by Gilbert Pipard until Easter 1185, and by Bertram de Verdon thereafter.[16] Ranulf III was belted earl in 1187,[17] and knighted at Caen by Henry II on January 1, 1189.[18] On the third day of the following month, Henry gave him Constance of Brittany, widow of his own son Geoffrey and mother of Henry's grandson Arthur of Brittany; with the marriage came *jure uxoris* the titles earl of Richmond and duke of Brittany.[19] Since this marriage had far more important ramifications for Ranulf's career on the continent than in England, I shall reserve a discussion of this unhappy match until the portion of this chapter which treats of the earl's role in Normandy and Brittany.

It is sufficient here to emphasize that Henry II must have held Ranulf in great favor to grant him his own daughter-in-law and grandson. He may well have thought to make Ranulf the stepfather of a future king. The earl of Chester was at this time about nineteen years of age, but his vast and widely dispersed holdings, hundreds of knights' fees, high lineage, and lofty titles exceeded his years in importance.

Before the year was out, Henry II was dead, his place on the English throne taken by Richard I, Lionheart. The only indication of the new king's early relations with Ranulf is unfortunately legendary. The annals of a Cistercian house translated by Ranulf in 1214 state that the earl had accompanied the king on crusade, was captured with Richard, and, "hearing he was to be sold, escaped and remained overseas for a long time."[20] Not only is this story unconfirmed by other sources, but Ranulf's itinerary can be traced sufficiently to demonstrate that he could not have been in the Holy Land with Richard; nor did he attest any of the king's charters when the monarch was on crusade, although he attested fairly frequently for Richard in England and in Normandy. While Ranulf did crusade in 1218–20, he was never captured, insofar as surviving evidence indicates.

When the young earl did appear in his first English role of national importance, his conduct exemplified two characteristics which were to mark his entire public life: loyalty to his sovereign and military prowess. As is well known, when Richard was a captive in the Holy Roman Empire as a result of a series of misadventures on his way home from the east, Prince John, in collusion with Philip Augustus of France, played the traitor and went into rebellion against his absent brother and monarch. When Richard returned to England, Ranulf was one of his loyal men. While John's great castle of Tickhill was invested by Hugh du Puiset, the doughty bishop of Durham, and the stronghold at Marlborough by Hubert Walter, Ranulf, along with his brothers-in-law Earl David of Huntingdon and Earl Ferrers of Derby, besieged Nottingham castle, then held for John against the royalist forces. Nottingham held out until Lionheart arrived; he joined the besieging forces on March 25, 1194, and three days later the fortress surrendered through the intervention of Hubert Walter, archbishop of Canterbury.[21]

On the thirtieth of March, the triumphant Richard convoked a council at Nottingham; Ranulf was among the great assembled there, with such notables as Eleanor of Aquitaine; the two English archbishops; six bishops (including Hugh of Durham); Ranulf's brothers-in-law of Derby and Huntingdon; Hamelin Plantagenet, earl of Surrey; and William Longsword, earl of Salisbury. The agenda of this council need not concern those primarily interested in Ranulf III of Chester, but for one item: the council fixed a date for the second coronation of King Richard.[22] This solemn pageant was staged at Winchester on the seventeenth of April.

Coronations in medieval England were splendidly festive, emphasizing not only the majesty of the king but also his close relationship with his magnates. In an age when symbolism meant much, the ceremonial of the twelfth-century coronation embodied (beyond its religious elements) what was virtually a secular liturgy. Preceded by prelates and followed by great barons, the king, crowned and vested, made his solemn entry in procession before Mass beneath a canopy carried by the earls of Norfolk, Wight, Salisbury, and Derby. Immediately before the king, the three swords of state, ancient symbols of royal majesty, were borne in golden scabbards, one by William King of Scots, the second by the king's uncle Hamelin of Surrey; the third, the blade Curtana, was borne to the king's left by the twenty-four-year-old Ranulf of Chester.[23] After Mass the company retired for a great feast with their king.

As is so often the case, we know what happened but not why it happened. In this case, why was Ranulf chosen to carry the sword Curtana? He was not a member of the coronation party in 1189, and would not be recorded as more than an observer at the coronation of 1199. Nor was he a participant in the coronation of Henry III. His successor as earl of Chester, John the Scot, bore Curtana in 1236 at the coronation of Queen Eleanor of Provence because he was earl of Chester.[24] The *Liber regalis*, believed by its editor to derive from the reign of Edward II, also attributes the right to bear Curtana to the earl of Chester (the other swords are carried by the earls of Huntingdon and Warwick), and this was still the custom at the coronation of Charles I.[25] In analyzing the right to bear swords at the coronation of a monarch, J. H. Round hypothesized that the swordbearers at the first coronation of Richard I—the king's brother, Count John of Mortain; David, earl of Huntingdon; Robert, earl of Leicester—were chosen because of their high status. Turning to the 1194 coronation, Round thought that William carried one sword because he was himself a king, Earl Hamelin another because he was the king's uncle, and Earl Ranulf Curtana, either because of his recent expeditions on Richard's part against the adherents of John or because he was lord of "the greatest of English palatinates."[26] One guess is as good as another in the absence of evidence, but it is more than doubtful whether Chester was a palatinate at this time,[27] and others (such as Earl Ferrers and David of Huntingdon) had also distinguished themselves on Richard's behalf. Might it be significant that Earl Ranulf and Richard Lionheart shared a common great-great-grandfather in King Henry I? This would set Ranulf apart from others who had distinguished themselves on Richard's behalf. That John the Scot bore Curtana in 1236 and that subsequent earls of Chester did the same argues only that Ranulf established a tradition, not that he followed one. Perhaps we are best to stay with the rather vague statement of Gervase of Canterbury that *"tres vero comites nobiliores Angliae portaverunt tres gladios in vaginis aureis"*—the nobler earls carried the swords.[28] No evidence indicates why Ranulf III rather than another earl was chosen for the great honor.

By Michaelmas 1194 Ranulf had followed his king to Normandy; the pipe roll noted his absence in quitting him of scutage laid for the king's ransom because he was in the Norman campaign.[29] Notices of the earl in England while he was abroad until 1199 are few, and of such a nature that they do nothing to illuminate the life story of Ranulf. Yet the accumulation of lands, titles, and knights' fees so characteristic of his public career in the thirteenth century had begun in 1198, when he inherited the southern Lincolnshire honor of Bolingbroke as the closest heir of William III de Roumare. William's great-grandfather was Roger fitzGerold; after Roger died, his widow Lucy married Ranulf I of Chester. William III's grandfather, William I de Roumare, was therefore the half brother of Ranulf II, the grandfather of Ranulf III. Bolingbroke answered for approximately sixty-eight knights' fees,[30] and its acquisition substantially enhanced the earl's already powerful position in the county.

It was, then, as one of the ranking magnates that Ranulf's support was important to Prince John when Richard Lionheart was slain at Châlus.[31] The shifty and capricious John was neither the sole candidate to succeed his late brother nor necessarily the one with the best claim; Arthur of Brittany was the son of Geoffrey, older brother of Richard and of John, who had died in 1186. Arthur, as the son of the older brother, had a strong claim, possibly stronger than John's as younger brother of the late king. And Arthur was the stepson of Ranulf III of Chester.

Historians have been in agreement concerning Ranulf's political position in May of 1199. William Stubbs said that Ranulf "had always hated" John, that "[his] policy halted between the temptation of being stepfather to a king and the hatred of his unfaithful wife."[32] Dom Pierre-Hyacinthe Morice thought that Ranulf "sighed for the rank from which he had fallen" and so supported John; his allusion here is to the end of Ranulf's ducal title coming from the dissolution of his marriage with Constance of Brittany.[33] All who have dealt at length with the question of why Ranulf came to support John's claim have stressed his selfishness; in their view, Ranulf's primary political motives were purely opportunistic. Sidney Painter found Ranulf one of "a group of powerful barons who wished to force [John] to purchase their support."[34] J. C. Holt suggests that the earl's policies were "largely determined by his desire to extend his interests into Lincolnshire and northwards from this earldom into Lancashire."[35] No one has suggested that Ranulf might have made his decision to support John on the basis of principle.

Then, too, students of John's reign stress his hostility to Ranulf. Frank Barlow wrote that John "cold-shouldered the earl of Chester in the north,"[36] while Painter stated baldly that "John saw very clearly that the one man most dangerous to the royal authority in England was Earl Ranulf."[37] As Brian E. Harris points out, "the evidence for these assertions seems rather thin."[38] But I am getting ahead of the story.

Lionheart's death in April of 1199 necessitated an immediate decision on the succession. Arthur had been recognized by the nobles of Anjou and Brittany, while the Norman baronage tended to favor John, the brother of the late king and an adult, over Arthur, his nephew and a child. Hubert Walter, archbishop of Canterbury, and the great William Marshal,[39] accompanied by Geoffrey fitzPeter, assembled a large group of barons and other *homines regni* at Nottingham to obtain their fealty for John.[40] Whether, as Roger of Howden suggests, John's advocates doubted that these men were faithful to John is far from certain; perhaps they simply had not yet committed themselves in the succession question. Perhaps they had not yet had an opportunity so to do.

The group included Ranulf, his brothers-in-law of Derby and Huntingdon, Roger the constable of Chester (himself a man with extensive holdings in Yorkshire and Lancashire), Earl Richard de Clare, William de Mowbray, and William de Stuteville. The chronicler tells us that all present swore to support John *contra omnes homines* upon being promised that John would do them justice. Roger of Howden's language makes it clear that the magnates mentioned above were among a large number of earls, barons, and others, and he mentions only William I, king of Scots, as presenting any formal demands for satisfaction of claims due him by right. I cannot agree with Holt that Ranulf "tried to bargain for [his] loyalty at John's accession."[41] He may well have done so, but there is no firm evidence that he in fact did; such evidence exists only for King William, brother of Ranulf's brother-in-law David of Huntingdon.

John, already recognized as duke of Normandy, was crowned at Westminister on the twenty-seventh of May. While Ranulf was among the dignitaries present, there is no evidence that he took part in the coronation ceremony.[42] Ranulf was still with the new king on June 7, when John issued a "constitution" instituting reforms in fee schedules charged by his chancery.[43] John's policies toward the baronage[44] obviously affected Ranulf, by this time the "leading peer of England, and the last survivor of the aristocracy of the Conquest."[45] Ranulf, of course, held a large position in English affairs; what more did he want?[46] The traditional view is best expressed by Painter. Ranulf's "rapacious eye wandered greedily all over northern England. Nor did he lack extensive and rather plausible claims." Painter's description of these ambitions derives first from the charter granted in 1153 by Henry Plantagenet as duke of Normandy to Ranulf's grandfather.[47] By this charter, Ranulf II was granted the royal demesne lands in Staffordshire as well as the overlordship of all but a few fees therein, the castle and borough of Nottingham, the borough of Derby and the other lands adjacent, several important baronies (including Tickhill, Eye, Lancaster, and Peverel of Nottingham), important possessions already held by the earls of Chester in their Norman lands, and numerous other specified holdings. Painter noted that Ranulf held none of these English properties in 1199; but his father Earl Hugh also had held none, and Ranulf II was dead before the charter's terms became effective. Further, the charter was neither confirmed nor reissued by any subsequent king, nor does an *inspeximus* appear in any later chancery enrollment. That Ranulf may have wanted these grants is possible; that he had a right to them is dubious. Painter also thought that Ranulf had an unsatisfied hereditary claim to Lincoln castle and to the honor of Richmond; the latter is clearly incorrect, since he was not the widower of Constance of Brittany but her former husband. Her current spouse had a sound claim, and in fact Guy de Thouars was invested with the honor by John. As Harris has shown, even upon Guy's death Ranulf had no claim as of right on Richmondshire.[48] Painter also thought that the grant of the honor of Camel, part of the Roumare lands, was a "foolish proceeding" that was "bound to annoy Ranulf exceedingly," but F. A. Cazel has demonstrated that Ranulf had no hereditary claim to Camel.[49] Painter also argued that the grants made to William de Ferrers were not made to please Ranulf but to "wean the earl of Derby away from his dangerous brother-in-law," but we do not in fact know why John did so favor William. Nor is there any reason to assume that William would be receptive to efforts to detach him from Ranulf. As well, Painter found John "doubly foolish" to offend Ranulf when one considers conditions in Normandy—only he, Robert of Leicester, William Marshal, and Hamelin de Warenne, of the great English barons, had important Norman possessions. Now, King John had many shortcomings, if fewer than traditionally ascribed to him,[50] but foolishness was not one of them.

Of course, there were reasons why a suspicious king should regard Ranulf with mistrust. He was, after all, the stepfather of John's rival, Arthur. He had more landed power and knights' fees than any other English baron, and commanded an active and powerful military force. "When one considers the ambition, greed, energy, and military reputation of the master of all this power, it is easy to understand John's position [of hostility]."[51] Further, as Holt noted, Ranulf was associated with some of Arthur's affinity in Normandy.[52] Painter was correct in saying that the earl's "general policy" was to acquire "anything he could get, anywhere, but he was especially anxious to build up his power in the shires adjacent to Chester."[53] I argue this not on the basis of Ranulf's actions from 1199 to 1204, but rather on subsequent events, particularly those falling to the period 1212–18, and a similar policy should be noted for Lincolnshire as well. But there is no necessary reason why ambition should conflict with loyalty, and I find no primary evidence that Ranulf bargained with John for his support, nor that the assumed enmity of John for Ranulf in the period from his coronation to late 1204 has any demonstrable basis in fact. As will appear below, and as Harris has concluded independently,[54] John's isolated acts against Ranulf were based upon very rational considerations. When John did take action against the earl, the incidents were of short duration and of no lasting consequence. Historians of the reign agree that Ranulf and John got on well together in and after 1205,[55] but I would argue that Ranulf was loyal to John in the first five years of that unhappy reign as well: not only is there no convincing evidence to the contrary, but one of the dominating principles of Ranulf's entire public career was loyalty to his sovereign. It is unlikely that the principle would have characterized his behavior from 1188 to 1199, lapse for five years, and then for the rest of his public life be consistently followed. In short, I do not agree with Holt's contention that "from the accession of John to the winter of 1204–1205 Ranulf . . . was among John's most dangerous and suspect vassals."[56]

Certainly there is no English evidence to substantiate Holt's judgment; to the Norman situation I shall turn shortly. Ranulf passed from England to Normandy in the early summer of 1199, not to return until the turn of the year 1204 (except for a time early in 1201). Thus—alas for his biographer—one of the most interesting records of Ranulf's life is fictitious. In April of 1200 Fulk fitzWarin, a minor landholder in Shropshire and Gloucestershire, rebelled against King John. In the *Geste of Fulk fitz Warin*,[57] Earl Ranulf occupies an important and withal plausible place as sympathetic to Fulk in his rebellion yet loyal to King John.[58] The *Geste* shows Ranulf as a mediator in the quarrel; after the reconciliation of John and Fulk, he accompanies the former rebel to Ireland. But chronology makes Ranulf's supposed role in the affair impossible. The continent provides the setting for more interesting and more important events in the first quarter-century of the life of Ranulf III, among them his first marriage, to Constance of Brittany.

When this uncomfortable union took place, Ranulf III of Chester was already a powerful landholder in southwestern Normandy, where the ancestral Norman lands of his line shared a common border with Brittany. The earl's Norman holdings had enfeoffed 51⅞ knights by 1172, although they owed only 10 to the duke; by the early thirteenth century, lands were held of Ranulf for 71³⁄₁₆ knights' fees.[59] Hereditary viscounts of the Bessin and of Avranches, the earls of Chester also had held several Norman castles with their environs, notably Vire (Calvados), Barfleur (Manches), and Jacques de Beuvron (Avranches), as well as other scattered lands.[60] But although Ranulf was a great Norman and English landholder, a man of standing in the baronage, he was not a king's son. While there is no evidence on this issue, perhaps this is one reason why Constance of Brittany disliked the marriage to the young earl which had been arranged by her former father-in-law, Henry II.[61] The union was blessed on February 3, 1189. This widow of Geoffrey Plantagenet never was compatible with Ranulf, nor he with her. Possible reasons are many, but evidence is lacking to permit more than hypothesizing. All we know is that they endured a disagreeable relationship for ten years, a relationship which was characterized by the earl's capture and imprisonment of his wife in 1196.

In any case, this was not intended to be a love match. Constance brought to her husband political stature beyond that which he already enjoyed. While it is true that the marriage "added greatly to his importance . . . as a French rather than an English potentate,"[62] it is also true that his importance in England was enhanced by his wife's English lands of Brittany, the great honor of Richmond, which in her lifetime answered for 140 knights' fees.[63] As C. T. Clay pointed out, Ranulf styled himself duke of Brittany and earl of Richmond even when addressing charters which did not deal with lands held *jure uxoris*.[64]

The political complications arising from the marriage were as turbulent as the personal ones. The unruly Bretons abhorred Ranulf, regarding him as a usurper and a tyrant, a tradition followed by modern Breton historians of the Middle Ages.[65] According to A. de la Borderie, the Bretons drove the "fell" Ranulf from Brittany shortly after the death of Henry II, supporting Constance and Ranulf's fey stepson, Arthur of Brittany, as against the earl's own pretensions to Breton power.[66] Kate Norgate's wry judgment rings true: the marriage of Constance and Ranulf "would have furnished an excellent means of securing the Norman hold upon the Breton duchy, if only [Ranulf] himself could have secured a hold upon his wife."[67] Constance and her people were fractious with Ranulf and with Richard Lionheart, but their seemingly good relations with Philip Augustus of France were predicated on their wish to use the king against their enemies. The Bretons were adept at fishing in troubled waters and equally adept at ensuring that they themselves did not become the big catch.

By the mid 1190s Richard was ready to use force against

the duchy. In March of 1196 Constance emerged from her refuge there intending to parley with Lionheart, but while on her way to the king she was captured by Ranulf at Pontorson and then imprisoned in his great stronghold at Jacques de Beuvron, there to languish for more than two years under the custody of her "odious spouse."[68] The Breton lords assembled at S.-Malô with Arthur, who had been recognized as duke, to deliberate upon their response to Constance's imprisonment. Efforts to reach agreement with Lionheart failed and were followed by his ravaging of the Breton frontiers. Predictably, the Breton response was to adhere to Philip Augustus, whereupon Richard devastated Brittany. It was an untidy situation.[69]

In 1199 Richard Lionheart died, and Ranulf's marriage ended in the same year. No evidence survives to explain how the miserable union was dissolved, or on whose initiative. Some sources present Constance as the aggrieved party, citing consanguinity or Ranulf's alleged adultery.[70] The charge that Ranulf was adulterous inspired one chronicler to drag in yet another example of the lechery of King John; it was said that John had in fact dallied with Constance, and that Ranulf "often warnid King John for taking the Daughtters of diverse Nobile Men, and deflouring them."[71] Others allege that Ranulf had taken the initiative in the dissolution of his relationship to Constance,[72] some adding that in divorcing Constance Ranulf was following the example of his king's abandonment of Isabelle of Gloucester.[73] Painter and W. L. Warren thought that there had been in fact no formal dissolution of the marriage.[74] Perhaps each had ample cause for unhappiness with the other.

Within a year Ranulf was again married. Like his first marriage, the second was clearly political; unlike the first, this one lasted until the end of the earl's life. The Breton barony of Fougères lay in the northeast corner of Brittany, directly adjacent to Ranulf's Norman lands, which had been raided during his previous Breton problems. Obviously, the friendship of the ruler of Fougères was of value.[75] Between late 1199 and the autumn of 1200, the earl married Clemencia, widow of Alan de Dinan, sister of Geoffrey, lord of Fougères. Not only did the match bring security to Ranulf's Avranchin borders; it also brought kinship through marriage with the powerful Fulk Paynel (who held in the Côtentin) and with William du Hommet, constable of Normandy. Apparently there was some disagreement over the dowry, since a composition dated October 15, 1200, mentions contention between Ranulf and Geoffrey in setting forth the terms of the marriage agreement. By this concord, Ranulf received the Vale of Mortain in Normandy, Long Bennington (Lincolnshire), and an annual proffer of one hundred pounds Angevin to last for five years, as well as other considerations.[76] Clemencia's uncle William du Hommet never paid the seventy-five marks remaining from the two hundred pounds Angevin proffered the king of England in 1200 for his consent to the marriage.[77] Ranulf's second marriage, like his first, was barren; this was, it was said, because the earl had divorced his first wife.[78]

While a man of action such as Ranulf of Chester probably had a role in the continental campaigns of Richard Lionheart, it was not so conspicuous as to attract the attention of the chroniclers of the battles. Indeed, in these campaigns he appears for the reign of Richard only as standing surety for the king's observance of the treaty made in July 1197 between Lionheart and Count Baldwin of Flanders at Les Andelys.[79] His first appearance in the Norman affairs of King John was also as a surety for John's observance of a treaty with Baldwin, on August 18, 1199.[80] As noted (pp. 9–12), it is the received opinion that Ranulf and John were at odds until the loss of Normandy. I find no evidence of this. John's first official notice of Ranulf, on September 23, 1199, was the grant of Castle Semilly (arrondissement S.-Lô) to the earl.[81]

While it is not certain why this grant was made, other than the possibility that the gift was the consequence of royal favor toward the earl, it probably was in some way connected with the marriage of the earl to Clemencia, since she was the niece of the constable of Normandy, who was heir to Gervasia de Sai, in whose lands the fortress lay.[82] In the following year, Ranulf made fine with the king of one hundred pounds Angevin for having the lands of the honor of Sai, which also lay with the house of du Hommet.[83] This does not appear to me to be evidence of bad feeling between John and Ranulf. Fines for favors could be refused as well as accepted. In September of 1200 Ranulf was a pledge for one hundred of the six hundred pounds Angevin proffered by Roger de Planes to the king, that Roger might have the widow of Richard de Reviers.[84]

As Harris points out, the frequency of the earl's attestations of John's instruments does not argue for enmity between the king and the earl in late 1203 and early 1204. I also agree with Harris's argument that John's suspicions of Ranulf in the spring of 1203 were solidly grounded,[85] contrary to the view of the scholars cited in his article. In April John, informed that Ranulf, Fulk Paynel, and others were prepared to withdraw from his affinity, hastened to Castle Vire to await the earl and Fulk. On the Saturday before Easter, Ranulf and Fulk had an audience with the king in the presence of his barons and convinced him of their loyalty. The earl surrendered Castle Semilly to John and provided sureties in the persons of William du Hommet and Roger de Lacy, who pledged to deliver to the king the lands which he held of the honor of Chester should the earl prove disloyal. Semilly was restored to Ranulf by letter patent less than a month after the incident.[86] Painter identified the real reason why John's suspicions were quite rational: writing of his marriage to Clemencia in 1199 or 1200, he noted that "Ranulf and his new relatives could seriously compromise the safety of a large section of John's continental possessions."[87] Nor was the threat theoretical. The house of Fougères had early in the year deserted John's cause for that of Philip Augustus. It is a commonplace that family ties frequently meant family policies. Fulk Paynel did eventually adhere to Philip Augustus. Ranulf's holdings were more extensive and more valuable in England than they were in Normandy, and material self-interest alone would dictate Ranulf's loyalty to John; one can nevertheless understand why John might well demand sureties from Ranulf for his continued loyalty. In any case, the incident was quickly past and is survived by no evidence of continuing ill feeling on the part of either. To the contrary, the earl was given custody of the tower of Avranches at the end of May.[88] Ranulf himself must have realized the validity of the king's action, since he apparently neither protested nor took hostile action. It is a further sign of John's favor that he lent Ranulf two hundred marks in May 1204 for Ranulf's part of the one-thousand-pound ransom of the earl's constable, Roger de Lacy, who had been taken captive at the fall of Château-Gaillard.[89]

By January of 1204, Ranulf of Chester had returned to England. He did not depart again until February of 1214, when he returned to take part in the campaign to recover Normandy. When the duchy was lost in 1204, his extensive Norman landholdings were lost as well; as Powicke wrote, "Ranulf's feelings when the fall of Normandy was imminent cannot have been pleasant. He had much to lose."[90] Yet he was soon to be compensated for the loss of his Norman holdings by vast English acquisitions which made him England's most powerful lord in landholdings and in knights' fees. While Ranulf had spent more years in Normandy than in England since attaining his majority, he was to spend most of the remainder of his life in the island kingdom, where he was to become the leading magnate of the realm.

II.
LOYALIST BARON

After the loss of Normandy, King John spent most of the years remaining to him in England. No longer could grievances against abundant governance be launched against a justiciar or viceroy ruling in the name of an absent king who doubtless would correct grievances if only he knew of them: John was home, and he visited all parts of his kingdom with some frequency, ruling as well as reigning. As is well known, John's troubles overcame him; chief among them were the conflict with Innocent III over the archbishopric of Canterbury, the disaffection of many barons leading to Magna Carta, and the civil war ensuing. In all three, Earl Ranulf of Chester played an important role, in the baronial unrest and in the civil war a central one. A significant figure in the first five years of John of England's reign, Ranulf III of Chester became a dominant figure by its end.[1]

Even if Painter is correct in believing that John was fearful of a general baronial uprising in the period 1203–5,[2] evidence for the thesis is lacking in John's relations with Ranulf except for an incident falling in December of 1204. The earl first appeared in the records after his return to England as the recipient of royal favor, a quittance of money owed because his men of Chipping Camden (Gloucestershire) had violated the forest law.[3] Four months later, in October, Ranulf's possession of certain lands of the fee of the countess of Warwick in Yorkshire was recognized.[4] The sole indication of John's putative ill feeling and suspicions toward the earl of Chester erupted on December 14. A letter close to the sheriffs of Lincolnshire, Nottingham, Yorkshire, Leicestershire, and Warwickshire directed that Ranulf's lands and possessions in their counties be seized and that his men holding in the specified counties be forbidden to perform the services that they owed to the earl.[5] The letters allege Ranulf to have been favorable to the cause of Gwenwynwyn, John's opponent in Wales through the king's alliance with Llewelyn, to whom he had married his own daughter. J. E. A. Jolliffe suggested that Ranulf and his brother Roger had committed themselves to Gwenwynwyn, to an uncertain extent.[6] The only evidence to support this statement is John's own letter, although it is certainly likely that Ranulf would favor the southern prince against Llewelyn, who was raiding Ranulf's lands along the Welsh border. In any case, within six days the two distrained men received a safe-conduct from the king that enabled them to come before John and give security for their loyalty.[7] Painter observed that "it is impossible to say whether Earl Ranulf was aiding the Welsh prince because of his annoyance with John or whether he had simply been too slow in following the rapid turns of the king's policy in Wales."[8] Ranulf may well have seen Gwenwynwyn as a counterbalance against his then enemy Llewelyn. That he opposed John's Welsh policies is likely, but I cannot agree with Holt that Ranulf nearly rebelled in December.[9] Nor, considering Ranulf's own relations with the Welsh, does it seem irrational and pathologically suspicious of John to have distrained Ranulf pending the giving of guarantees for his fidelity. No later evidence survives to show that John considered Ranulf of Chester anything other than what he was: one of the most stalwart supporters of a king sorely in need of loyal captains.

Earl Ranulf of Chester was a man for whom great losses

were followed by greater gains. The dissolution of his wretched first marriage terminated his English title earl of Richmond, held *jure uxoris*. John's loss of Normandy was accompanied by Ranulf's loss of his ancestral continental possessions.[10] In compensation for the loss of his Norman lands, Ranulf III received Dovedale (Derby) and, more important, the lands of the honor of Richmond in Richmondshire.[11] Of course, Ranulf had no claim as of right on his former wife's English holdings, which had been given to Earl Robert of Leicester when Guy de Thouars adhered to Philip Augustus in September of 1203.[12] Robert died in 1204, and on March 6, 1205, John bestowed the rich holding on Ranulf III, reserving the 9¾ fees withheld from Robert of Leicester.[13] The honor of Richmond in Richmondshire answered for 40½ knights' fees when in Ranulf's possession in 1210–12.[14] Whether King John had, as Painter suggested,[15] thought to encourage rivalry between the earls of Leicester and Chester by his grant to Earl Robert is not clear; such a policy would have been a reversion to the similar aim of King Stephen. In any case, by early March 1205, the Richmond lands in Yorkshire were safely in Ranulf's hands, enlarging the base of his power in northern England. Holt is correct in stating that John's motivation is unclear,[16] but I agree neither that John felt threatened by the earl nor that Ranulf's support could be purchased; rather, it is likely that the king granted Richmondshire to the earl as compensation for his Norman losses, as the Worcester annalist suggested, and as a reward for Ranulf's loyalty at a time when disloyalty was rife among those who held on both sides of the Channel. Obviously, John's self-interest dictated that one of his most loyal supporters be enfeoffed in the north, where, along with Ranulf's brother-in-law William of Derby and the earl Warenne, the earl of Chester became a bastion of royal power.[17]

Nor were Richmond and Dovedale the sole marks of royal favor coming to the earl during his first year back in England.

John pardoned Ranulf the debt of 353 marks owed by his father to Aaron the Jew of Lincoln, whose accounts upon Aaron's death in 1185 were assumed by the crown for collection.[18] The king also quit Ranulf of scutage in Nottinghamshire and postponed payment of scutage in all the earl's English lands.[19] The earl was probably an exchequer baron in the Michaelmas term of 1205; the other pipe-roll mentions of Ranulf in this year are unremarkable, showing scutages owed and reflecting the king's need for palfreys in preparation for the coming attack on the Continent, which never occurred. The earl's exchange of a palfrey for a lamprey which the king gave him seems rather a poor bargain for the earl; John forgave Ranulf the debt during the following year.[20] At November's end Ranulf was named by John as a member of the party to escort William, king of the Scots, to York in the coming February,[21] joining the earl of Salisbury, the Earl Marshal, the constable of Chester, and others. In April of 1209 Ranulf again was delegated to conduct William the Lion to England, this time in the company of his brother-in-law of Derby, his constable, and Eustace de Vesci, among others.[22] Further evidence of King John's favor toward Ranulf is found in a number of small grants that preceded the windfall of the years of rebellion. Lands of the earl's fee in Nottinghamshire and Buckinghamshire were given him in 1205, as were a house, vineyards, rents, and the custody of the land of Robert de Muskham, in the following year.[23] In 1213 the king ordered the sheriffs of Devonshire and Buckinghamshire to seise the earl with the manors of Ipplepen and Witleford, claimed *jure uxoris*.[24] Two mandates direct that Ranulf's ships receive favorable treatment and be licensed to trade,[25] and two further orders granted Ranulf timber, as well as deer for the earl's park at Royñg.[26] To cheer the earl's evenings, John presented ten casks of wine to Ranulf.[27] The pipe roll for 1208 records the royal pardon of Ranulf's debt of two marks incurred in a forest offense, and the praestita roll for 1212 reveals that King John paid a gambling debt of two shillings and fifteen pence to the earl.[28] Now, all this is rather unremarkable, bearing no hint of the earl of Chester's startlingly sudden re-emergence as a prominent national figure in 1209.

Ever since the reign of the Conqueror, relations between England—more precisely, great English magnates of the marches—and Wales had been troubled.[29] The Conqueror had endowed the first earl of Chester, Hugh of Avranches, with Flintshire and a portion of Denbighshire; relations between the earls of Chester and the native lords of north Wales were thereafter sore, the seasons of war aflame with border raids until the 1220s. So ambitious a king as John, himself a former marcher lord, was unlikely not to intervene in internal Welsh factional feuds. His opportunity seemed to have come when, in 1209, his crushing of the powerful Braose family roiled the Welsh border and threw political stability among the marcher magnates into a splendid confusion. The king's son-in-law, Llewelyn ap Iorwerth, the Great, began to extend his power from Snowdonia southward into Powys. As Austin Lane Poole noted,[30] John continued to favor the Welsh prince until 1210, despite a foray against him in the spring of 1209. In January of that year, the king ordered the sheriffs in whose areas of jurisdiction Ranulf of Chester held fees to make certain that the earl's knights obeyed his call to serve against Llewelyn.[31] Although John with a host moved into Wales, little came of the invasion, and the king returned to England after talking with the Welsh prince.[32] Llewelyn was again in the king's favor, accompanying him on an expedition against the king of Scots, and in October he renewed his homage to John.

But in 1210 Llewelyn and his father-in-law were again in the field against one another, and Ranulf III followed his king's pennons to war. Little is known of the campaign, which was led by Ranulf; Geoffrey fitzPeter; Peter des Roches, bishop of Winchester; and the king's half brother William Longsword, earl of Salisbury.³³ In the ravaging of Ranulf's lands, Llewelyn destroyed his own castle of Degannwy; this was of little avail, as the earl rebuilt it, and raised Holywell in Flintshire and Treffynon in addition.³⁴ Gervase of Canterbury remarked upon the savagery of both sides in this expedition.³⁵ It is to this campaign that I suspect the rather raucous story of Earl Ranulf and the bawds is to be assigned. Ranulf, it is said, was contained in his castle at Rhuddlan by the Welsh and sent to Roger de Lacy for immediate assistance. The constable of Chester, himself without proper fighting men, called upon those present at the midsummer fair in Chester to assist their lord, as a consequence of which a "tumultuous horde of the fiddlers, players, cobblers and debauched persons" hastened to Ranulf's relief. Deceived by the din into thinking that a large host was hurrying to the earl's assistance, the Welsh raised the siege and fled. Ranulf is said to have rewarded the constable and his heirs with authority over such rabble in Cheshire; Roger's son John de Lacy, then earl of Lincoln (1232–40), assigned the rights to his steward, Hugh de Dutton.³⁶

Less entertaining, but more important, was the English aggression of the following year; John's invasion of Wales did not succeed, owing to the familiar problems encountered by a traditionally organized fighting force in conflict with guerrillas who melt into the mountain fastness. Undeterred, in the summer of 1212 John again mobilized an army of Wales, with the careful preparation so characteristic of his later years; as Painter has written, the logistical planning followed by the hanging of twenty-eight Welsh hostages indicated that the king had determined to crush Llewelyn's power rather than to conduct a desultory campaign concluded by diplomacy.³⁷ Yet the expedition was cancelled on August 16, because of the king's reaction to tales that a baronial conspiracy was incipient.³⁸ Ranulf's last recorded appearance in Welsh affairs in John's reign fell to June of 1213, when he was one of the five named addressees of a letter patent from the king announcing a truce with the Welsh, negotiated by the papal legate Pandulf. While originally confined to a two-month period, the comparative peace endured until the great revolt of the spring of 1215, when Llewelyn adhered to the insurgents.[39]

The major dramas of King John's later years were interrelated (although for clarity's sake they will here be presented, insofar as Ranulf of Chester was directly concerned, separately): the long quarrel with Pope Innocent III over the Canterbury incumbency, the plans to invade the France of Philip Augustus and thus recover the lost Angevin lands north of the Loire, and the king's increasingly poisoned relations with his barons of England. Archbishop Hubert Walter, a faithful and ingenious servant of Henry II, Richard Lionheart, and John, died in mid July of 1205.[40] Hubert had been a devoted royal official, and John wished to replace him as archbishop with a like man, John de Grey, bishop of Norwich, who had made himself useful, too, to Henry II in the Becket dispute. Clashes of interest between a king and the monks of Christ Church, Canterbury (who had the right to elect the archbishop), were not something new to the reign of King John. The Canterbury monks, moving in the shadows and with questionable legality, elected their subprior Reginald to the archbishopric, hoping thus to thwart both the royal nominee and the Canterbury suffragans, who were contesting again for the right to participate in the election. John had allowed an appeal to be carried to Rome, but when he learned of Reginald's election, he compelled the parties to the appeal to end their contest and the chapter to elect the archbishop with the concurrence of the bench. Not surprisingly, John de Grey was elected. Innocent III took cognizance of the case in 1206, invalidated the elections both of Reginald and of John, and advanced the name of Stephen

Langton, cardinal and professor at the University of Paris.[41] Despite John's determined opposition to the papal appointee, Innocent consecrated Stephen in June 1207, thus negating John's veto over the nomination.

While John could no longer prevent the consecration of Langton, he could still close England to his new archbishop. With the support of the baronage and of many of the episcopal bench, the king moved to defend what he perceived as his rights, expelling the monks of Christ Church in July 1207. In response Innocent threatened to impose the interdict on England and Wales, closing churches to the faithful. Although John offered a reasonable compromise, efforts to reach agreement between the two contending parties failed, and in the early spring of 1208 the penalty was announced.

The interdict lasted until 1214, and, while inconvenient, it did not succeed in bending the English king to accept Stephen Langton as his archbishop; to the contrary, it permitted John to exploit the church financially, and at first he did so with great enthusiasm. Yet, while his successful defiance of Innocent III may indeed have added to his prestige, lengthy quarrels with the church ultimately were politically and socially unhealthy. Hence, while other troubles mounted, the king decided that the time had come to reconcile England once more to the papal obedience, and he accepted, in 1212, terms which had been proffered in the previous year. The diplomacy of the two antagonists progressed rapidly toward a resolution of the burry situation. A longlasting state of confrontation tends to become incapable of rational solution, yet 1213 was a productive year in Anglo-papal relations. Once having decided to convert the most formidable of his opponents into a protector, the excommunicate king moved with determination and vigor. In February, Innocent had demanded that John confirm the submission, made the previous November by his representatives in Rome, by June 1. The king met the papal legate Pandulf on May 13 and so agreed; two days following, the king made the startling concession of England and Ireland to Innocent III, receiving them again as the pope's man, owing an annual payment of one thousand marks sterling. Ranulf attested for the king on this occasion, as he did when the arrangement was confirmed in October.[42] The earl of Chester was among the eleven earls and other great men receiving a command from the pope that they not use John's relations with Innocent as an excuse to cause difficulties within the realm.[43]

These men, who included William Marshal, Geoffrey fitzPeter, William Earl Ferrers of Derby, William Longsword, and William of Arundel, were designated by Stephen Langton to assure the security of expatriate English clergy upon their return to England following the solution of the quarrel between king and pope.[44] Consequent upon the settlement of the dispute with the church were two letters patent from the king to Hugh of Welles, bishop of Lincoln, asking his return to England, explaining that the church and her prelates were now in the royal security and promising restitution to him; Ranulf attested both,[45] as he had the May 2 charter of John guaranteeing his peace to the clergy and laity of Christ Church, Canterbury.[46]

Ranulf's role in the resolution of the Langton controversy continued into 1214. The settlement of the many fiduciary aspects of the contest with Innocent III found Ranulf III a guarantor that the payment promised by John would in fact be realized.[47] Owing to the successful presentation of the case for John's inability to pay, his financial obligations as viewed from Rome on the eve of the interdict's relaxation were in fact never fulfilled.[48] King John returned from the luckless continental campaigns in the fall of 1214, shortly thereafter (November 12) issuing his charter which granted freedom of election to the churches of England. This instrument, attested by Earl Ranulf, was reissued on January 15 of 1215, confirmed by Innocent III on March 30.[49] The royal charter promised freedom of election to all churches and monasteries in England, reserving specifically only the custody of vacancies belonging to the king and the custom of seeking the king's license to elect, which, he promised, would never be denied, nor would the royal assent to clerical election, without reasonable cause.

Ranulf's role in the foredoomed invasion of France in 1214 is not particularly significant insofar as surviving records indicate.[50] He attested an agreement between John and the turncoat French baron Renaud de Dammartin in May 1212 that the king would make neither truce nor peace with Philip Augustus without Renaud's consent, and at month's end Ranulf again attested, on the king's behalf, the pact made by the monarch with Hugh de Lusignan, count of LaMarche, which provided that Joan, John's daughter, would marry the count.[51] It is ironic that this proposed marriage to Joan never took place; rather, Hugh later married John's widow, Isabelle of Angoulême, the breaking of whose betrothal to Count Hugh had given Philip Augustus the pretext to begin his assault on John's northern French possessions in 1202. Ranulf had crossed with his king to Poitou, returning with him in mid October. No account survives of the earl's conduct in battle or as captain; he is recorded only as one of the royal negotiators, along with Hubert de Burgh, with the experienced diplomat to the papacy Alan Martel and others, who negotiated the truce with Philip Augustus that was to last until 1220. Increasingly more significant was Ranulf's rapid emergence as a leading loyalist magnate in the troubles which followed the great baronial revolt of 1215–16 and the promulgation of Magna Carta.[52]

All important historians of the revolt have recognized his pivotal role; Stubbs thought that John "trusted [Ranulf] more entirely than any other Englishman,"[53] although Holt reminds us that "John might be thankful for the support of an earl of Chester or Derby, but it was the men of his own making who really ensured his political survival and the acceptance of his son after his death."[54] While there is much truth in this judgment, I find it difficult to believe that either John's political survival or the continuity of his dynasty could have been assured without the active support of such magnates as Ranulf and William Marshal, earl of Pembroke.

Certainly Ranulf's strength was acknowledged in his time and since. Margaret Wade Labarge has stated that Ranulf's "lands and castles were dotted all over England, and his revenues and knights' fees made him the most powerful lord in the realm after John himself."[55] Painter explained more fully that the earl of Chester, while not possessed of the prestige radiated by the Earl Marshal, yet excelled him in feudal strength; with the Earl Ferrers of Derby, he controlled Cheshire, Staffordshire, Nottinghamshire, and Derby. To these men should be added, as staunch supporters of the king among the most wealthy and powerful of the magnates, the earls of Surrey and Arundel and the lords marcher of south Wales.[56] Not only had Ranulf a position of great power and influence; he used his resources and leadership effectively in unwavering support of his monarch. Holt has noted that "there is not a single instance of a rebel holding land of the earldom of Chester [in Chester] except where, as in the case of ... John de Lacy, he also held baronies or important mesne tenures elsewhere."[57] Even in Lincolnshire, only a rough half dozen of the earl's men were in rebellion.[58]

The causes and course of the rebellion and of the civil war of 1215–16 need not here be discussed in detail.[59] The impersonal causes were few and in bold relief: John's quarrel with the church and its resolution on terms fundamentally favorable to himself, the loss of Normandy and the failure of the continental campaigns of 1214 to recover his ancestral lands north of the Loire, the unstable financial situation left him by the reckless Richard Lionheart with the resulting crushing exactions by an ably run exchequer, and a government overefficient and overzealous in obeying its master's commands. Less easy is it to state with confidence the personal factors involved in the revolt. The character and personality of the king have been dissected, psychoanalyzed, twisted, defended, ferociously attacked—yet the king remains an enigma,[60] in large part the victim of stereotypes and of received conventions. That John was unpleasant, cruel, bawdy, and highly intelligent is obvious. The baronial leaders of the rebellion—Robert fitzWalter, lord of Dunmow, and Eustace de Vesci, lord of Alnwick—seem no better as human beings. Both were bounders.[61] They stand in sharp contrast to the great loyalist barons, men of integrity, character, and loyalty. The earl's fidelity attracted the attention of contemporaries as well as rewards from John. In early March 1215, Walter Mauclerk, John's emissary at Rome, noted in a letter to the king the loyalty of Ranulf, as did Walter of Coventry writing of events of August.[62] The only sources which allude to Ranulf as anything other than completely loyal to his monarch are too late to be acceptable as evidence, although they may have some value as demonstrating that the earl's reputation as a man of great importance in the realm had begun to enlarge beyond history and to edge toward legend. Both the author of the *Eulogium*, composed at Malmesbury Abbey in the fourteenth century, and the fifteenth-century chronicler Henry Knighton, present Ranulf as reproving the king, as a spokesman for morality and justice. Their lack of command of fact is demonstrated by the assertion that Ranulf was most concerned about John's failure to abide by the laws and statutes of the reign of Edward the Confessor; this had not been an issue since the Coronation Charter of Henry I, and the pale Edward's laws and policies were completely disregarded in the baronial revolt and the civil war which followed. Properly so; they would have been a total anachronism. The monk of Malmesbury presented Ranulf as rebuking the king for having sipped of sexual liberties with the wives and daughters of the English nobility, but especially for failure to uphold the good old law of St. Edward.[63] Henry Knighton amplified generously upon this pleasant story, adding that Ranulf himself was threatened with disinheritance because he often had made bold to tell the king how the monarch had disgraced himself by his errors; to the charges of the *Eulogium*, Henry added that Ranulf reproved his king for his crimes against the church, and that John had moved against his people without lawful judgment. Henry puts an address in Ranulf's mouth which begins, "Why, o King, do you do evil to your people [*plebe*, not magnates]? Why do you transgress the law of God?" He added that the Magna Carta was issued in alarm at Ranulf's admonitions.[64] But there is no contemporaneous evidence of Ranulf's public reproof of his sovereign.

The maneuverings and conspiracies leading to Magna Carta in June of 1215 are not recorded as involving Ranulf on either side; indeed, he was conspicuously absent from the sources in the months preceding Runnymede, either as a counselor of King John or as a confidant of the rebellious barons (which assuredly he was not). Since the late spring and summer of 1215 mark the occasion of much attention's being paid to Ranulf in the narrative sources, it is curious that few notices of him at this time would appear in the record sources. It is probable that Ranulf, while supporting his king, did not approve of the course of events leading to the Charter; certainly he did not approve of it "in its more revolutionary aspects."[65] Record evidence proves him to have been with the king only on January 3 and 9–15, February 8, and April 12 and 22, 1215, before the sealing of the Charter. Whether this absence from the king indicates the earl's aloofness from the growing crisis or his preparing to engage in it is impossible to say.

In giving his kingdoms in fief to the pope, John drew about himself the protection of Innocent III, who actively thereafter interceded for John against his enemies both domestic and foreign, as a proper lord should have done for his vassal. In March of 1215 the wily king added a further ecclesiastical shield to his armory: he took the cross, joined by Earl Ranulf; William de Ferrers of Derby, Saher de Quency of Winchester; John de Lacy, constable of Chester; and others.[66] Thus John, who grew daily in cunning, armed himself with the crusader's privileges, most important of which were the protection of himself and of his property by the great pope. As it turned out, his ploy did him no more good than identical privileges did for his late brother Lionheart when he was captured and held for ransom in the empire. While there is no way to judge the earl's motives in becoming *crucesignatus*, or even whether he originally intended to go to the East, he did in fact become a crusader in Egypt, conducting himself with valor and distinction in the siege of Damietta in 1218.[67]

As the mutterings of rebellion grew more pronounced across the spring, John of course took whatever countermeasures he could; among them were the granting of strongholds to his supporters in order that his own position might thereby be strengthened. The first such grant to Ranulf of Chester was made on May 20, 1215, and confirmed on August 1, the fortress of Newcastle-under-Lyme with its manor and all appurtenances.[68] The earl was to hold this for the token service of one knight; the grant of the castle was the first of many rich benisons bestowed upon Ranulf in King John's last months.

Yet Ranulf, faithful follower of the king though he was, had no recorded role in the events leading to the sealing of Magna Carta. He attests no royal charters or letters in May or June of 1215, and is recorded in no chronicle as being a royal counselor at this time, although he was instrumental in the reissues of the modified Magna Carta in the early years of Henry III's reign. As Holt points out, "the Charter of 1215 was the work of King John's enemies. The re-issues of 1216 and 1217 were the work of his friends and supporters.... They had fought [in the civil war] not so much to destroy the Charter as to preserve Angevin control of the throne, to protect all the benefits they had received hitherto as friends and supporters of the king and to preserve their influence in local politics."[69] Roughly contemporaneously with the royal charter, Ranulf issued the so-called Cheshire Magna Carta.[70]

Hardly was the Great Charter sealed when the rebel barons occupied London and huffed mightily against the loyalist barons, among them Ranulf of Chester, William Longsword of Salisbury, the Earl Warrene, William count of Aumâle, Henry earl of Cornwall, William d'Aubigny earl of Sussex, and others. Matthew Paris tells us that the rebels had threatened the loyalists who had not joined them, warning that they would overawe them, level their castles, and ravage their lands if they failed to do so. Only the earls of Aumâle and Sussex defected.[71] Surely to threaten the earl of Chester was a foolish gesture; Ranulf was to fling himself into combat with gusto and with skill. Painter pointed out that, in the summer of 1215, Ranulf took ready advantage of the unstable situation and of targets of opportunity in order to enrich his holdings.[72] I see no reason to assume cynically that Ranulf was bought by the enormous grants which soon fell to him; rather, there was here a coincidence of loyalty and of self-interest, as well as a recognition by John of political realities.

In July 1215 half of the great honor of Leicester was acquired by Ranulf, to be held in custody for Count Simon III de Montfort.[73] Ranulf had in all likelihood requested this rich prize from the king, claiming it by blood descent; his mother was Bertrada de Montfort, daughter of Simon II de Montfort; the earl was thus a nephew of Simon III. The honor had been seized into the king's hands in 1207 as a consequence of Simon's electing to follow Philip Augustus when the barons holding on both sides of the Channel had to choose which suzerain to follow. Ranulf held the honor until Simon's death in 1218 on the Albigensian Crusade, when it was again resumed by the crown, to be restored once more to Ranulf a year and a half later. Shortly after the grant of Leicester the king ordered Ranulf's brother-in-law, the Earl Ferrers, to release Nicholas de Verdon's hostage when Ranulf should have vouched for Nicholas's fidelity.[74]

Ranulf was less lucky in August, when John commanded Brian de Lisle to seise him with the great castle and forest of the Peak (Derbyshire).[75] As Painter noted, the mandate was never obeyed; he also pointed out that Ranulf and his brother-in-law of Derby controlled the countryside in Staffordshire, Derbyshire, and Nottinghamshire, and coveted as well the area's royal castles.[76] Ranulf held Newcastle-under-Lyme, but he and Earl William never did acquire the Peak and Bolsover in fact. Holt felt that the failure of Brian to obey the king indicates that John was no longer in control of his officials.[77]

By late December, Earl Ranulf had joined King John in the field as he swung from Newark to Pontefract Castle, held by John de Lacy, son of that Roger who so distinguished himself as the captain defending Château-Gaillard in 1204 and constable of Chester as was his father. John offered his obedience to the king, promised his fidelity to John and his descendants by the then queen, and gave his brother as a hostage for the performance of his obligations, the failure of which would result in eternal loss of his possessions. Ranulf, who had interceded for his constable, attested the instrument by which John de Lacy made his submission.[78] Ranulf then captured Richmond castle; on January 6, 1216, John ordered the constable of that castle to do whatever Ranulf ordered on the king's behalf.[79] Painter is probably correct in thinking that the earl seized Middleham castle at about the same time he took Richmond. Ranulf accompanied the king on his retaliatory campaign against the Scots; at Berwick, he attested the charter by which the rebel baron Gilbert fitz Renfrew made his submission to the king.[80] At the end of the month, the earl received another generous grant, custody of the castle and county of Lancaster.[81]

Not only did this grant place a thoroughgoing loyalist in command of the area, but Ranulf had some hereditary claims on the honor of Lancaster.[82] In the reign of King Stephen, Roger of Poitou's honor of Lancaster had been divided by the king; the southern portion (what will appear below as the lands "between Ribble and Mersey") was granted to Ranulf's grandfather, Ranulf II; his mother had been the enigmatic Countess Lucy, who had claims to the honor, although Stephen's charter granting the southern part of Lancaster to Ranulf II made no mention of a hereditary right on the earl's part.[83] At the same time Ranulf gained custody of Lancaster, he also was granted the lands and castle of Thomas of Moulton; Thomas, formerly sheriff of the king, held of the honor of Richmond.[84] In February his men, and those of his steward for Bolingbroke, Walter of Coventry, were taken into the king's protection, as were the earl and his servant.[85] Ranulf apparently remained in the west or northwest as the king's campaign in the north wound to success at the end of February.

April 13, 1216, was not a sinister date for Earl Ranulf; on that day, the earl was granted custody of Bridgenorth castle and of Shropshire and Staffordshire, in which counties he was to be obeyed "as earl, as sheriff, and as royal official."[86] Earl Ranulf was quit of his accounts in these two counties and in Lancashire until spring of 1218 because of the expenses he had incurred in maintaining royal castles,[87] as well as for other debts. Ranulf now controlled a range of contiguous counties in the west and northwest of England, an immensely powerful position of support for the king, as well as of prestige and of might for himself. Painter judged that Ranulf in late 1215 "was in a position to take the offensive against the king's enemies. Moreover as such an offensive would be highly profitable to himself, he was almost certain to conduct it."[88] Now, he was in an even stronger position to take the field.[89]

By the spring of 1216, what had been a baronial rebellion had become a civil war, the loyalist barons contending against those who would replace John with Prince Louis, called the Lion, husband of Blanche of Castile, John's niece. John and his supporters, lay and ecclesiastical, moved with determination and vigor to shore up the royal cause. Actually, the baronial party which had offered its loyalty to Prince Louis fought in desperation, its ranks continually and steadily leeched away by defections to the rightful king. Louis, backed by ludicrous claims to the English throne, landed in England in late May to pursue a foredoomed—and not very seriously pressed—campaign. The first phase of Louis's campaign gave promise of victory, as he moved steadily westward, John falling back before.[90] Indeed, so did Mars seem to smile upon the French prince that John, alarmed at both defections and military failure, ordered Ranulf on June 5, three days after Louis's arrival in London, to destroy Castle Richmond if it could not successfully be defended against the king's enemies.[91] Some leading earls adhered to Louis, including those of Warenne and Arundel, William of Aumâle, and the king's half brother William Longsword of Salisbury; they were joined by William Marshal the younger. William pressed claims upon Louis, particularly the right to be styled marshal. Young William made the error of taking Worcester for Prince Louis; his father, strongly displeased, ordered him to leave, which he did just as a force commanded by Ranulf and Faulkes de Breauté seized the city.[92]

While the earl of Chester was absent when John died of dysentery in Newark Castle on October 18, he was among the mourners when the royal corpse was interred at the cathedral church of the Blessed Virgin and St. Wulfstan at Worcester.[93] Ranulf was among the three earls (the others were William Marshal and William of Derby) named as executors of John's will, an instrument which allowed the executors wide discretionary powers in seeing to the satisfaction of wrongs done by John to the church, sending relief to Palestine, assisting the king's sons in recovering and defending their inheritance, rewarding the king's friends, and distributing offerings to the poor and to conventual bodies for the repose of John's soul.[94] The document, which does not adhere to a common form, gracefully says of Ranulf and his co-executors that they were "faithful men . . . without whose counsel, were they at hand, I would not, even in health, ordain anything; and I ratify and confirm whatever they shall faithfully ordain and determine."

As Ranulf, earl of Chester, entered a new phase in his career, it is fitting to consider why he displayed such conspicuous loyalty to such a disagreeable and unpleasant king as John. I think attempts to explain this "relic of the Conquest" solely in terms of ambition, of material and tangible gains assessed in terms of long divisions and fine fractions, are wide of the mark. Holt and Warren seem to have understood Ranulf's nature. Holt, writing of Ranulf and his stalwart old comrade-in-arms William Marshal, stated that they "seem to have placed the king's favour and their loyalty to him before any attraction they may have felt to the rebel barons' programme."[95] Warren put the same judgment in other words: "When the time came to line up for or against the king, their oaths of allegiance counted for more than remembered grievance."[96]

III.
A PINCHPENNY PATRON

Earl Ranulf's public career entered a new phase with the death of John and the accession of Henry III. Therefore this turning point is a logical place to interrupt the narrative biography of the earl and to turn to analytical treatment of two topics not readily amenable to chronological discussion: his patronage of religion and the governance of his wide-ranging lands.[1]

Ranulf III of Chester was by 1205 secure in his familial and personal position, and in himself. Wealthy and powerful, he might be expected to have been an important and generous patron of the monastic order; wealth and power are less important in themselves than in how they are utilized. The records do not show him openhanded to religious houses, however, nor do they show that the church, whether monastic or secular, influenced his conduct in any manner susceptible to documentation. He was conventionally religious, but his many admirable qualities derive more from his standards of noble and manly behavior than from the civilizing and gentling influence of the church. For Ranulf, following the way of Christ probably meant following his Lord's paths on crusade, rather than in his daily life. If it be true that where a man's treasure is, there also is his heart, his heart was not in religion, except in its final resting place at the Cistercian abbey of Dieulacres.

To what extent does Earl Ranulf exemplify the traditional

explanations of motives for patronage? Medieval men patronized monasteries for various reasons: tradition, which appears in Ranulf's close ties to St. Werburgh, Chester, the family's Benedictine foundation in his *caput*, although in no other case; prestige, of which Ranulf had a superfluity; devotion, of which there is little evidence in his case; spiritual benefits, such as masses for the repose of his and his ancestors' souls, which seldom appear as a motivation in the earl's charters to religion; and economic benefits for the patron, which abound. By Ranulf's time, a comparatively peaceful era when English barons seldom turned their murderous savagery against houses of religion or other defenseless prey, patronage was no longer motivated by remorse and guilt occasioned by the pillage and rapine so characteristic of earlier decades. The founding of an important monastery is one thing which one must not expect of Ranulf; Bennett Hill, discussing the English Cistercians and their patronage, noted that after the reign of King Stephen founders of white-monk houses were not of comital rank.[2]

Further, there were few major new monastic houses founded after the early thirteenth century; Dom David Knowles suggests that "the number of existing monasteries of the old model [that is, monks, not friars] was so great that . . . saturation point had been reached in the country at large."[3] That the Norman earls of Chester, Ranulf's ancestors, were substantial patrons and founders of monastic houses does not necessarily argue that he should follow in their footsteps. Rather,

> by the end of the twelfth century almost every considerable family had acquired some interest in an established religious house, so that instead of founding a new one, the average English baron was content to add to the endowments of an existing monastery, to provide for the support of an additional monk or canon . . . , or merely to leave his body to be buried beside those of his ancestors. . . . If he has inherited the patronage of a religious house, there was no need to found a new one.[4]

Ranulf founded only one house, Dieulacres, and even that act was a translation of the pre-existing house at Poulton.

Alienation of land, property, and money to religion was an economic as well as a religious decision. As Susan Wood points out, patronage

> might be at once an act of penance, an investment in lordship, and a great man's conventional act. Its value as an investment varied.... It would turn largely on how else the land could have been used: its degree of cultivation, its possibilities as an estate for the lord himself, and his current need or opportunity to endow fighting men. Probably the scale was always tipped by his assumptions about prayer or purgatory, and by the social prestige of owning a great church (this prestige, like the privileged position of a monastic estate, itself depending on other laymen's assumptions).[5]

The Cistercians received more individual gifts from Earl Ranulf (forty, including seven confirmations) than did any other order; the reason is patent. Hill's sad judgment illuminates Ranulf all too well as a Cistercian patron: "Barons endowed the Cistercians because it cost them virtually nothing to part with the paltry things they gave."[6] The earl gave only one grant of property (aside from confirmations) to a Cistercian house other than Dieulacres—this was a grant of land in Macclesfield forest to Combermere for making a grange, with what must have been a very large pasture (1190–92/3).[7]

Founded in 1146 as a daughter of Savigny, Poulton had by Ranulf's time become unsuitable for the Cistercian way because of Welsh disturbances in that part of Cheshire. Ranulf III's family had long held a special relationship with Savigny, and he had issued a charter in 1200–1203 taking the abbey and its possessions on both sides of the channel into his protection.[8] For him to take an interest in Poulton was logical: it was threatened, it had a relationship with a great abbey of which the earl's family was patron and protector, it was located in Cheshire, and translating an extant house was cheaper than founding a new one. The *Annals of Dieulacres Abbey*[9] ascribe Ranulf's motives in establishing the abbey to a dream in which his grandfather Ranulf II appeared to him and told him to go to the parish of Leek (Staffordshire), where the earl was to establish a Cistercian abbey on the site of a church dedicated to the Blessed Virgin. He was to restore the church building and increase the possessions of the monks of Poulton, there to be translated, and the house would be adorned by a ladder of angelic prayer as well as work toward the salvation both of Ranulf II and of the dreamer. Awakening, the earl told his countess of his dream. *"Deux encres!"* she responded, and thus the new house received its name. Ranulf attended the laying of the abbey's first stone; the necessary buildings were not completed (or restored) until about 1220.[10]

Ranulf's foundation charter, although conveying no property, placed the abbey, its property, and its appurtenances in his own hand, custody, and protection.[11] Founded on May 1, 1214, Dieulacres was the beneficiary of many grants from Ranulf and his barons, but none can accurately be described as generous. The most valuable grant was its founder's gift of the manor of Leek, with appurtenances, and his own heart when he should die.[12] Gifts of land beyond the manor of Leek were not lavish; the *Annals of Dieulacres* states that Ranulf purchased the manor of Rossall (Lancashire) for seven hundred silver marks from the king for his monks of Dieulacres;[13] it is certain that the king ordered the earl, as sheriff of Lancashire in August of 1216, to deliver seisin of the manor to the monks,[14] and that in 1228 he granted the livestock in the pasture at Rossall to Dieulacres. But I believe the *Annals* incorrect in ascribing to Ranulf the gift of seven hundred marks to Henry III; to argue from silence, he does not appear on the pipe rolls as accounting for this amount in any of the seven years which the annalist alleges to have been the term for the fine to be paid in installments. Further, such generosity does not conform with the pattern of the earl's consistent parsimony. The records also dispute the Dieulacres house writer, for the unpublished Fine Roll for 1228 shows a different story. There we find the abbot of Dieulacres making fine with the king for seven hundred marks to have all the land of Rossall, with appurtenances, and to pay for it in stated installments. Ranulf is listed as a pledge for the payment of three hundred marks of the sum, with others of his barons, including John the constable of Chester, Henry de Audley, Alured de Suleny, and William de Cantilupe.[15] It would be pleasant to support the annalist's confidence in Ranulf's oblation, but it would be out of keeping for the earl and out of joint with the records. Perhaps the incident may serve as well as a warning against counting on the accuracy of a narrative source without verification, where possible, against record evidence.

The Dieulacres monks had perhaps planned to build a new abbey while Ranulf yet lived, for he granted them the manor of Rudyard (Stafford) with its appurtenances for the building of an abbey; as with the earl's other grants to this house, the gift was in frankalmoin, free and quit of all services other than spiritual.[16] The move, if contemplated, was never made. Ranulf's benefactions to his monks in the parish of Leek are otherwise typically frugal. Between 1226 and 1228 Dieulacres received four bovates with their appurtenances in Cocsuche,[17] and between 1229 and 1231 the town of Byley with quittance of court and of other secular duties.[18] The earl granted two churches to this house, those of Leek (between 1217 and 1223) and of Sandbach (between 1229 and 1232).[19]

Ranulf's donations of land and property to houses of the Cistercian order may seem miserly; they were prodigal when compared with grants to other orders. St. Werburgh, Chester, was a Benedictine house which had been the special object of his family's patronage for generations; to it, the earl gave three charters conveying land or other tangible property, nothing more in this category. It is probably, although not certainly, this Ranulf who gave the abbots of St. Werburgh a house in each of his manors in order to facilitate their attendance at his court free of customary encumbrances.[20] Again a probable grant is that of half a bovate of land at Sibsey (Lincolnshire) with its appurtenances.[21] The last is a quitclaim of all the earl's enclosures in Quarndon (Derbyshire) and other places, and of all St. Werburgh's lands in Derbyshire.[22] The Benedictine abbey of Shrewsbury received land and other rights in Wolston (Lancashire),[23] and Ranulf III is the likely donor of a parcel of land in "Chindredewich."[24] To the Benedictine nuns of Chester, Ranulf gave a manor in Wallerscote (in Delamere forest, Cheshire).[25]

Other orders received even fewer benefits. The Austin canon house of St. Mary, Montmorel (diocese of Avranches), received a small site in his ancestral town of S.-Jacques de Beuvron between 1188 and 1199,[26] and the Austins of Wellow (Lincolnshire) held two acres in frankalmoin of his gift.[27] Ranulf III's gift of two virgates of land in Seabridge (Staffordshire) to the Austins of Kenilworth was not without strings; he exchanged it for the prior's recognition of his right to the advowson of a moiety of the church of Stoke, following ample litigation.[28] It is probable that the Franciscan house at Coventry, extant by 1234, had received the land on which the friars erected their friary from Ranulf in his manor of Cheylesmore.[29] The final probable grant by Ranulf III of land was to the Hospitallers, ten bovates in Maltby (Lincolnshire).[30]

Ranulf of Chester was not generous with grants of land to the religious orders; neither was he a sacrificing donor of money grants. The vast majority (of a small number) of such gifts were given to Benedictine houses. The comital foundation of St. Werburgh rejoiced in an annual grant of eight shillings fourpence a year from the receipts of the sheriffs of Chester (of which twenty pence were to be given to Ranulf III's leper hospital of St. Giles, Chester), of ten shillings which they were to convey to St. Giles and use to feed a hundred poor folk on the anniversary of the death of Earl Hugh (Ranulf's father), and of the desmesne tithes of Rhuddlan and its fisheries and of the earl's mills at Englefield (Flintshire).[31] The black-monk house of Coventry received the annual tithe of all the earl's property and possessions in Coventry,[32] the Benedictines of Montebourg (diocese of Coutances) were the recipients of the tithes of a mill at Trévières,[33] the nuns of Polesworth (Warwickshire) received ten marks per year for the soul of Robert Marmion senior,[34] and Spalding (of which Ranulf was the patron) received various tithes in the honor of Bolingbroke (Lincolnshire) before 1200.[35]

The Cistercian house at Stanlaw received an annual grant of twenty shillings in about 1206,[36] the Breton canons of Fougères tithes of the manors of Twyford (Derbyshire) and West Kington (Wiltshire),[37] and Roger, precentor of Salisbury, enumerated tithes at Wilsford (Wiltshire) in about 1229.[38] Nor did Ranulf overextend his resources when making oblations to hospitals. St. John's without the Northgate (Chester) was founded by the earl in the early 1190s[39] "for the sustentation of poor and sillie persons"; to this institution he granted alms of an unspecified amount and maintained three beds.[40] The earl also established the lazar-house of St. Giles at Boughton (Cheshire), and granted its denizens twenty pence from the rent of ten shillings given to Chester Abbey.[41] The leper hospital of the Holy Innocents (Lincoln), founded by one of the earl's ancestors, received an unusually generous grant; thirty-three shillings sixpence, as well as part of the income of the town of Bracebridge and a mill.[42] The most humanly interesting of Ranulf's money grants was his grant of a penny a day to Wimark, the anchoress of Frodsham (Cheshire). When the gift initially was made does not appear, but the oblation continued to be honored, if sometimes to fall into arrears, until 1278, when this solitary disappeared from the pipe rolls, on which her pension had been enrolled since Chester was *in manu regis* following the death of Earl John the Scot in 1237.[43] One would like to know why Ranulf endowed this anchoress. She may have been the earl's most expensive single benefaction, for even if he established the gift in 1232, the year of his death, she collected a penny a day for forty-five years. The monasteries which he patronized may have envied her good fortune.

Alienation of lands and of money was an act which deprived the donor—negligibly, in this case—of current income and current resources. Alienation of agricultural, commercial, judicial, and forest rights rather granted away expectations of future profits; with these Ranulf was less covetous. Unfortunately, there is no statistically valid way to determine the value of such grants, although it is apparent that they were worth less to the earl than to the houses which received them; small sums mean more to the poor who receive them than to the rich who give them away. Even so, the earl must have slept through the gospel on the day when the story of Dives and Lazarus was intoned. Again, Ranulf favored the Cistercians more than other orders, and again the force of Bennett Hill's judgment concerning the minimal cost to the patron for their paltry gifts is demonstrated.

Dieulacres received only two grants in matters relating to agricultural economy; even so, that is one more than any other monastery. In 1226/27 this house was given quittance from multure in the earl's mills at Chester;[44] more generous might appear the grant of mills at Leek and Cheadle,[45] but this grant of 1217–29 was in exchange for lands elsewhere. The white-monk house of Garendon received a grant of common of pasture for all its herds in Barrow-on-Soar (Leicestershire), except in the earl's park;[46] but this was not a purely charitable gift. Hill[47] has shown that grants of common were to the grantor's economic benefit, since he would, as a result of the grant, have more and better sheep and fertilizer as well. Combermere was granted land in Wincle, in the forest of Macclesfield, for pasture early in the reign of Richard I.[48] Bardney Abbey, a Lincolnshire Benedictine house, received two mills and the tithe of another from Ranulf;[49] the nuns of Chester, freedom from multure for grain to be ground for their own use in the mills of Chester;[50] and the black monks of Spalding, a water-mill at Scamblesby.[51] This is the extent of the earl's grants concerned with agricultural income. As with his grants of land and money, he repressed his desire to devote his vast resources to the benefit of those less well endowed with this world's goods than himself.

Grants of immunity from toll were of obvious benefit to the houses which received this boon from Ranulf III, but it is probable that such grants were not without interested concern for the economy of Cheshire as a whole, since it is possible to argue from analogy, applying Ephraim Lipson's judgment of such quittances' importance on the national level to that of Cheshire. He writes, "Immunity of outsiders from payment of toll facilitated the growth of commercial intercourse, encouraged the development of internal trade, curtailed the monopoly of the gild-brethren, and helped break down the customs barriers of the boroughs—thus paving the way for national economic unity."[52] Only one such grant by the earl lay outside Chester, that of 1201 for the Cistercian house of St. Mary (Aulnay; Calvados), a charter which restricted the grant of immunity from tolls only to those things belonging to the monks throughout his lordships.[53] All but one of Ranulf's quittances of toll in England was to a Cistercian house: for Basingwerk,[54] Bordesley,[55] Combermere,[56] Dieulacres,[57] Stanlaw,[58] and to the Benedictine house of St. Werburgh.[59] Ranulf made two grants of free boats to fish in the Dee at Chester, to Combermere[60] and to Poulton.[61] While the gift of boats free to fish the river without hindrance must have been useful to these Cistercian houses, since fish was so important a constituent of the monastic diet, the grants represented no measurable loss to Ranulf. A grant of quittance of forinsec service lying upon land which the monks of Stanlaw held at Acton is the last of the earl's charters relating to matters rural:[62] no estimate of the value of this gift can be established in economic terms. I will discuss Ranulf's numerous forest charters to religious houses in the following chapter, together with his other forest grants. Excluding them, the sum total of his alienation of land, money, and economic privileges, other than those arising from concessions of judicial rights, appears to have been niggardly indeed. The data base is too poor to permit quantification, yet generosity is not the virtue which springs most readily to mind when one hears the name of this greatest earl of Chester of the Norman line.

Judicial rights conceded embody matters both of interest and of importance. Again, Ranulf's grants in this area cost him little and were of principle value to the monks and nuns who received them as reliefs from burdens and nuisances. Four grants of judicial rights were made to Dieulacres; all are quite specific in their content, and three append the judicial grants to a charter of general protection. The first (1214–17) bestowed quittance of "shires, hundreds, pleas, plaints and customs and all earthly service and secular exaction," and required that the monks be impleaded only before the earl or his justiciar.[63] To these grants, the second (1214–17) adds relief from "tallages, passage, pontage, multure in all the earl's mills, pannage in all his woods, *sallinis*, murage, toll and all aids and mises, customs and demands" for all their land, both present and future.[64] By the last (1217–25) the white monks of Dieulacres were quit of "shires, hundreds, pleas, plaints, aids, army, customs and all earthly services and secular exaction."[65] Dieulacres's other grant of judicial privileges, not found in a charter of general protection, occurs in the earl's grant of the town of Byley (1229–32), to which he added freedom from "shire, hundred, and all pleas, puture of serjeants, and of all demands and customs belonging to the earl and his heirs."[66]

St. Werburgh received only one grant of judicial rights, appended to a charter permitting the monks to extend their buildings (1208–15); the earl gave them, in the new land described in the charter, quittance from watch and toll and from the taking of ale and of all customs.[67] Combermere's judicial grants, which follow Ranulf's confirmation of grants (1230) made to that house by Hugh Malbank and his son, were the most extensive given any monastic house. The long list includes court, toll, the assize of bread, service, hue and cry, *blodwita* (a fine for bloodshed), chattels of felons, forfeitures and felonies, measures (probably the right to prove measures), and amercements for all kinds of human transgressions. These rights were to apply to all their lands, while the grant of the right to have a gallows, of *infangentheof* and *utfangentheof*, applied only to the manors granted by the Malbanks and confirmed in this charter. As well, in an unwonted burst of generosity, Ranulf granted quittance of all tolls, of feeding the earl's servants, of pursuits of county and hundred, pleas and plaints, murage, pannage, passage, pontage, scutage, work in construction and custody of castles, and of all works and services throughout his dominions; nor were any of the earl's officials to exercise jurisdiction in their lands without special permission from the earl, without his particular warrant or that of his justiciar.[68] Greenfield, an obscure house of Cistercian nuns in Lincolnshire, was granted remission from suit of court in the earl's court at Greetham.[69] Ranulf quit the Austin canons of Norton (Cheshire), in a charter falling to the period 1202–17, of shires, hundreds, and other pleas in his domains and prohibited his servants from seeking hospitality of the canons or from "in any way vexing them."⁷⁰ A grant to Rocester, an Austin house in Staffordshire, has not survived; the gift of judicial rights may be inferred from a royal confirmation of 1246 to that house of "all liberties and free customs which Ranulf, Earl of Chester, granted them by charter."⁷¹

With the grants of judicial rights, then, there is a continuation of the pattern established in the more narrowly economic sectors of Ranulf's benefactions. These grants were alienations which cost Ranulf very little in economic terms and relieved their recipients of nuisance and bother rather than of major obligations. The quittances of various sorts were not uncommon; even such a comparatively rare franchise as *utfangentheof* was enjoyed by all those who held of the honor of Chester.⁷² The right to the chattels of felons, a high franchise, was a "rather common ecclesiastical privilege."⁷³ While I wish to reserve for the following chapter a discussion of the constitutional and feudal contexts of Ranulf's grants, it is appropriate here to point out that the alienation of franchises, those privileges "that could in theory be derived from no source except a royal grant,"⁷⁴ was common among barons of Ranulf's day and before. The lawyers' theories do not conform to the fact, and hence the award of the right to judge in life and limb (carried with *in-* and *utfangentheof* and the grant of a gallows) is not evidence of any unique constitutional or feudal standing for the earl. Nor were such franchises unusual.⁷⁵ As well, *infangentheof* seems to have been of little economic importance, although quite obviously in a disorderly age it would have been of considerable value for the swift punishment of manifest thieves, and thus a contribution to public order on the local level.

For a monastic institute to be placed under the protection or patronage of Ranulf was not a casual relationship; the earl took his responsibilities seriously. While Susan Wood is correct in her judgment that "the patron's protection of his house was largely for the preservation of his property," she is equally right to stress intangible motivation for protection and intercession, "a matter of affection, pride, and family tradition."[76] Already in the first decade of his majority, when still the husband of Constance of Brittany, he asked Richard fitz-Nigel, bishop of London, to assist the canons of Fougères (diocese of Rennes) in gaining possession of the church of Cheshunt (Hertfordshire), then held by one Master Osbert; should this not be done, Richard was asked to see that Osbert gave a pension to the canons in recompense.[77] Between 1200 and 1204 the earl issued a charter granting a carucate of land in Long Bennington (Lincolnshire) to the abbey of Savigny; the instrument also took the house and its monks into his protection "as of his own demesne."[78] It does not appear that the earl's relationship of protector was ever invoked by the house. Likewise, the patronage of the priory of Humberstan (Lincolnshire; Tironian Benedictine) did not involve the earl in the need for intervention in the house's affairs; the sole notice of his patronage here falls to 1226, when a new prior was elected, confirmed, and installed with the license and assent of the earl.[79]

The ancestral black-monk house, St. Werburgh, Chester, was under the earl's special protection.[80] Within five years of attaining his majority, Earl Ranulf intervened in a resounding quarrel within the house. Robert of Hastings, a monk of Christ Church, Canterbury, had been installed as abbot with the aid both of Archbishop Baldwin of Ford and of Henry II in 1186, while Ranulf was yet a minor.[81] Apparently the monks of St. Werburgh resented the fact that Robert was not of internal provenance; the house annal attributes the monks' success in ousting him, in 1194, after much litigation and contention, to St. Werburgh herself as well as to the "glorious earl Ranulf."[82] No such patronal intervention occurred with Ranulf's own foundation of Dieulacres; while the abbey was under his protection, there is no record that he intervened in the internal affairs of the house.[83] This was not the case with the remaining house of which Ranulf was patron, the alien Benedictine priory of Spalding (Lincolnshire).

Spalding lay in the Roumare fee (the honor of Bolingbroke) and had come into Ranulf's protection in 1198 when he inherited the honor.[84] Dependent on Croyland Abbey when it was founded in 1052, Spalding was twenty-four years later made an alien priory dependent on St. Nicholas of Angers. In 1189, Spalding and Croyland commenced a typically lengthy dispute over possession of a marsh upon which the abbot of Croyland claimed the monks of Spalding had encroached.[85] Each house appealed to powerful friends and protectors, as was the custom of medieval religious houses.

Spalding turned to Ranulf of Chester; he "diligently fostered the side of Spalding as their patron and advocate . . . for he asserted that what was done to them was done to him," when he attended King John's Christmas court at Argentan.[86] Ranulf's intercession temporarily impeded Croyland's case, although after much indecision Spalding became the eventual loser. Lady Stenton attributed the hesitation in awarding the case to Croyland to the probability that "the court might well hesitate to offend the earl of Chester, especially at a critical junction in the reign."[87]

In 1230 Ranulf again exercised his right of patronage in a dispute in which the abbot of St. Nicholas, Angers, appointed a prior to whom the monks objected.[88] The earl originally had agreed to the appointment of John, prior of Kirkby, but on the protest of the monks he sent a second letter to Hugh of Welles, bishop of Lincoln (within whose diocese Spalding lay), revoking his original support of Prior John. The bishop presumably supported Ranulf's rights of patronage, since the earl thanked him for his concern in seeing to it that these rights were upheld.[89] The quarrel seemed settled by "peace made real and perpetual" by final concord on April 20, 1232, in the presence of both the earl and the bishop.[90] While the terms of the concord lasted only a decade, the next composition had the effect of ending Spalding's status as an alien priory.[91]

Ranulf's strenuous intercessions on behalf of the houses of which he was patron raises an obvious query: Why did he expend the time and energy, perhaps even the concern, on these squabbles? I suspect he did so because his role as patron demanded active support when his house was in need. He was active on behalf of his monks because he was expected to be so. Surely, as also indicated by his generosity with gifts of rights and quittances and his relative parsimony with grants of land and money, there is little evidence of personal religious devotion. Ranulf's motivations appear to have been secular in the absence of positive documentation to the contrary, but it may be that conventional religious acts and benefactions were the expression of genuine religious motivation.

IV.
FEUDAL LORD AND EARL OF CHESTER

Not only would a discussion of the administrative structure of Cheshire and of the internal organization and estate management of Ranulf's lands and household at the turn of the thirteenth century be inappropriate in a biography, but aspects of the subject are in press for the Victoria History of the county.[1] Yet it would be deficient history totally to omit the topic, since whether Ranulf was an earl palatine is a question of substantive importance for an understanding of his standing and power in England. Had Ranulf been an earl palatine, one would expect to see evidence of this special status reflected in his charters and in his exercise of comital jurisdiction within Cheshire (no one has ever maintained that he exercised semiregal powers beyond the county).[2] Yet his borough and forest charters, while interesting in themselves, confer quite similar boons within and without the county. Thus they cannot be utilized to demonstrate special authority in Cheshire.

While Ranulf founded—rather, translated—only one monastery, he was the founder of four boroughs.[3] The foundation charters are much alike in their terms. The earl's charter for the burgesses of Frodsham (Cheshire) grants to each a burgage tenement in the borough and an acre in the fields, for which the burgess was to render a nominal annual payment of twelvepence. To this basic grant Ranulf added quittance of toll on all merchandise moved by land or water (except for salt), pasture for their cattle in his forest and marsh, and whatever wood from the forests the burgesses needed for building. As well, the earl granted that for no plea excepting pleas of the sword (see below, pp. 63–67) were the burgesses to be impleaded in any but the borough court; and those in his mercy were to be quit for twelvepence, unless the offense was committed on a Sunday—then the amercement was sixty shillings and a halfpenny of gold.[4] The other Cheshire borough founded by Ranulf was Macclesfield, established in 1220, according to tradition; while no charter has survived, there was a release from all services in return for an annual payment to the earl of twelvepence.[5]

The other two boroughs owing their origins to charters of Earl Ranulf were Leek (Staffordshire) and Salford (Lancashire). The burgesses of Leek held each a half acre of land with a house within the borough and an additional acre in the fields. In addition, they were permitted to take timber from the earl's forest of Leek for their buildings and for fuel, and were granted common of pasture and freedom from all tolls in Cheshire but for that on salt. Finally, the burgesses were quit of rent for the first three years of their tenure (after which they were to pay twelvepence annually), quittance of tolls at markets and fairs, freedom to dispose of their burgages to whomever they wished (but *nisi religioni*), and freedom to elect their own reeve with the earl's assent.[6] The burgesses of Salford, established between 1230 and 1232, received similar liberties: the annual quitrent of twelvepence, the grant of an acre of land, the right to elect a reeve from among themselves, and the freedom to dispose of their burgages as they wished except to a religious establishment. The customary quittances of pannage and of all tolls but for salt and the grant of their own court and of common pasture complete the charter.[7]

Thus the four charters establishing boroughs are virtually identical in their terms. They conform with Adolphus Ballard's list of "distinguishing characteristics" commonly found in borough charters of Ranulf's period, which include, as well as burgage tenure and a borough court, "payment of a [small] money rent . . . in satisfaction of all demands and services . . . ; the tenant in burgage had full power of sale and devise; . . . the grant that all the inhabitants of a vill should thenceforth hold their houses by a free burgage appears to have had the effect of raising that vill to the rank of a borough. In many places the burgage tenement consisted of a house in the town and some lands in the fields." Among the other common rights he found that of cutting timber "usually limited to such as was required for repairs to the houses and for firing," as well as that of common pasture; he also wrote that "sales [of property] to religious houses were forbidden in several boroughs."[8]

Ranulf bestowed other confirmations and rights of a mercantile nature, but no further borough foundations are to be found. Most charters of this class relate to fair and other trading rights. Shortly after attaining his majority (1190–92), Ranulf granted to the citizens of Chester their liberties and free customs as held in the days of his ancestors and in a further grant, gave the same privileges to the merchant gild of that city;[9] another charter of limited interest grants that the burgesses of Coventry were to hold of the earl as freely as did those of Lincoln.[10] A last Chester charter granted to its citizens that none coming into the city to trade might do so without the citizens' consent except at the two named fairs.[11]

Lords would not have founded boroughs in their lands so freely were they not of obvious economic importance; they were centers of commercial activity, and Ranulf saw their financial importance to himself, as did most English lords of his period. Ranulf also exhibited a strong interest in gathering grants of fair rights from John and Henry III, for example, at Leek, Coventry, Campeden, Navenby, Chartley, Wainfleet, and Chauton.[12] It may seem odd that kings were willing to alienate such lucrative franchises as the right to erect markets and fairs, but Lipson points out that while "grant of a market or fair was essentially a royal prerogative, . . . in a feudal organization of society the sovereign was easily induced to alienate the royal rights of the Crown, and no privilege perhaps was more lavishly conceded than the grant of fairs and markets."[13] Ranulf's interest in these matters is easily explained: tolls and other charges laid upon those who bought or sold at these markets were a source of income worth encouraging.[14] That profit may follow commerce also explains why the earl received other grants from the king permitting merchants under his protection or from his lands to trade in other places in England and in Ireland.[15]

Ranulf was less concerned with commerce than with a more traditional feudal economic and jurisdictional right, the management of forests. The earl held vast tracts of forest both in Cheshire and in its surrounding counties. As would be expected, surviving records reveal more of legal and jurisdictional interest than they do of economic and social history of the forest; the principal interest of the earl's surviving forest charters is whether their terms support the conclusion of Sidney Painter that palatine lords "handled their forests as the king did his."[16] The pattern of his forest charters to religious houses again shows his special consideration for Chester Abbey (two charters) and for Whalley and Coventry (three grants each). The other houses—Birkenhead, Dernhale, Dieulacres, Repton, and Revesby—received one grant each.

St. Werburgh (Chester) received quittance of puture in its Wirral Forest lands except for feeding six foot foresters; the four demesne manors of the abbey at Sutton, Eastham, Bromborough, and Irby were released from any form of puture obligation. The other grants gave pannage and right of common in the earl's forests of Cheshire and Englefield (Flintshire).[18] Stanlaw, the Cheshire Cistercian house which moved to Whalley (Lancashire) in 1296, received of the earl disafforestation of Stanneygrange as well as the exemption thereafter from all forest pleas and services.[19] Ranulf also gave the white monks of Stanlaw quittance of pleas concerning beasts of the forest, as well as of oversight by foresters and other officials,[20] and quittance of puture at their manor of Wynlaton.[21] The Coventry forest charters show an exchange; the earl's grandfather, Ranulf II, had granted the monks permission to send two carts per day into his forest to take wood to be used for building repair, firewood, and for the repair of hedges.[22] Ranulf exchanged for one of these carts 280 acres of wood and waste in Exhall and Keresley (Warwickshire), then delineated and defined the area exchanged and quitclaimed it to the monks.[23]

Ranulf III's other forest charters for religious houses are largely unremarkable: quittance of puture of sergeants, except for six foresters, for Birkenhead, a Benedictine priory in Cheshire;[24] Dernhale received pasture, reasonable estovers and other easements;[25] Dieulacres acquired quittance of pannage in all the earl's lands in Cheshire;[26] to the Austin canons of Repton the earl gave the right to send a cart daily into his woods at Tichnall (Derbyshire) to transport wood for their own use as fuel,[27] and to the Cistercians of Revesby (Lincolnshire) the grant of warren in certain enumerated properties.[28]

Ranulf's forest grants to secular figures and corporations are similar to those to religion. In the forest of Macclesfield, he gave William de Vernon, justiciar of Chester, various liberties including pannage and license to assart, and to nine named townships the right to take oaks in their own demesne lands without view of the foresters.[29] The men of the forests of Delamere, Murdrem, and Wirral claimed in 1351 that Ranulf had granted that his foresters should not prevent them from taking material for the repair of houses and hedges, nor from freely disposing of their deadfall,[30] and the freemen of Wirral had a charter of Ranulf quitting them from maintaining sergeants of the peace other than six walking foresters, with the specific understanding that the recipients of the grant themselves assume the responsibility for maintaining the earl's forest.[31] Ranulf bestowed upon his knight John Arden exemption from puture and from pleas of the forest in his fee of Aldford (Cheshire),[32] and upon his chancellor Peter the Clerk pannage rights and freedom from puture in his manor of Thornton-le-Moors (Cheshire).[33] To Thomas Dispenser the lord of Cheshire granted disafforestation, free warren (which bestowed upon its recipient the exclusive right to take hare and fox), and exemption of all forest services in the baron's manor of Barrow; to William Gerard he gave the right to gather wood for various purposes.[34] The last forest grant is a general one to his barons of Cheshire, found in the earl's Cheshire Magna Carta. The privileges bestowed include the right to assart their lands in the forests of Cheshire, to recultivate lands which had been taken out of cultivation, to take wood to repair houses and hedges without the view of the foresters, and to dispose of estover as they wished.[35] These, then, form the corpus of forest charters of Ranulf III of Chester. What do their contents tell us of the way in which Ranulf III used his power, and of the nature of his forest jurisdiction?

Modern studies of the medieval English forest are few;[36] hence, analysis of the forest charters of Ranulf III must necessarily be tentative. The forest, "a definite tract of land within which a particular body of law was enforced, having for its object the preservation of certain animals *ferae naturae*,"[37] was important not only for its holder's jurisdictional authority and income from forest pleas, but also because forest land in the thirteenth century was becoming more valuable than it had been "as one of the few remaining reserves of reclaimable territory."[38] Nor were all forests royal; that Ranulf of Chester held forests with the concomitant authority inherent in their possession had nothing to do with any alleged palatine status, since private forests were by no means uncommon.[29] G. J. Turner's judgment that "it is impossible to describe with any accuracy the laws which obtained in the chases of private forests of the thirteenth century" remains true, but it is clear that private forests were often managed in the same way, and by officials and courts with the same nomenclature and functions, as those of the king. And of course the possessors of forests were ambitious to enlarge their rights over them; in this Ranulf was typical, as in his granting of numerous exemptions from the forest law.

The forest exemptions given by Ranulf were of the same order of economic importance as his monastic patronage discussed in the previous chapter: they were gifts which cost the giver little but were of great benefit to the recipient, either in economic terms or in terms of release from nuisance and bother. Partial or full quittance of jurisdiction of the earl's foresters must have been a welcome exemption, since these officials not only had wide jurisdiction to enforce forest laws but also had rich opportunities to abuse their positions.[40] Quittance of puture—the obligation to feed foresters—was simply relief from a bothersome obligation; as well, the seven grants of pannage exemption cost the earl little, since pannage income was "rarely of much importance."[41] Quittance of pleas concerning beasts of the forest must have been gratefully received by the monks of Stanlaw; pleas concerning these animals (such as poaching and inquests into the manner of their deaths if found dead in the forest) touched the red and fallow deer, the roe, and the boar.[42] Obviously to be quit of inquests into such matters was an important and welcome privilege. So too the grant of the right to take living wood or deadfall from the forest was valuable to those who received it and useful to the earl who gave it, since debris was cleared from his forests and some tree harvesting accomplished, and, as shown in his borough charters, Ranulf was generous with permission to take wood for the repair of hedges and houses.

While it is the received opinion that afforestation and disafforestation were royal rights, there has not been sufficient study of baronial forests to establish this opinion; even if it were true, M. L. Bazely and Turner have shown the frequency of the exercise of such rights by nobles, whether on the basis of franchise or of prescriptive use. And while Painter believed that "authorization to make parks and warrens and to hold fairs and markets" were privileges which "could in theory be derived from no source except a royal grant,"[43] private parties had erected these preserves since the early Norman period in England. Besides, there is some disjunction between theory and practice in any case, as is evident, for example, in the exercise of the franchise of *infangentheof* (theoretically a royal right) by most knightly English landholders in the twelfth and thirteenth centuries.[44] It is likely that the status of the Cheshire forests developed as the king's notions of royal forests were becoming fixed; there may never have been any recorded grant by a monarch to an earl of Chester. Probably the lord of Chester simply imitated the royal forest and was unchallenged in so doing. Royal forest courts were forced to recognize many other anomalies and privileges on the grounds of custom when the claimants could not produce charters to substantiate their claims. With two legal structures in the process of formation, it is doubtful that the situation was very tidy. Despite the lack of a royal charter, it may be significant that neither Henry III (ca. 1225) nor Edward I raised any problem about Chester in the argument over confirmation of the charters, although both challenged any unauthorized exemptions from the forest law and structure.[45]

I find no evidence in the forest charters of Ranulf III of

Chester and Lincoln to support the view that he handled his forests any differently than did other nobles. Rather, Ranulf appears to have handled his forests both as other lords holding such districts did theirs *and* as the king did his; hence there can be no demonstration based on this argument that Cheshire under Ranulf was a county palatine.

Ranulf's charters dealing solely with Cheshire, other than those discussed previously, would provide much the strongest evidence for his exercise of uniquely privileged authority; yet they do not establish it. Since I have discussed elsewhere the general problems with the literature on medieval English palatinates,[46] it is unnecessary to repeat the arguments there presented, except as necessary to establish a context for the *acta* of the earl. Briefly, most historians of twelfth- and thirteenth-century England assume the palatine status of Cheshire, at least toward the later years of the period. The first record reference to Chester as a palatinate occurs in 1293, and references thereafter are frequent.[47] Andrew W. Lewis's argument concerning the French royal domain in Ranulf's time applies to the earl's alleged palatine powers: since the term was absent in the early thirteenth century, so was the concept. Part of the difficulty in defining whether Chester was a palatinate derives from scholars' lack of agreement as to how a palatinate was to be defined; definitions range from a lordship whose lord had the right to judge in life and limb to the vast claim that the territory comprehended was a semiregality. But, as Gaines Post points out, the regal powers of a palatine lord, even at their broadest, were limited: "A great feudal franchise or liberty in England, such as the palatine earldom of Chester, was in theory no longer a feudal immunity in the old sense; rather, it was a delegation of the royal jurisdiction for the administration of justice in a part of the realm, and the earl remained subject ultimately to the king's power and right to do justice and maintain the peace."[48] Yet another recent writer has pointed out the limits to the powers of the earl of Chester; wide as they were, Geoffrey Ellis states, "the Earl remained a tenant-in-chief of the Crown. When a minority occurred, the earldom was taken into custody. When heirs failed the earldom escheated to the Crown. When the Earl was 'out' against the Crown, his earldom was resumable by the Crown, and once was resumed."[49]

Whatever one wishes to call Cheshire, however, it is apparent that it "was not a normal English county."[50] The most recent commentator on the question of Chester's status under Ranulf III presents an eminently sensible conclusion: "It is impossible to define the exact extent of the earl's powers in Cheshire. All that can be said is that, with two exceptions, kings of England did not apparently think it politic to interfere in Cheshire affairs."[51]

Unfortunately, it is also impossible to determine whether Ranulf III's power in Cheshire, and vis-à-vis that of the king, owed more to his special status or to his outstanding personal abilities. Harris, discussing ways in which Cheshire exhibited special status, is cautious and circumspect. Cheshire, he notes, was absent from the pipe rolls except during unusual periods when its earl was a minor or in rebellion. Its sheriff was neither appointed by nor responsible to the monarch. Itinerant justices did not include the county on their eyres. The shire did not make returns to the various military inquests undertaken from time to time, and it had peculiar legal customs.[52] All of this is unexceptionable; all of this, however, does not add up to semiregality. Harris and others who argue palatine status for Cheshire in the early thirteenth century seem to me to retroject inappropriate concepts and categories into a period where they had no reality; palatine status probably was a real category by the 1290s but did not exist around 1200.[53]

The quasi independence traditionally claimed for Cheshire did not in fact approach that of the Welsh marcher lordships. Cheshire records antedating the shire's annexation to the crown in 1237 are too sparse to support dogmatic statements, but it is apparent that Ranulf III's high position and powerful standing in the realm owed more to his own character and endowments, and to his widely distributed holdings, than to constitutional status. Certainly John the Scot, his successor, did not enjoy the influence and power exercised by his uncle. That having been said, it should be added that the abilities and characters of the men who headed medieval institutions greatly influenced the institutions themselves; the most obvious example of this truism is the precipitate collapse of ducal authority in Normandy when the feckless Robert Curthose succeeded his mighty father, King William. Further, Cheshire institutions—whether palatine or not—were developing rapidly during the early Angevin period, as were those of other great lordships. As well, the great Cheshire administrators of Ranulf III were dead by the end of his own lifetime, thus leaving the young Earl John with a largely inexperienced cadre; gone were Peter the Clerk, Philip of Orby, Roger the Constable, William de Vernon, and the others. Thus one can make no airtight argument against Ranulf's great authority on the basis of the lack of its continuity.

I agree with Cazel that "the rights of palatinates [in the early thirteenth century] were still in the process of being developed."[54] Record evidence from Ranulf's tenure of the earldom does not clearly show whether he had any institutional status calling for special notice. There are references to lands held of the sword of the earls of Chester rather than of the Crown, but his allusion seems to have no particularly exalted meaning; one could just as well have said that he held of the honor of Chester rather than of the king in chief. The earliest reference to the sword of the earl of Chester occurs in an encomium rather than in a specific sense.[55] Claims that certain holdings are of the earl's sword appear well after Ranulf's death.[56]

Ranulf's charters dealing with feudal matters are by and large not distinctive, granting lands in return for knights' fees or fractions thereof, or for other considerations. Only one of the earl's charters dealing with feudal matters has been discussed in the context of palatine lordship—the so-called Cheshire Magna Carta.[57] As was the case with John's charter of 1215, this document was not known as Magna Carta at the time of its issuance; but while the circumstances surrounding the issuance of John's charter are well known, it is not at all apparent why Ranulf issued his own charter, which deals with matters feudal, legal, financial, and social. Tait thought that "the exceptional conditions of the palatinate would make a separate charter practically inevitable."[58] But this statement does not really explain its origins. Further, in the text of the Runnymede charter the only franchises or polities treated separately are Wales, London, and the March. Holt says that "it is probable that [Ranulf's charter] was issued because Magna Carta did not run within the franchise of Chester,"[59] but he presents no evidence for the opinion. Certainly the earl's charter was not a copy of Magna Carta: although they overlap at certain points, at others they are mutually inconsistent. And if a separate charter had to be issued for Chester, why was not the Magna Carta simply duplicated by Ranulf's chancery? There is no evidence of baronial unrest or discontent in Cheshire under Ranulf III; hence the charter would not seem to have been forced by dissatisfaction with Ranulf's rule in the shire. There is similarly no evidence that Cheshiremen were less than loyal either to the king or to the earl; there would hence be no need for Ranulf to "buy off his own barons" in order to give John his support on the national level.[60] If the Cheshire charter was related in some way to the earl's imminent departure for crusade without direct heirs of the body, the text does not say so. All that can be said certainly is what the charter itself says by way of explanation of its origin: Ranulf, having taken the cross, has responded to the petitions of his barons by issuing the present charter. Was this clause perhaps intended to ensure that the earl did not take advantage of the crusader's respite? The Cheshire Magna Carta, then, contrasts significantly with that of King John: it was granted by petition, not forced by revolt; and it was local, not national, both in its terms and in its importance. Moreover, the earl's charter concluded with some petitions denied; these concern wreck and fish of the sea, hunting with bows and dogs in the earl's forests, agistment of swine, and amercements in Nantwich. The charter, like the king's, also required the earl's barons to grant the provisions of the instrument to their men and tenants.

The feudal chapters of the charter (3, 4, 10, 11, 12, 13, 14, 15, and 18) are unremarkable. They require that as many knights should be fielded as the fee owed and that proper equipment should be owned by all who performed service in the field. Barons were not to serve beyond the eastern limits of Cheshire except by their own consent and at the earl's expense.[61] Villeins were exempted from military service, and those who resided in Chester for a year and a day were to become free. The rights of widows and heirs were guaranteed. Finally, when knights from England owing castleguard at Chester castle stood their tourns, the men of Cheshire were not obliged to be present unless there was a threat of invasion. There is nothing here which can be adduced as evidence that Chester was a regal franchise under Ranulf III. More ambiguous in this regard are the judicial aspects of Cheshire administration.

As Stewart-Brown noted, certain aspects of Cheshire judicial administration in the thirteenth century were highly unusual. The earl or his justiciar presided over the court of Chester, which was subject neither to royal itinerant nor to forest justices, and the procedures followed were similar to those used in court royal. Writs ran in the earl's name rather than in that of the king, and they were issued and sealed by the Chester chancery; yet, except for insignificant matters prevailing in local custom, royal law was enforced within the shire. As well, the sheriff of Chester was a comital rather than a royal official.[62] Several features of Chester justice in Ranulf's time are of particular interest.

Stewart-Brown thought that Ranulf III had given Chester its own register of original writs,[63] but he based his opinion on late-thirteenth-century evidence. In a case falling to Easter term of 1278, a writ was challenged because it lacked a phrase "which is of the substance of the writ." But a party replied that Ranulf III "had delivered to [Chester] a register of original writs and in that register that word [*que mortua est*] neither was nor is, nor up till now has it been used in the county court of Chester."[64] Lacking corroborative evidence, this statement may be rejected, since even the first surviving *royal* register of writs dates from 1227. Another instance from legal record of a procedure peculiar to Cheshire justice lies in a record of a case in Michaelmas 1199, where an essoin *de malo lecti* was denied because the ill person lay in Cheshire, "where no view touching any one's sickness is made, nor is it the custom."[65] This does not, of course, imply the existence of a separate register of writs; perhaps such a register is implied—but no more—in a writ of Ranulf to his justiciar which refers to "my writ of mort d'ancestor."[66] In any case, even if Ranulf did in fact give the county its own register of writs, it apparently has not survived. A register purported to be one of medieval Cheshire has been shown "not [to be] a Register specifically made for use in Chester ..., [although] it was made for a man with Chester interests." Further, "it is in no sense an official Register, and only by minor emendation is it in any sense a Chester register."[67]

The Chester court was a court of record,[68] unlike the earl's court at Grantham (Lincolnshire).[69] Lady Stenton may have been too cautious in suggesting that "in the earldom of Chester no attempt had yet [1199] been made to introduce the new rules of procedure developed in Henry II's reign."[70] The county court in Ranulf's time had introduced three legal reforms coming from Henry's reign: the writs of *darrein presentment* and of *mort d'ancestor*, and the final concord.[71] That Chester under Ranulf had the privilege of return of writ does not mean that the earl had the right to exclude the substance of royal justice;[72] the king's writ ran in liberties which issued their own writs.[73]

Henry de Bracton thought that only the king and those to whom he delegated such authority could handle pleas dealing with judgment of life and limb;[74] no charter survives showing that the king did in fact grant this franchise to an earl of Chester. Bracton, however, is a late source for Ranulf's lifetime, and he wrote in a century which saw rapid legal development; he was, moreover, a royalist theorist, and his theoretical dicta did not always conform with the facts.[75] Judgment in life and limb was commonly exercised by the English baronage in the twelfth and early thirteenth centuries,[76] and (as seen above in forest administration) the absence of a charter in a period when prescriptive tenure of rights was still common proves nothing about Ranulf's right to judge in life and limb. The earl of Chester exercised the right to pardon for felony; so, too, did the lords of the Welsh marches, the bishops of Durham, and Earl Reginald de Dunstanville of Cornwall.[77]

Charters issuing from Ranulf III after 1200—but from no earl of Chester before that date—mention pleas of the sword, equated by writers from Dugdale to the present with pleas of the crown elsewhere in England. The equation is probable, if not certain.[78] All six charters employing the term reserve pleas of the sword and to the earl; there is no evidence that he ever granted the right to take such pleas to others, even to the highly favored Peter the Clerk.[79] Yet he alienated other judicial privileges frequently, as shown in the previous discussions of his charters to boroughs and to religious houses. To laymen Ranulf granted certain quite similar legal privileges, although few alienations encompassed judgment in life and limb. First, a charter of questionable provenance: if the charter was issued by Ranulf III, he freed William Gerard of the annoying burden of suit of court.[80] Robert Lancelyn and his heirs were granted that they be free of attendance at shire and hundred courts in their holdings at Poulton and Bebington and that they need not answer except before the earl or his justiciar for any matter punishable by forfeiture.[81] Peter the Clerk received freedom from all pleas and plaints (except from pleas of the sword) along with commercial rights.[82] John Ardern, in his fee of Aldford, received the splendidly alliterative grant of sac and soc, toll and team, *infangentheof* (which presumably Ranulf would not have granted had it been something special for him or a peculiarly royal right), liberty of the duel and the ordeal by fire, and quittance of suit of county and hundred courts.[83] The Cheshire Magna Carta granted to all Ranulf's barons the right to try all pleas but pleas of the sword, to bail their own men when arrested unless sued by the sacrabar, and to receive strangers loyal to the earl in their lands. The charter also limited certain fines and gave safeguards to the barons' men when impleaded without witnesses.[84] In the vill of Thornton-le-Moors, Peter the Clerk was granted quittance of suits of county, hundred, and forest courts, as well as of pannage and puture.[85] Ranulf granted to Richard de Davenport, the earl's chief forester for Leek and Macclesfield, and to his heirs, freedom from suit of court at Chester, and of the hundred courts at Nantwich and Middlewich and from serving on juries.[86] While all this demonstrates Ranulf III's power to grant quittances of certain legal obligations constituting a costly nuisance, they do not indicate any special jurisdictional authority.

Such is not the case with the grant of *infangentheof*, or of the other grants to religion of similar rights to judge life and limb. Crown theory—which "does not cover the facts"—held that "no delegated rights could be granted away by those to whom they had been delegated."[87] The point was made with force by the royal sergeant Hugh Louther in a *quo warranto* hearing of 1293: Ranulf III had not been an earl palatine with the authority to confer rights which belonged solely to the Crown's gift.[88] Although originating sixty years after the death of Chester's greatest earl of the Norman line, and therefore to be used with caution, Louther's argument points to an element of palatine rights: one who alienates the right to judge in life and limb (the plea dealt with rights of this nature claimed by the abbot of Dieulacres) shares in the regal dignity, and must be either the royal person or an earl palatine. But, as seen above, theory and fact are in this instance no kin. Louther's opinion must be treated as strictly that, an opinion. His statement cannot be used as conclusive evidence that Ranulf III was not an earl palatine.

Nor can any evidence presented in this chapter be used to prove conclusively that he was anything other than a feudal lord of great power and considerable independence of conduct. No certain conclusion is possible in the question whether his independence came from constitutional status or from personal prestige, great resources, and skillful use of position. Yet, the evidence supports Barraclough's opinion that the earl's court "owed much to royal example," as, in all likelihood, did Ranulf's forest management.[89] Barraclough may be correct in attributing a developing semiregal authority to Ranulf III of Chester after 1200, but I suspect that growing definitional clarity over time better explains the genesis of the palatinate of Chester than do events of its rule by Ranulf III. While there is no way to prove the assertion, I think it likely that the earl's changing, although not yet palatine, status followed upon the loss of his Norman lands; like John, he was now in England for most of the rest of his life. And, again like John, he may well have concentrated his ambitions and policies on strengthening the foundations of his authority.

V.
"GREATEST BARON OF THE REALM"

The death of King John ended neither the baronial rebellion nor the civil war; nor did it end the prominent place of Ranulf of Chester in English political life. To the contrary, the circumstances of the accession of Henry III, a boy of nine years of age, and of the accession to power of a regency headed by Earl William Marshal, magnified the opportunities for the earl to wield his authority and to assume the ever larger place which he held in affairs of war and of state. It is likely that Ranulf attended the coronation of young Henry at Gloucester on October 28, 1216. Painter writes as if the earl did not arrive until the ceremony had passed, basing his narrative on the *Histoire de Guillaume le Maréchal*.[1] He did not explain his reasons for rejecting more numerous, and contemporaneous, English sources which name Ranulf among those who convened at Gloucester on the twenty-seventh of October; in addition to the earl of Chester, the assembly included the papal legate Gualo, Bishop Peter des Roches of Winchester, Bishops Jocelyn of Bath and Sylvester of Worcester, the Earl Marshal, William de Ferrers of Derby, and John Marshal.[2] Yet the author of the *Histoire* had no apparent reason to derogate Earl Ranulf, whose puissance he acknowledges; certainly the narrator of the biography does not attempt to enhance the role of the Marshal by means of Ranulf's absence.

In any case, Ranulf was an active participant in the ceremony of October 29, when he and the other magnates did homage to young Henry and established a regency under the Earl Marshal to rule during the king's minority. The Marshal had not wished to take counsel on the matter of the regency without Ranulf, since "to run the risk of offending [Ranulf] would have been nothing short of idiotic."[3] Historians agree on the status and standing of the earl of Chester during Henry's minority. Discussing Ranulf's qualifications as a possible regent, Painter found him "in the forefront of the English baronage in respect to rank, power, and prestige" and compared him with William Marshal in his "untarnished record of loyalty to the house of Anjou and in his experience as a captain."[4] F. M. Powicke judged him "the greatest baron of the realm" and "the most outstanding in dignity among the loyalists."[5] Turner wrote, shortly after the turn of our century, that "modern historians have spoken hardly of Ranulf, Earl of Chester," whom he thought to have been "a great man, who served John splendidly and faithfully."[6] His support of Henry III was fundamental, in the opinion of Bertie Wilkinson, who thought the king "might never have survived but for two great lords in particular," William Marshal and Ranulf of Chester, "the greatest magnate of the land."[7] It is, however, perhaps an exaggeration to say that the earl "was a powerful but unofficial member of King Henry's Regency."[8]

Powicke felt that Earl Ranulf's support was so essential to the survival of the boy king that he listed this factor as one of the four reasons why disintegration of the realm did not occur during the minority: "the sagacity of Stephen Langton and his episcopal colleagues, the intervention of Pope Honorius III, the quick-witted determination of the justiciar [Hubert de Burgh], and the restraint of the earl of Chester," adding that "it is but just to lay stress upon the loyalty of Earl Ranulf and to pay tribute to a man who never let his pride and prejudices destroy his mental balance."[9] Yet Ranulf and his associates were human, not lofty idealists; as Ralph Turner said, "[William Marshal] and his supporters . . . took steps to set the crown securely on the young king's head, yet at the same time they sought the power and profitable perquisites that go to men surrounding the seat of power."[10] Even the great Marshal, earl of Pembroke, a man who epitomized all that was best in knightly society and ideals, did not overlook targets of opportunity as they arose.[11]

After the magnates had done homage to Henry Plantagenet, serious deliberation ensued concerning the regency. Painter believed that a handful of men who had been steadfast in their support of John were realistic possibilities for the regency—they included the papal legate Gualo, Peter des Roches, Hubert de Burgh, William Marshal, Ranulf of Chester, and his brother-in-law of Derby.[12] In the council which discussed the regency, the Earl Marshal demurred from the responsibility, suggesting instead that the younger Ranulf assume the onerous obligations of the post, Alan Basset having averred that the regent must be either Ranulf or William. The lord of Chester refused with dignity: "No, Marshal, that cannot be. You are so good a knight, so fine a man, so feared, so loved, and so wise that you are considered one of the first knights in the world. I say to you in all loyalty that you must be chosen. I will serve you, and I will carry out to the best of my power all the tasks you may assign to me."[13] I find this brief statement attractive; Ranulf appears loyal, realistic, strong. Even if the precise words attributed by the author of the *Histoire* to Ranulf are an invention, his characterization of the earl conforms to what we know of his personality and policy. I further suspect that the manly deference in the reported words reflects a sense of security in self and in position, a self-confidence natural to a magnate whose titles and resources were melded with a history of personal accomplishment and sturdy integrity.

I have above alluded to the somewhat inflated picture of Ranulf, drawn by Ellis, as an unofficial regent; Powicke is more probably correct in making him a member of an intimate and informal council attendant upon the king and his *rector*, the marshal, its core drawn from the executors of John's will.[14] Whatever his official status, Ranulf's central importance in the conduct of English affairs during the minority is patent. It was essential for the regent to appeal for as broad a base of support for the new king as possible. Hence, on November 12 the Magna Carta was reissued, by the advice of the legate, eleven bishops, four earls (with Ranulf named second only to William Marshal), Hubert de Burgh, and numerous others.[15] Holt's analysis of the political value of this reissue is worth quoting at some length.

> The Charter of 1215 was the work of John's enemies. The reissues of 1216 and 1217 were the work of his friends and supporters.... They had fought [in the rebellion and civil war] not so much to destroy the Charter as to preserve Angevin control of the throne, to protect all the benefits they had received hitherto as friends and supporters of the king and to preserve their control of office and their influence in local politics. None of this precluded them from acknowledging that many of the demands of the original Charter were just and reasonable. The rebellion of 1215 failed but much of its programme had succeeded. The men chiefly responsible for this were the great loyalist barons of John's reign ..., backed by the old king's agents ... and by the curialist bishops and the papal legate. There is nothing to suggest that these men reissued the charter simply to accelerate the return of peace. It is more likely that with John now dead they could at last express their real views.[16]

"Loyal to the core and well able to appreciate the claims of order and justice"[17] Ranulf doubtless was; he was also willing to receive the more tangible rewards of fidelity—indeed, in at least one instance he apparently took to himself the portion of the honor of Richmond which had been retained by the Crown when the earl received the remaining fees.[18] But this was a minor matter, overshadowed by the growing might of the earl resulting from royal grant. He was appointed sheriff of Lancashire, Staffordshire, and Shropshire in April 1216, holding these posts nearly until the end of the minority; he last rendered his account through deputies at the exchequer at Michaelmas 1223.[19] On May 23, 1217, Ranulf was created earl of Lincoln;[20] his grandfather Ranulf II had held the earldom after 1129, although the inheritance was divided between that Ranulf and his half brother, William I de Roumare, who had been belted earl in 1141. In 1198 William I's grandson, William II de Roumare, died, ending his line; his death occasioned the grant of the honor of Bolingbroke to Ranulf III in that year.[21] The comital title followed a scant three days after the great royalist victory at the "Fair of Lincoln."[22] Ranulf accounted for the third penny of royal pleas in the county of the shire, styled earl of Lincoln as well as of Chester, until Michaelmas 1232.[23] Upon his death the earldom passed to John de Lacy, Ranulf's nephew.[24] In June, Ranulf received the gift of all the lands of the king's enemies in the county which were of his own fee; he is first recorded accounting for the third penny at Michaelmas of 1218.[25] On the eighth of August 1217 he received the honor of Lancaster, which he now dominated, since he was already sheriff.[26]

The great honor of Richmond had been given by Prince Louis to Peter of Dreux, duke of Brittany, who panted after the recovery of this fee which he claimed *jure uxoris*; as Painter said, "this can have been little more than a pleasant gesture," since Richmond castle and the lands of the honor north of the Humber were "firmly held by that staunchest of loyalists, Earl Ranulf of Chester."[27] The earl received grants in 1217 and January 1218 pertaining to lands and rights of the honor in Lincolnshire, East Anglia, and Cambridgeshire.[28] Ranulf's Yorkshire lands of the honor were ordered surveyed in May of 1218; perhaps an order dated the following month, to Henry of Pont Audemer, is the result of the inquest, since it orders the payment to Ranulf of twenty-three pounds in compensation for expenses incurred in the maintenance of Richmond castle by knights of the honor of Richmond outside Yorkshire.[29] Peter of Dreux's interest in acquiring the honor was not abated by the failure of the French invasion. In May of 1218, the month when Ranulf of Chester departed England on crusade, the duke of Brittany returned to England to press his case with the Earl Marshal; he was rewarded in January of 1219 by the grant of all the lands of the honor of Richmond, saving the service of thirty fees, south of the Humber.[30] Other grants of landed property were insignificant when compared with those discussed. The earl had held ten knights' fees, and as well was granted a manor, of the honor of Leicester.[31]

If the doughty Ranulf gathered in gifts, it could be argued that he had earned them by his exploits in battle in 1217, as well as by his past loyal service to the Angevin kings of England. On January 14, 1217, Ranulf was among several prominent men mentioned in a letter patent which "deserves a place in [English] constitutional history [as an] example of community of action." The earl, along with the Earl Marshal, the Earl Ferrers, William Brewer, and others, swore to ransom any defenders of royal castles who should be captured by the rebels.[33] As Powicke noted, "the stability of Henry's cause rested in the end on the joint guarantees which his wealthier vassals were willing to give." Ranulf gave more than financial support; at February's end, a letter patent assured the men of Rye that an army was marching to their relief; in the host was the earl of Chester.[34] Although the Marshal had hoped to relieve the town, William found that it had fallen and that Prince Louis had evaded his strategy.[35] The force then turned inland and seized castles holding for Louis in Hampshire, Surrey, Sussex, and Wiltshire. Late in April, Ranulf became more prominent as the royalist host mounted ever-increasing pressure against the insurgents. Along with the Earl Ferrers, William de Forz, Robert de Vieuxpont, Brian de Lisle, Philip Marc and others, Ranulf of Chester led a force which invested Saher de Quincy's great stronghold of Mountsorel. The castle, defended under the command of Henry de Braibroc, resisted stoutly the best efforts of the besiegers, "stone for stone, javelin for javelin." Yet superior force told, and the besieged eventually were obliged to send for succor to the earl of Winchester, then in London. Saher led a relief expedition commanded by himself, Robert fitzWalter, the count of Perche, and the marshal of France (Walter de Nismes); devastating the countryside on the way, the force arrived at the castle to find that Ranulf and his associates had already raised the siege and retired to Nottingham castle.[36] His stalwart conduct in the siege of Mountsorel earned the earl passing notice from a contemporary poetaster.[37]

Greater glory awaited Ranulf of Chester before this particular campaign ended in triumph for the royalist forces.[38] When Saher de Quincy and his cohorts arrived at Mountsorel to find the siege raised, they proceeded to Lincoln, where a host loyal to Louis of France wearied of protracting an unsuccessful siege; the rebels moved to assist the besiegers. Learning that the insurgent host had moved to reinforce the attackers, the earl of Pembroke moved decisively to join battle, arriving with his men early in the morning of May 20. The Earl Marshal divided his forces for the attack, the five battles commanded by himself, Faulkes de Breauté, William Longsword, the bishop of Winchester, and Earl Ranulf, who had earlier apparently refused to join in the attack unless he were given the right to strike the first blow in the onslaught. The loyalist army fought under crusading privileges bestowed by the papal legate, Gualo, who had anathematized the adherents of Louis the Lion. The count of Perche made what Painter called a "fatal blunder" in not offering battle against the outnumbered royalist forces in the open, remaining within Lincoln in the assumption that his men could take its castle before the Marshal and his force could relieve it. Lincoln castle stood against the west wall of the city, and communication with its defenders was possible through the postern gate; Peter des Roches entered, surveyed the situation, and discovered a loosely blocked gate on the west wall of the city. On his advice, the castle defenders were reinforced; that part of the army entrusted to the command of "the headstrong" Earl Ranulf had wearied of inactivity and was hurling itself at the north gate of Lincoln. Unable further to contain himself, the regent and the other three battles of his force breached the west gate, while the earl of Chester, a man "conspicuously lacking in sheeplike qualities,"[39] thundered with his division through the north gate. Ranulf's further role in the Fair of Lincoln is not recorded in the sources, other than his capture and subsequent imprisonment of Maurice de Gant.[40] It was, of course, a glorious day for royalist arms, and a fatal one for the ambitions of Louis the Lion. Three days after the battle of Lincoln, William Longsword was ordered in the king's name to deliver Mountsorel to Earl Ranulf;[41] but when the earl and his brother-in-law of Derby reached the castle, they found it undefended and destroyed the fortress.[42]

A rather puzzling letter from Pope Honorius III to the legate Gualo issues from July 8, 1217. Turner wrote that "in the spring of 1217, it was proposed that [Ranulf] should be appointed the Marshal's coadjutor. The pope raised no objection to the man, but refused to allow the responsibilities of the office to be divided. These are facts which point unmistakably to the high esteem in which Ranulf was held."[43] Honorius had advised against appointing Ranulf as the Earl Marshal's associate in power, fearing both that the earl of Pembroke would be offended at the suggestion that he share his power, and that divided authority would be an unwise political tactic.[44]

Prince Louis's ambitions to be monarch of the English declined speedily following the Fair of Lincoln; for the Lion's cause, everything seemed to go wrong, by land and by sea. No fool, Louis cut his losses on September 11 in a *forma pacis* sealed at Lambeth. Among those attesting the document was Ranulf, associated with Gualo, the young king, the Earl Marshal, Hubert de Burgh, William Longsword, and the Earl Warenne.[45] The terms of the concord display the moderation and sense of political realism so characteristic of the regent, later paralleled in the Lord Edward's settlement of the civil war of the Montfort period. Before September's end, Louis the Lion had departed English soil, never to return.

The regent had similar success with the traditionally troublesome Welsh; as the eminent Welsh historian John Edward Lloyd noted, the year 1218 ended in unaccustomed peace.[46] The *Annals of Chester*, under the same year, informs us that peace was made between Ranulf and Llewelyn; no evidence survives to indicate recent hostilities between them at that time, although the statement may be related to the fact that the Welsh prince supported the rebels against King John.[47]

Ranulf of Chester had taken the cross with King John; in the first week of June 1218, he left for the crusade, although he did not reach the Holy Land.[48] One would like to know what motivated him. Was the earl uncommonly devout, was he in search of adventure in far-off lands, had he the wanderlust, was he escaping an unhappy domestic situation, had he merely tired of the troubled English political scene, was he atoning for some grievous sin for which he had taken the crusader's oath in expiation? Or had he simply, in an excess of enthusiasm, become *crucesignatus* with his king, only to find himself obliged to a course of practical action which he in fact found repellent or whimsical? It is highly improbable that his thirst for battle had been slaked insufficiently by the turmoil of the years 1215–27; Earl Ranulf was a man who fought well and with enthusiasm, but he seems not the type to seek out battles which did not have to be fought. In any case, the earl of Chester and Lincoln was a significant figure on the Fifth Crusade.[49]

The history of the Fifth Crusade has been written by Thomas C. Van Cleve and Steven Runciman; it remains here only to discuss the role of Ranulf of Chester in the enterprise. He appeared heroic in battle, wise in advice. Among the other English barons departing with Ranulf in April of 1218 were Saher de Quincy, earl of Winchester; William, earl of Arundel; the redoubtable constable of Chester, John de Lacy; and the renegade Robert fitzWalter. All acquitted themselves well in battle, but only Ranulf appears in the guise of counselor in questions concerned with the siege of Damietta and its aftermath. Not suprisingly, his advice was sensible and pragmatic. And, not surprisingly, it was ignored.

The crusade had been carefully and well planned; that it came to grief was largely the responsibility of the strong-willed Spanish legate Pelagius, a man who had a genius for snatching defeat from the jaws of victory equalled only by his obstinate refusal to heed the advice of experienced warriors, such as Earl Ranulf, and of those familiar both with the climate and with the nature of the Moslem enemy's style of warfare. Innocent III had intended that the leadership of the crusade remain in the hands of the church (Pelagius) rather than of secular commanders. But the legate, although strong-willed, was wrong-willed, a man to whom rigid principle meant more than success, to whom common sense was alien. He was also a man who believed that, since God was on his side, failure was not possible.

Van Cleve wrote that "chivalrous society no longer responded with enthusiasm to the call for a holy war, and did not provide the necessary leadership. Mercenary motives persisted among those who took the cross."[50] Certainly the first judgment does not apply to Ranulf, although true in general. It is impossible to say whether the second opinion describes the earl of Chester; there is simply no evidence, although certainly there is no indication that his motives were in fact anything other than religious.[51] Whatever Ranulf's motivation for crusading, the Battle of Damietta had been well underway before the earl arrived; the first elements of the crusading forces had reached the Egyptian city on May 27, 1218. Before the arrival of the earl of Chester and his party, the hinterland of the city had fallen to the initial elements of the crusading force, soon augmented by a French contingent. Throughout the winter, Moslem and Christian forces thrust and parried, the Christians generally victorious, to the point that the Moslems sought a negotiated peace, the principal terms of which were a return of the kingdom of Jerusalem to Christian hands in exchange for Christian evacuation of the lands occupied in Egypt. Despite evident Saracen anxiety to seal the truce, Pelagius, contrary to the advice of experienced lay crusaders, declined the offer, and "the Christian refusal of the Moslem terms sacrificed the attainable to the visionary."[52] Toward the end of August, an ill-conceived attack upon the Moslems was kept from being turned into a rout of the Christians by the earl of Chester, King John of Jerusalem, the crusading orders, and others who threw themselves into the fray in timely fashion to save the remainder of the host. In part owing to what he hoped would be the salubrious effect upon the besieging forces of his victory, and in part owing to the misery of his own followers in Damietta, the sultan twice again offered peace terms; Pelagius twice refused them. It was in the late summer that St. Francis arrived in Egypt at the crusaders' stronghold; perhaps Ranulf met him, or at least he may have seen the friar. The earl of Chester was among those who urged the legate to accept the second peace offer, which—not without reason—Pelagius refused.[53] In any case, Damietta fell to the Christians in early November. Although the sources do not so indicate, Ranulf was probably in the successful host; since he did not return to England until the summer of 1220, he was probably among those pilgrims who left the East in the spring of that year.

On his return journey, Ranulf is said by a Dieulacres chronicler to have experienced an intervention of a type not uncommon to medieval voyagers in peril.[54] A fierce storm arose one night, heavily troubling the sea. The other passengers were in terror; Ranulf inquired the time as midnight approached and the ship's master urged him to "commend yourself to God, for the tempest grows stronger . . . and we are in danger of our lives." Ranulf withdrew to himself, and shortly the storm abated. On the following day, the captain asked him why the weather had calmed; the earl explained that "at midnight and thereafter my monks and other religious which my progenitors and I have founded in diverse places" had offered the Office for himself and his companions, thus stilling the turbulence. When Ranulf arrived in Chester on August 16, 1220, he was received with joy and with honor.[55] Hardly was the earl back in England when, consulted, he gave his "emphatic approval" to the proposed marriage between William Marshal the younger and the king's sister Eleanor.[56] Following his return, however, Ranulf played a negligible role in national politics, but for Welsh affairs and for the crisis of the resumption of the royal castles in 1223. Rather, the sources reflect a continuing interest in lands, offices, and fees.

Ranulf's interests in the honor of Richmond were protected in his absence on crusade, despite the maneuverings of Peter of Dreux, duke of Brittany, who characteristically had attempted to turn his support of Louis the Lion in 1216–

17 to advantage with the Earl Marshal at a time when the *rector* of the realm was pursuing his wise policy of reconciliation and moderation toward those who supported the French prince in his quixotic pursuit of the English crown.[57] Despite Peter's successful quest for the lands and fees of the honor lying south of the Humber (reserving thirty fees retained by the monarch), the earl's holding, the honor of Richmond in Richmondshire, with its great castle, was maintained intact. In November of 1217 he was seised with all domains and appurtenances of the honor in Lincolnshire, Norfolk, Suffolk, and Cambridgeshire, an order repeated in June of 1218.[58] He was compensated for the grant to Peter of the lands south of Humber by the grant of part of the profits of the rich fair of Boston.[59] Ranulf's officials, in his absence, had successfully excluded the authority of the royal sheriff from Richmondshire, arguing that the king's writ would be enforced by the earl's bailiff.[60]

Since 1215 Ranulf had acted as custodian of half of the honor of Leicester for Simon II de Montfort.[61] Upon the death of Simon in 1218, the lands were taken into the monarch's possession and entrusted to various keepers, then regranted to Ranulf in 1220, a grant enlarged by letters patent in 1227 to last for his life's term.[62] His shrieval power in the honor of Lancaster was augmented by a January 1221 grant of custody of the honor's lands within and without Lancashire to be held at the king's pleasure.[63] Ranulf also held the lands of his minor nephew, John the Scot, earl of Huntington and his own future successor as earl of Chester, until John became of age.[64] Other marks of royal favor were less grand, yet no less indicative that Ranulf continued to stand high in the king's esteem, or rather in that of his guardians, until late in the summer of 1223. In the spring of 1218, Robert Marmion died, and his heirs were given possession of his estates; the Robert Marmion (one of two brothers so named) who stayed in England was, with his *maritagium*, in the custody of the earl of Chester. In 1222 Ranulf acquired custody of William Marmion and of his land at Thornton (Lincolnshire).[65] The pipe rolls show many quittances from scutage and other debts owed the crown, suggesting that the powerful and the influential received financial benefits from the exchequer rather than (in general) paying what they rightly owed.[66]

While peace was made between Ranulf and Llewelyn in 1218, and while the Welsh prince was present among those who welcomed the earl home to Chester from crusade,[67] Llewelyn's stormy relations with marcher lords and with the monarch continued to be fitful.[68] Since 1220 the prince had conducted a running feud with William Marshal, son of the great William, whose ambitions and interests clashed with those of the Welshman. As Lloyd pointed out, the danger in relations between the Welsh and the marchers lay in the fact that "petty local quarrels were certain to draw the great men into their toils and ultimately to involve the king and the prince in a conflict on the grand scale," although Llewelyn "maintained . . . the most cordial relations, amounting to a veritable alliance with Ranulf," who "had a fellow-feeling for a great territorial lord whose franchises were threatened by the activity of the central government, and his warm support of Llewelyn relieved the prince from all fear of hostilities along the Cheshire border."[69] This fellow-feeling was recognized formally by the marriage of John the Scot with Helen, Llewelyn's daughter, in 1222; the final concord negotiated at the time between the prospective father-in-law and Ranulf gave John a grant of lands in Warwickshire, Worcestershire, and Shropshire as well as a thousand silver pounds and other considerations.[70] While trouble had been threatening late in 1222,[71] Llewelyn's raid into Shropshire early in 1223 provoked the king and his justiciar, Hubert de Burgh, to intervene. The young Marshal landed from Ireland in force in mid April, following Earl Ranulf's strenuous prior mediation with Henry III for Llewelyn.[27] Although Llewelyn's most important landed interests were not in peril, William generally had the upper hand in the fray, and the summer's attempts by the king and court to mediate the quarrel were unavailing. In mid July, Owen and Griffin, the sons of Gwenwynwyn, late lord of Powys, who had been in the custody of Earl Ranulf, joined the king at Gloucester, where all the former tenants of Gwenwynwyn were urged to adhere to these sons and to the king.[73] Matters worsened to the point that the host was raised and an expedition launched against Llewelyn. Reconsidering his position in the face of successful campaigning by the royal forces, he made peace on October 8,[74] thus ending another turbulent episode in Anglo-Welsh relations of the thirteenth century.

Domestic politics occupied the attention of the earl of Chester to the end of the minority. When the great Earl Marshal died in 1219, "the ablest and most powerful of the English barons, Earl Ranulf, was in distant Palestine, and there was no one to take his place."[75] Hubert de Burgh, justiciar of England, moved adroitly to fill the leadership vacuum with his own undoubted talents, and Ranulf's well-known hostility toward Hubert may date from the justiciar's succession to the seat of power.[76] Ralph V. Turner noted that the great loyalist barons "had long distrusted Hubert . . . , feeling that he was a greedy upstart," and that they "held [him] responsible for the policy of resumption of royal castles."[77] Perhaps the reasons for Ranulf's dislike of Hubert are not so apparent. Did Ranulf fear the justiciar's growing power in Wales and the March, and might that be connected with the earl's friendship for Llewelyn? Was it a question of old blood against new? Was it that Ranulf (and other nobles) felt that they had a better right than the justiciar to guide the crown? It is possible that personality conflict also was a factor in their bad relations, since Hubert was far from lovable.[78] In any case, Ranulf did not get on at all well with the justiciar, and very real issues embittered their relations between 1220 and 1224.

The moderation and wisdom which characterized Ranulf's

policy earlier in the minority continued to dominate his behavior, although he was sorely strained in this attitude in 1223. As Powicke believed, Ranulf was

> loyal to the core and well able to appreciate the claims of order and justice. As events were to show, he could not allow himself to become a rebel against constituted authority, but he refused to admit that the king's closest governors and advisers had a greater right than he had to rule England. He had great sympathy with men like Fawkes de Breauté, and did not see why they should be disturbed.[79]

Since Magna Carta and the following civil war, the monarchical position had been upheld by Henry's supporters among the barons and by royal servants. Powicke pointed out that

> these men naturally expected to be rewarded rather than dismissed after the restoration of peace, and for some time they were left undisturbed. It was obvious, however, that normal and responsible administration under the direction of court and exchequer would be impossible if foreign adventurers acquired a prescriptive right to hold royal castles and dug themselves into the shires.[80]

It was equally obvious that the royal castles must be in the control of men dependent upon the royal administration; the number of castles involved was not small—of roughly a hundred castles held for the king, a third were royal fortresses. Not all who held important strongholds and shrievalties were foreign captains who had been loyal to John and to his son: Ranulf, earl of Chester and Lincoln, also held key fortresses and shires, as did his brother-in-law of Derby. The native barons wished to retain their custodies because "control of the castles assured the magnates of a continued role in the royal government."[81] Yet, the loyalty of such men as Ranulf notwithstanding, Powicke's opinion remains valid:

> England . . . was at this time exposed to a great danger which has received too little attention from later historians. This was

nothing less than the permanent distribution of political power among the loyal supporters of King John. It was not confined to the consolidation in office of foreign adventurers; it extended to men of impeccable standing in the old Anglo-Norman baronage, into which the new-comers could easily have been absorbed.... The danger that a vested interest in royal castles and local administration might grow up could not be lightly regarded, so long as half a dozen barons and military experts ruled from their strongholds nearly a score of shires in the midlands and west of England. The fact that they were for the most part tried men, and, according to their code of honour, trusty men, increased rather than mitigated the danger.[82]

Nor were the dangers of growth of possessory interest in royal castles by their custodians merely theoretical, a nightmare conjured up by such men as Hubert de Burgh to justify their own drive to power; practical precedents existed for the Crown's apprehension. William Marshal, as regent, moved warily, preferring persuasion to domination; yet, even during the earl's incumbency of the seat of power, Philip Marc had delayed for nearly a year in responding to the 1217 precept to relinquish the castles of Newark and Sleaford. William de Forz failed to respond to a 1218 mandate to surrender Sauvey and Rockingham until June of 1220, and even went so far as to revolt at the end of 1220 over the Crown's insistence that he deliver Bytham castle to its rightful possessor, William de Coleville; he was forced to obey the Crown's will in February of 1221.[83] In the summer of 1220 young William Marshal held Fotheringay in defiance of royal mandate until November. Earl William de Ferrers of Derby relinquished castles Bolsover and Peak in 1222, with what grace we are not informed.[84] King John's foreign mercenary castellans—Engelard de Cigogné, André de Chanceaux, Philip Marc, Faulkes de Breauté, Peter de Maulay, and others—also remained a problem. For example, there was outcry when Peter was relieved of Castle Corfe in 1221. Thus events of the years 1218–

22 demonstrate both an increasing determination on the part of the Crown to repossess the castles and a reluctance on the part of their custodians to relinquish them. So important had the royal policy and the opposition thereto become that Pope Honorius III felt obliged to intervene.[85] So, too, did the prelates of the English church, led by Archbishop Stephen Langton, who firmly supported the central government in the matter of resumption.

At Henry's second coronation (May 1220) the barons present took an oath to surrender their custody of royal castles and wardships when it so pleased the king and if necessary to bring pressure upon those who refused to give up their custodies,[86] a further "step toward resumption."[87] Among other papal letters dealing with the topic is one of April 29, 1221, addressed to Peter des Roches, Hubert de Burgh, Ranulf of Chester, and others of the king's counselors, to see to it that the wardships and escheats, retained by men taking advantage of Henry's minority, be restored to him;[88] further papal letters upholding Henry's official stance on his castles and other rights were to follow, increasing both in frequency and in urgency. The ominous tension worsened at the Christmas festival of 1221, where Ranulf—acting, it is alleged quite probably, with the foreign castellans—participated in "disgraceful outbursts of passion."[89] Obviously the interests of the court party and of the custodians were increasingly at odds. The situation was doubtless complicated by the fact that most of the castellans were loyal to the royal house; had they been rebellious, the situation could have been much more easily dealt with, as the example of William de Forz's rebellion showed and as that of Faulkes de Breauté was to show. Early in January Archbishop Stephen convened a council at London, which ended the immediate crisis through the threat of excommunication of those who disturbed the realm and impugned the interests of the king; yet this postponed, rather than solved, the problem of the castles, offices, and wardships. The whole Christmas affair is obscure both in its origins and course; Norgate thought that we know nothing of "the subject and origin of this quarrel," although it seems apparent that it was connected with the policy of resumption; she erred, I think, in saying that we do not know who the foreigners were—clearly, they were the alien castellans and sheriffs with whom Ranulf felt affinity. She was, however, correct in stating that what Ranulf "did, or threatened to do, or was suspected of intending to do, is absolutely unknown." She advanced the suggestion that the whole incident may have been personal, which I would question, but she was probably sound in her opinion that there was probably no "actual or even supposed design of political disturbance or rebellion" on the part of the earl of Chester and those who looked to him for leadership.[90] Ranulf and his adherents are an instance, before the later development of the practice and doctrine of loyal opposition to the Crown, of a policy which elsewhere in Europe would have seemed a self-contained contradiction.

Until the late autumn of 1222, other problems diverted attention from that of resumption, particularly those of relations with Wales and with Poitou and France; yet, while these seemingly more pressing issues forced themselves upon both the Crown and upon its loyal opposition, they also made the solution of the domestic difficulties more necessary. The question of resumption slumbered until November of 1223, when the infection in the body politic of England finally suppurated. In April of that year, Pope Honorius III had declared Henry III of sufficient age to control both his seal and the "free and quiet" disposal of his kingdom; Roger of Wendover paraphrased a (probably) later papal letter which emphasized the resignation of possession of lands and castles to the crown from private hands.[91] Yet a further papal letter—November 20, thus written too late to have affected the course of events in England before early to mid January of

1224—stated that Ranulf, among others, had been instructed to yield his castles to the Crown; this directive noted that the earl and the others named (Hubert de Burgh, Faulkes de Breauté, Peter des Roches) might nonetheless be the most reliable custodians of their offices.[92]

On November 4, the king had commanded Ranulf, Earl Gilbert de Clare of Gloucester, William de Forz, John the constable of Chester, Faulkes de Breauté, Engelard de Cigogné, and others to come to Gloucester in early December in order to talk about current problems; it is perhaps indicative of the state of mutual distrust that the king granted them his protection while they were on this mission.[93]

The justiciar had resumed repossessing castles in the autumn, when Walter de Lacy and Ralf Musard were forced to surrender their castles and shrievalties (Hereford and Gloucester, respectively); Ranulf, Gilbert of Gloucester, and the count of Aumâle strongly and futilely objected, unable even to speak with the king.[94] Ranulf and his adherents, including the foreign custodians of castles and offices, attacked the justiciar's fortress, the Tower of London, in late November. The king returned to London on November 28, and the attackers moved to Waltham; thereafter Stephen Langton mediated between the king and the castellans, following which a discussion between the two sides was arranged. Again the polarity of the parties was exacerbated: the king, the justiciar, and the archbishop "represented professional royal government" as opposed to Ranulf and his associates, amateurs who represented "continued dispersal of power among the magnates."[95] Yet those who opposed the justiciar "may reasonably be supposed to have acted as they thought best for the good of their country"; the baronial party thought that the king could do no better than to be served by "faithful men willing to do his work for him in their own areas."[96]

At the meeting held in early December, tempers flared,

particularly between Hubert de Burgh and Peter des Roches, who supported Ranulf and his party. The only serious outcome of this meeting, which otherwise ended indecisively, was the subsequent decision of the council to effectuate the papal grant of the previous April; shortly thereafter Colchester castle was given in custody to the bishop of London.[97] The problem of resumption was not to fester for very long, for it had now reached a point where Archbishop Stephen felt obliged to take decisive action. So intense was the animosity of Ranulf and his fellows against Hubert that they celebrated Christmas at Leicester rather than with the king at Northampton. On the following day Langton excommunicated, without specific names, "all disturbers of the king and of the kingdom and invaders of holy Church"; emissaries were then sent to Leicester, to the earl of Chester, making it quite clear that he and his "accomplices" were the intended subjects of the anathema.[98] Probably feeling that he had resisted as stoutly, and as long, as he could, Ranulf and his following surrendered their royal castles and custodies to the king on December 29, after being assured that the royal policy would apply to all and respect everyone's interests.[99] Stephen Langton was true to his word, since the following redistribution of castles and offices seems not to have been made with regard to past attachments. On the following day, Ranulf was ordered by letters patent to surrender the castles of Bridgenorth, Shrewsbury, and Lancaster, as well as his shrievalties over Shropshire and Staffordshire (a joint office), and the custody of the shrievalty and honor of Lancaster.[100]

While it is true that Ranulf "no longer ruled by the Severn,"[101] there was one outstanding exception to the peaceful success of the government's policy of repossessing the castles, that of King John's old Norman soldier, Faulkes de Breauté.[102] Faulkes had served the king and his father well, and in consequence had been rewarded generously with offices, lands, and other emoluments; while he had stood with Ranulf in opposition to the royal policy of repossession, he cooperated with the archbishop in turning over his royal castles to custodians. But in 1224 the royal justices began to implead him for numerous novel disseisins, most of them the result of his abuse of his own shrieval offices. The veteran knight heeded neither royal nor judicial summonses; on June 17, the mounting crisis was brought to a confrontation by Faulkes's brother William, who captured an itinerant justice who had been hearing cases against Faulkes, bearing him to imprisonment at Bedford Castle, which Faulkes had held of the gift of King John since its hereditary constable, William de Beauchamp, rebelled in 1215. Faulkes had in fact himself captured it in the following year. The king and his advisors could neither disregard nor negotiate such an affront to the royal dignity as the capture of a crown justice. The royal host laid siege to Bedford, an engagement which was to last until August 14, when the castle finally fell to the attackers. Ranulf's loyalty to the king was demonstrated in his appearance among the besieging forces, even if briefly; his sympathy for Faulkes was shown in his giving him refuge in Cheshire. The earl both refused to support the knight with arms and interceded for him with the king; Ranulf also prevented Llewelyn from intervening with force in the rebel's cause. Ranulf's ambiguous position was, of course, known to the king; hence the earl had been excluded from the royal council at Bedford.[103] Early in August, while the siege still held, Ranulf wrote to the king on Faulkes's behalf, assuring the monarch at the same time of his own continued loyal service.[104] Henry had, thought the earl, erred in attacking Faulkes and in thinking him guilty of plotting against the king; rather, Faulkes endured the king's wrath until it should be assuaged by his own efforts and those of his friends. But the king's anger was not assuaged; he followed rather the advice of those who reminded him that had he acted sternly against William de Forz when Bytham castle was besieged in 1221, the example would have prevented Faulkes from defying him so boldly. Hence, the fate of Faulkes and the defenders of Bedford became the example for other potential rebels to ponder.

In the same year, 1224, through ambassadors, the earl asked the papal court to send a legate to England, stating forcefully that he and his associates should have their castles restored and be admitted once more to the king's council.[105] The pope did not respond as asked, possibly following the counter arguments of Langton's representatives at Rome; nor did Ranulf further press the matter.

Ranulf's continued role as mediator between his king and his old companion-in-arms is suggested by a letter from Pope Honorius III in mid July of 1226, in which Honorius asked the intercession of Ranulf and others of the royal council to bring peace between Faulkes and the monarch he had so faithfully served in the young king's testing time. Mortality ended the problem, as Faulkes died before the end of the year, dispossessed, embittered, deprived in his view of his reward for services long and faithfully rendered.

Throughout the whole crisis over the castles, the conduct of Ranulf III of Chester exemplifies the opinion of Reginald F. Treharne:

> The role of the barons in thirteenth-century politics . . . shows them at their best. Henry's minority placed heavy strains upon their loyalty: repeatedly severe demands were made on them to surrender powers which they had come to regard as their rights, in the interests of peace and orderly government. . . . These years mark a very important stage in the political education of the English baronage, and Earl Ranulf of Chester, the leader of the responsible majority of the baronage after the death of the great Earl Marshal, well embodies the triumph of the sense of duty and responsibility to a national ideal over the promptings of private advantage, personal prestige, and class interest.[106]

VI.
PRUD'HOMME

It is part of the human condition that life overflows with clutter. Ranulf III in the years 1224–32 was involved in squabbles over advowson[1] and in court cases of no intrinsic importance;[2] he was also a pledge for his brother-in-law the earl of Derby, for Walter de Lacy, for Faulkes de Breauté, and for William fitzHamon.[3] The marks of the king's patronage were less impressive than in previous years, although there is no indication that Ranulf was held in any less favor by his monarch. His custodies fell both in number and in importance,[4] gifts from royal forests for the earl's building were spare,[5] and royal grants of land were both sparse and small.[6] There were of course some exceptions to this last generalization. Least among them was the grant of the three Yorkshire wapentakes of West Gilling, Hang, and Hallikeld in 1229.[7] Peter of Dreux, who shed loyalties as easily as a serpent sheds its skin, abandoned Henry III and shifted his allegiance to Blanche of Castile in March of 1227; in May, Henry III conceded to Ranulf that part of the honor of Richmond which he had held of the gift of King John, in terms similar to those of his father's charter.[8] Finally, Henry granted to the earl all the royal demesne in Lancashire between the rivers Ribble and Mersey (southwestern Lancashire), that is, Liverpool and the three wapentakes of Salford, West Derby, and Leyland.[9] This generous territory was to be held for forty shillings or a mewed goshawk annually; upon Ranulf's death the lands passed to the earl of Derby.[10] Ranulf rounded out this great holding by the purchase, from Roger, son of Ranulf de Mersey, of his lands between Ribble and Mersey for two hundred marks and the annual render of a pair of white gloves or a penny.[11]

The mature earl of Chester played a somewhat reduced role on the national and international scale of politics as well after 1223. Since he was only in his fifties (he died aged either sixty-one or sixty-two), advanced age does not account for this relative decline in activity, nor does diminished vigor, as his conduct on the French campaigns of 1230–31 demonstrates. His health seems to have been sound until shortly before his death.[12]

Ranulf, as a lay witness second only to the justiciar, attested the February 11, 1225, reissues of Magna Carta and of the Charter of the Forest, an event of great importance in the constitutional history of England, the first royal boon exchanged in return for a grant of taxation by the polity.[13] The content of the charters is identical to that of those of 1217, except for the statement that the instruments were issued, not by the advice of the king's advisors, but in return for the grant of taxation by the king's subjects. Powicke wrote, "The concession of the charters was part of an agreement to which everybody in the realm was regarded as a party. The form of what historians term a feudal contract was given a richer content, the idea, namely, that society was the expression of mutual obligation."[14] The reissue thus both marked an expansion of the concept of what was comprehended in the community of the realm and constituted a precedent for the later parliamentary tactic of withholding approval of taxation unaccompanied by redress of grievances.

While, as I have noted, the aid of 1225 did not run in Cheshire, Ranulf himself laid a tax in his home county to finance the building of Beeston and of the keep and curtain wall of Chartley castles, as well as for construction of the abbey of Dieulacres.[15] Harris has raised an interesting question about Beeston: Why was it built?[16] He points out that it has an impressive appearance, sited as it is on an isolated hill in the Mid-Cheshire Ridge, but questions its strategic significance, noting that it is near no major contemporary highways, nor was it used more than twice in warfare. He wonders, "Could it have been built as a very costly gesture?" Was Ranulf making a show of strength in reaction to the political events of 1223–24? Perhaps this hypothesis, one of Ranulf growling against the royal policies, is supported by the fact that the earl did not attest royal charters between October 1223 and February 1225, and by his apparent withdrawal from national politics from January 1224 until the summer of 1227.

Earl Ranulf, in the summer of 1227, again took his place as the leader of the magnates of England.[17] The occasion was a petty squabble between the king and his younger brother, Earl Richard of Cornwall, over a manor which was a member of the honor of Cornwall. The manor was held by Waleran, styled the German, who held it of the gift of King John; Richard expelled Waleran and seized the holding. The king insisted that his brother return the disputed manor to its former possessor, and the earl refused, demanding judgment by the magnates. Henry was not pleased; his brother, fearing arrest, repaired to his friend the young Marshal at Marlborough. This private quarrel enlarged into a moment of some note in the constitutional history of medieval England when the greater magnates, including seven earls under the leadership of Ranulf, met at Stamford and gave their support to Richard. They also enlarged the scope of the dispute, calling into question recent enlargements by the king of defined territories composing royal forests. Henry, faced with determined opposition by the greatest lords of the realm, yielded. Bertie Wilkinson writes that nevertheless Henry "must have found it hard to reconcile himself to the action of the lords.

... the *universitas* had come to stay, as a permanent feature of English political life."[18]

Two years later Ranulf again led opposition to constituted authority, this time against the papacy, which in the spring of 1229 laid a tax of a tenth to help finance the rancorous conflict with Emperor Frederick II.[19] The machinery for collection was unusually efficient; hence the groans found in the narrative sources. Ranulf III refused to allow the papal gleaners into his home county; while William E. Lunt may have been correct in his cautious statement that we do not know the results of the earl's exclusion of the taxgatherers, I suspect that Ranulf was successful in protecting his Cheshire clergy from what he probably regarded as the depredations of the Fisherman's successor.[20] Matthew Paris noted the earl's deed with approval, and Wood utilized Ranulf's prohibition as an example of patrons protecting their religious houses "in their own interest as overlords."[21] Surely his stern refusal to permit taxation of his own people argues for sturdy independence of thought and of action.[22] So, too, did his opposition to the fortieth of 1232; in March of that year, Ranulf, speaking for the magnates in council, argued that the nonecclesiastical tenants owed no aid, since they had served Henry on the recent French campaigns.[23] The aid was at last granted the king in September; Ranulf had apparently failed in his advocacy, since the tax was laid upon all tenants-in-chief and subtenants.[24]

The truce which Ranulf had helped to negotiate with the French in 1214 had been renewed in 1220; upon its expiration in 1224, Louis the Lion again became an adversary of Henry III.[25] The French king's forces swarmed over Poitou, a county whose chief political characteristic was its lords' obstinate refusal to be ruled effectively by comital authority until its subjection by Alfonse of Poitou, upon whom it was bestowed by his royal brother when the count came of age in 1241.[26] Henry's counterinvasion guttered out owing to the firm resistance of Blanche of Castile, widow since 1226 of Louis VIII, the indomitable and overbearing mother of the great Louis IX. Yet another truce was sealed between England and France in the early summer of 1227; like its predecessors, it was to have a short life.[27] Henry III, whose ambition seemed always to exceed his resources and abilities, waited only two years before renewing the war, which stuttered along, interrupted by long periods of relative calm, until the sealing of the Peace of Paris in 1259. The ultimately futile adventure of 1230–31 was prepared both inefficiently and insufficiently, and—like most medieval wars—consisted primarily of an uncoordinated series of raiding expeditions which provided more excitement than positive results. Potential allies on the continent were few; thus the English king was compelled by circumstances to ally with Peter of Dreux, who thirsted for the recovery of the honor of Brittany in England (that is, Richmond), still held by Ranulf. From 1229 until the conclusion of the brief war, Peter adhered to the English king, doubtless because the French crown had responded to his Janus policy by besieging successfully his castle of Bellême early in 1229. Peter was an interesting and forceful man, but not a reliable one.

On July 27, 1229, the king ordered Earl Ranulf to meet him, accompanied by twenty knights, at Portsmouth preparatory to launching the great invasion, planned originally for October 13.[28] On the nineteenth day of September, the king ordered a ship readied for the earl to cross to the continent.[29] Yet, despite an imposing amount of preparation, the force was not ready to sail in October, and the frustrated monarch blamed the justiciar for the delay; while Hubert de Burgh had not been enthusiastic about the proposed venture, the king's enraged reaction to his administrator's supposed treasonous failure to have the host prepared to sail seems rather excessive. We are told by Roger of Wendover that Earl Ranulf and others intervened physically to prevent Henry III from slaying his justiciar.[30] The invasion was delayed until the spring of 1230. At the first part of May, Henry's army landed in Brittany to pursue a luckless campaign, ill led, ill provisioned, and seemingly directionless as to strategic goals. The earl of Chester accompanied his king to France.[31]

Apparently Ranulf did not accompany King Henry on his progress through Poitou to Gascony in the early summer, since he was with Peter of Dreux at Rennes in late June.[32] By August, Ranulf had received from Peter, and fortified, his ancestral castle in the Avranches, S.-Jacques de Beuvron, resulting in a corresponding loss of landed power in England.[33] When the earl had received the grant of Richmondshire, it had been given him in recompense for the loss of his Norman holdings; hence it was reasonable for King Henry to relieve him of the honor and to grant it in his stead to Peter of Dreux, who thus fulfilled an ancient ambition, first whetted by Louis the Lion's vain grant of Richmond to Peter in 1216.[34] Peter had persisted through the years in his quest for the honor of Richmond, tantalized by Henry's grant of those thirty knights' fees which had been retained by the king's regent, the Earl Marshal, in 1219.[35] Ranulf, of course, had had no claim on the honor other than royal grant since the severance of his marriage with Constance of Brittany; Duke Peter, on the other hand, claimed Richmond as the English holding which pertained to his duchy. The release of Richmondshire by Ranulf seems a poor exchange for Beuvron, but both the original royal grant to Ranulf and its subsequent confirmations make it clear that Richmondshire was to be held only until Ranulf's Norman lands should be recovered.

While the earl of Chester was at Beuvron, his young kinsman Simon III de Montfort came to him seeking the restoration of that part of the honor of Leicester which Ranulf had held since 1215; earlier, Henry III had refused to grant the lands to Simon because they were in Ranulf's custody.

Simon was accorded a sympathetic reception by the earl, who returned to England with him in 1231 and, Simon remembered, released Leicester to Henry III, in order that the king might then receive the homage of Simon for the holding.[36] Yet Ranulf had opportunity for some entertaining excursions before returning home. Late in September of 1230, he and Peter of Dreux spent a couple of weeks harrying in Anjou in what Painter called "little more than raids in search of booty."[37] In the following month, the king returned home (debarking at Portsmouth on October 28), leaving his forces under the leadership of the young William Marshal (upon whose death in April 1231 Ranulf became commander of the remaining host.)[38] The earl and the marshal, using S.-Jacques de Beuvron as their base, burned Pontorson in Normandy, held by Henry of Avagor; this was, as Painter wrote, a "dubious triumph," since Henry was the English king's man.[39] Attacking allies is poor strategy, and there is no evidence why Ranulf became an incendiary; it is most unlikely that he burned the town solely because of its association with his first wife, captured there in 1196 for imprisonment at Beuvron. Perhaps he and Henry had had a falling-out, or perhaps Henry was playing a double game, although no evidence survives to indicate this. The Norman thrust was followed by a sally into Anjou, where Ranulf burned the castles and towns of Gonner and Châteauneuf-sur-Sarte, returning with no losses.[40]

Warfare in medieval times lay dormant during the winter, but when spring came, could combat be far behind? By late June the forces of the king of France were threatening the duchy of Brittany; given the minuscule forces available to Ranulf and to Duke Peter, they did well in destroying the siege engines and capturing a number of horses in an engagement which Painter thought a "pleasant little skirmish."[41] Ranulf, as commander of Henry III's forces, was instrumental in concluding the truce sealed on July 4, which had been negotiated by Peter des Roches.⁴² Ranulf III of Chester had fought his last battle, and few months in this life were left to him. They were to be spent in Wales, and in England.

Upon his return to Britain in late July of 1231, Ranulf was welcomed with honor by Henry III at Painscastle; the king was in Radnorshire owing to yet another inflammation of his relations with Llewelyn, who had been burning and ravaging in South Wales and the March since April.⁴³ Yet the king and the earl shortly fell into a quarrel so bitter that Ranulf left the court and returned to Chester on August 21; Ranulf had attempted to explain the Welsh prince's position and the monarch had reacted petulantly. Quite possibly the earl had looked with approval upon Llewelyn's rebellion, since its primary target was Hubert de Burgh.

During the late summer and early fall of 1232, the downfall of Ranulf's old antagonist Hubert de Burgh was accomplished. While the earl of Chester did not live to participate in judgment against Hubert, it is rather ironic that his last public act was in the justiciar's defense.⁴⁴ Hubert had served his kings faithfully; yet he had made many enemies, none more important in the summer of 1232 than Peter des Roches, bishop of Winchester and now intimate advisor of King Henry. The great loyalist bishop had a long memory; he viewed Hubert de Burgh as a dangerous influence. Henry himself had begun to weary of Hubert—the scene in the autumn of 1229 when the king flew at his justiciar in a rage was an omen of things to come. The justiciar's dismissal, in part engineered by Peter des Roches and Peter de Rivaux (the bishop's nephew, possibly his son) and in part owing to fortunate events over which the bishop and his associates had no control, was compassed in August, when Hubert was deprived of his offices and castles. Ranulf and other great earls (Cornwall, Pembroke, Warenne, Ferrers) were in attendance upon the king, causing Henry to postpone a tournament since these earls (and the constable of Chester) could not attend.[45] Ranulf prevented the wrathful Henry from encouraging a mob from London to attack Hubert in Merton Priory, where he was in seclusion.[46] As Hubert fled later in the month to Bury St. Edmund's, he was dragged from sanctuary by a royal officer, provoking the church's intervention. Yet all was over for Hubert, and in November he threw himself on the king's mercy and lost all offices and all lands but for his own holdings.

It is likely that Ranulf felt the coming of his death, for (probably) in October 1232, he resigned the earldom of Lincoln to his sister, Hawise, widow of Robert de Quency; in her turn, she deeded the earldom to John de Lacy, constable of Chester and her son-in-law.[47] The greatest earl of Chester of the Norman line died at Wallingford, leaving "no peer in the king's dominions in territorial dignity and in weight of influence."[48] The narrative sources virtually all place the death of Ranulf on October 26, but record evidence would argue for October 25.[49] All chroniclers agree that he was buried on November 3, his viscera at Wallingford, his heart at Dieulacres, and his body at St. Werburgh's Abbey, Chester. While a not uncommon practice[50] in the thirteenth century, dismemberment of the dead was strongly condemned by Boniface VIII at the century's end.[51] The earl had two recorded monuments; one was the prayerful and respectful reaction to his death of the ancient enemy Hubert de Burgh, who read the entire Psalter for Ranulf's repose, standing before a crucifix.[52] The other was his epitaph at Dieulacres:

> Alas! Within this wall lies enclosed
> Beneath the hardness of marble the heart of the Earl
> Who once inspired all men with audacity;
> O Jesus, son of God, by whom all things
> In heaven are created, do not refuse
> To open the portals of Paradise to Ranulf.[53]

Yet the *Foundation History* of Dieulacres presents another side to the earl's passing; a multitude of devils rushed past the cell of a hermit, whereupon the holy man inquired to where and for what purpose they were congregated. The demons were, they responded, off to claim the soul of the sinful Ranulf. Returning a month later at the anchorite's request, they reported in frustration that, while Ranulf had indeed deserved damnation, the pandemonium raised by the mastiffs of the house had so shaken the dark kingdom that Satan was obliged to forfeit the soul of the earl in order to still the tumultuous dogs.[54]

The earl left no proper will; a testament drawn between 1229 and the earl's death directs that his heart lie at Dieulacres,[55] and Thomas, prior of Northampton, conveyed to John de Lacy and William de Cantilupe "a coffer with certain things therein for executing the will of" Ranulf.[56] Additionally, some weapons were delivered from S.-Jacques de Beuvron,[57] and there survive some documents relating to a holding of the honor of Bolingbroke.[58] Surviving evidence concerning the distribution of his vast holdings is incomplete.[59]

So passed Ranulf III, earl of Chester and Lincoln, from living into written history; like his fourteenth-century successor as earl of Chester, Edward of Woodstock, "he struck the keynote of an age."[60] But, unlike the Black Prince, he did not capture the popular imagination; Ranulf was, after all, a man lacking dash and glamour, he was not a king's son, and he did not fight in stunningly successful major battles. Yet he has a major place in the history of medieval England. He was a great baron, so essential an anchor of the Plantagenet dynasty that he was instrumental in its survival in 1215–17, a man who typified and exemplified the nobility of his age at their best, a warrior, patron, royal counselor, and crusader. He seems to have had no ideology but a pragmatic conservatism; he was a man more comfortable with ways and things of the past than with the changes taking place in England in the second and third decades of the thirteenth century. He seemed to have had no dominating principle but loyalty to his sovereign, whoever he might be, and no matter how unworthy of Ranulf's devotion. He was a man of great physical and mental courage, of political wisdom, of level-headedness, of integrity and independence, a man who conducted himself with dignity and with grace. The earl was acquisitive without being greedy, self-interested yet not ungenerous, stubborn but not unyielding. I cannot say whether he was a congenial man, a person with whom it would be pleasant to share an evening, nor can I even guess about his personal relationships with his family and friends; but it says something for him that even his enemies, such as Hubert de Burgh, obviously viewed him with respect and even with some affection. Ranulf of Chester embodied the qualities expressed in the chivalric conception of the great and grave knight, the *prud'homme*.

ABBREVIATIONS

The following abbreviations have been used in the Appendix and Notes.

Ann. Cestrienses	Christie, Richard C., ed. *Annales Cestrienses: The Chronicle of the Abbey of St. Werburgh at Chester.*
Ann. monastici	Luard, H. R., ed. *Annales monastici.*
Book of Fees	Great Britain. Exchequer. *Liber feodorum: The Book of Fees, Commonly Called the Testa de Nevill.*
Cal. Ch. Rolls	Great Britain. Public Record Office. *Calendar of the Charter Rolls Preserved in the Public Record Office.*
Cal. Close Rolls	Great Britain. Public Record Office. *Calendar of Close Rolls Preserved in the Public Record Office.*
Cal. Patent Rolls	Great Britain. Public Record Office. *Calendar of Patent Rolls Preserved in the Public Record Office, 1216–1377.*
Chs in the PRs	Mills, Mabel, and Ronald Stewart-Brown, eds. *Cheshire in the Pipe Rolls, 1158–1301.*
Chester Chartulary	Tait, James, ed. *The Chartulary or Register of the Abbey of St. Werburgh Chester.*
Chetham	Chetham Society. Remains Historical and Literary Connected with the Palatine Counties of Lancaster and Chester.
Curia Regis Rolls	Great Britain. Curia Regis. *Curia Regis Rolls Preserved in the Public Record Office.*

ABBREVIATIONS

FA	Great Britain. Public Record Office. *Inquisitions and Assessments Relating to Feudal Aids, 1284–1381.*
GB	Great Britain.
GC	Great Britain. Public Record Office. *The Great Cowcher Books of the Duchy of Lancaster.*
HKF	Farrer, William. *Honors and Knights' Fees.* Vol. 2.
Monasticon	Dugdale, William, ed. *Monasticon Anglicanum.*
Pipe Roll . . .	Pipe Roll Society. *Great Roll of the Pipe For . . .*
PRO	Public Record Office.
PRS	Pipe Roll Society.
RC	Record Commission.
RCHM	Royal Commission on Historical Manuscripts.
Red Book	Hall, Hubert, ed. *The Red Book of the Exchequer.*
RHF	Bouquet, Martin, et al. *Recueil des historiens des Gaules et de la France.*
Rot. chart.	Great Britain. Record Commission. *Rotuli chartarum in turri Londinensi asservati (1199–1216).*
Rot. litt. claus.	Great Britain. Record Commission. *Rotuli litterarum clausarum in turri Londinensi asservati.*
Rot. litt. pat.	Great Britain. Record Commission. *Rotuli litterarum patentium in turri Londinensi asservati, 1210–1216.*
VCH . . .	*Victoria History of the County of . . .*

APPENDIX
THE HONOR OF CHESTER UNDER RANULF III: A FEODARY

Historians have long acknowledged that the power enjoyed by the earls of Chester of the Norman line was owed less to their possession of Cheshire than to their holding the scattered lands of the great honor of Chester. The one systematic treatment of these holdings, the second volume of William Farrer's *Honors and Knights' Fees*, aimed both to identify the members of the honor and to trace their descent, but there are errors in his analysis of the fees: he deliberately excluded Yorkshire, and he did not separate the Chester holdings from those of the honor of Bolingbroke. This feodary in no way attempts to rework Farrer's monumental accomplishment; it attempts neither to trace the descent of the manors nor to discuss the history of the families who held of the honor. It aims rather at as complete a listing as the sources permit of all lands held of the honor of Chester and of the earl on which military service was owed, a list of the fees of the honor of Bolingbroke which Ranulf held from 1198 until his death, and concludes with a section treating of the earl of Chester's Norman fees and of his castles. Since feodaries exist for Cheshire itself,[1] I have not repeated that information here. This appendix is not a complete listing of the lands held of and by Ranulf III. I have not attempted an analysis of the members of the honor of Richmond (180–90 fees), which he held from 1188 to 1199, nor of those of that honor in Richmondshire (40¾ fees) which he held from 1205 to 1229 (with some breaks), nor of the 77 fees of the honor of Leicester, of which he was custodian from 1215 to 1231, nor last of the lands of the honor of Chester on which no military service was due.

APPENDIX

The table of knight's fees which precedes the detailed list of lands and fees requires some explanation. Column 1 of this table consists of fees shown in evidence contemporaneous with Ranulf III to be held of him (excluding the Bolingbroke fees, to be found in section 4). The second column contains those holdings provably held of the honor of Chester in the decade following the great earl's death; the third column indicates those lands lying in the honor after 1243 for which there is no contemporaneous evidence that they belonged to the honor under its Norman earls. The sums beneath each column reflect this division; and if the totals of fees derived from columns 1 and 2 are considered as forming the corpus of the honor of Chester in the early thirteenth century, it is clear that the earl of Chester enjoyed greater feudal power than has previously been thought.[2]

KNIGHTS' FEES OF RANULF III OF CHESTER OUTSIDE CHESHIRE

County	1170–1232	1232–42/3	After 1243	Total
Berks	2	1 $1/10$	—	3 $1/10$
Bucks	4 $3/4$	5	1 $1/4$	11
Derby	2 $1/2$	6 $3/4$	—	9 $1/4$
Glos	6	3	$1/4$	9 $1/4$
Hunts	1	1	—	2
Lancs	15	$1/2$	—	15 $1/2$
Leics	$1/2$	10 $47/60$	4 $1/8$ + $1/3$	15 $59/120$ + $1/3$
Lincs	52 $9/10$ + $1/46$, $103/120$	23 $17/20$ + $1/11$	4 $23/24$	81 $1/2$ + $2/5$, $25/33$
Nf	5	—	4 $1/6$	9 $1/6$
Northants	—	6 $29/30$	4	10 $29/30$
Notts	1 $7/12$	2 $1/3$	—	3 $11/12$
Oxon	6 $1/4$	13 $7/12$	—	20 $5/6$
Rutland	$1/2$	—	—	$1/2$
Stafford	15	6 $3/5$	—	21 $3/5$
Sf	—	7	1 $9/20$	8 $9/20$
Warwick	5	6 $5/12$	—	11 $5/12$
Yorks	2	—	4 $15/16$ + $5/9$	6 $15/16$ + $5/9$
Totals	121 $101/120$ + $1/46$	95 $1/20$ + $1/11$	24 $33/40$ + $5/9$, $1/16$, $7/12$	241 $1/20$ + $1/11$, $1/46$, $5/9$, $9/16$, $7/12$

Thus the holdings of the honor embraced about 122 knights' fees before 1232, about 95½ more before 1243 (total, some 217½), and in sum total, figuring in another 26-odd from the period whose sources fall after 1243, about 244. To these must be added the service owed within Cheshire, approximately 80 fees.

In the tabulations that follow, I have assumed that pipe-roll entries relating to the *servitium debitum* of the honor or of the earl without attribution of place name within the county are *not* identical with, nor do they comprehend, named members of the holdings, unless the number of fees owed for the two is identical. For a somewhat more conservative estimate of fees, the reader will wish to *subtract* all pipe-roll entries headed (in this list) "unidentified." He will also bear in mind that some lands on which military service was due, and which were acquired by Ranulf III, are included here if there is no known evidence that they escheated following his death (many are shown in the close roll for 1233 to have descended to his heirs). I have omitted those places which were acquired by Ranulf for a term of years, with which the second volume of the Great Cowcher abounds, and all lands of which he merely had the custody during the minority of an heir or while the tenant was out of favor with the king.

I. Fees held of the honor of Chester, 1170–1232.

County	Number	Place	Source
Berks	2	Unidentified	*Pipe Roll 7 John*, p. 65
Bucks	4½	Unidentified	*Pipe Roll 4 John*, p. 28
	2	Olney	*Book of Fees*, p. 19; *Red Book*, p. 173; *Pipe Roll 2 Henry III*, p. 65
	¼	Twyford	GB, PRO, *Close Rolls Henry III*, p. 164
Derby	2½	Markeaton	*HKF*, p. 29
Glos	6	Chipping Camden	*Book of Fees*, p. 49
Hunts	1	Coppingford	*HKF*, p. 27
Lancs	15	"Between Ribble and Mersey"; acquired by Ranulf in 1229 of the king	GB, PRO, *Cal. Ch. Rolls*, 1:101–2, and *Close Rolls Henry III*, p. 221; *Pipe Roll 14 Henry III*, p. 330, for the service.
Lincs	⅓	Aswardby, Sausthorpe, Langton	*Book of Fees*, p. 167
	¾	Bilsby	*Book of Fees*, p. 160
	1	Blyborough	*Book of Fees*, p. 190

I. Fees held of the honor of Chester, 1170–1232.—*Continued*

County	Number	Place	Source
Lincs	¼	Brinkhill	*Book of Fees*, p. 167
	⅖	Buckland	*Book of Fees*, p. 169
	1	Bucknall	GB, RC, *Rotuli curia regis*, 1: 31, 87
	1½	Calceby	*Book of Fees*, pp. 160, 161
	1	Claxby	*Book of Fees*, p. 168
	½	Claythorpe	*Book of Fees*, p. 161
	2	Conesby	*Book of Fees*, p. 189
	1	Derby, Haythby	*Book of Fees*, p. 189
	9/20	Dexthorpe	*Book of Fees*, p. 163
	2	Dunstall	*Book of Fees*, p. 191
	1	Farforth	*Book of Fees*, p. 175
	¼	Falsthorpe	*Book of Fees*, p. 160
	1	Fordington, Ulceby	*Book of Fees*, p. 163
	½	Fulletby	*Book of Fees*, p. 167
	¼	Fulstow	*Book of Fees*, p. 155
	½	Gainesthorpe	*Book of Fees*, p. 191
	¼	Hagnaby	*Book of Fees*, p. 161
	⅓	Hagworthingham	*Book of Fees*, p. 168
	1	Halton on Trent	*Book of Fees*, p. 189
	1	Hibbaldstow	*Book of Fees*, p. 191
	3	Humberstone	*Book of Fees*, p. 155
	2	Kilingholm	GB, PRO, *Cal. Patent Rolls, 1338–40*, p. 36
	2	Kingthorpe	*Book of Fees*, p. 173
	⅓	Mablethorpe	*Book of Fees*, p. 160
	½	Mablethorpe, Theddlethorpe	*Book of Fees*, p. 160
	⅓	Metheringham	*Book of Fees*, p. 178
	2	Newball	*Book of Fees*, p. 172
	2¼	Ormsby, Utterby	*Book of Fees*, p. 154
	⅝	Oxcomb	*Book of Fees*, p. 167
	1	Riby	*Book of Fees*, p. 155
	1	Salmonby	*Book of Fees*, p. 168
	1	Scotton	*Book of Fees*, p. 191
	1	S. Thoresby	*Book of Fees*, p. 161
	½	Stenigot	*Book of Fees*, p. 169
	½	Stenwith	*Book of Fees*, p. 185
	¼	Sutterby	*Book of Fees*, p. 164
	1	Swaby	*Book of Fees*, p. 160
	2	Thealby	*Book of Fees*, p. 189
	1	Thoresby	*Book of Fees*, p. 161
	½	Thrunscoe	*Book of Fees*, p. 155
	¼	Trusthorpe	*Book of Fees*, p. 160
	⅕	Ulceby	*Book of Fees*, p. 161
	½	Waddingham	*Book of Fees*, p. 191
	3½	Waddington	*Book of Fees*, p. 188; *Pipe Roll 4 Richard I*, p. 244

APPENDIX   109

I. Fees held of the honor of Chester, 1170–1232.—*Continued*

County	Number	Place	Source
Lincs	3	Walmesgate, etc.	*Book of Fees*, p. 107
	¾ + ¹⁄₄₆	Welton	*Book of Fees*, p. 163
	2	Wilsthorpe	*Book of Fees*, pp. 154, 169
	¼	Wintrington	*Book of Fees*, p. 189
	2¼	Wyun	*Book of Fees*, p. 154
Nf	5	Weybourne	*RBE*, p. 76
Notts	1	Broughton	*LF*, p. 230
	¼	Sutton upon Soar	*Chester Chartulary*, p. 59.
	⅓	Thorpe in the Glebe	*HKF*, p. 44
Oxon	¼	Great Tew	*Cal. Patent Rolls*, p. 26
	4¼	Pirton	*Pipe Roll 3 John*, p. 214
	3½	Unidentified	*Pipe Roll 3 John*, p. 214; *Book of Fees*, p. 102 (gives 2½)
Leics	¼	Mountsorrel	*HKF*, p. 62
	¼	Seagrave, Sileby	*HKF*, p. 72
Rutland	½	Aswell	*HKF*, p. 29
Stafford	1	Alstonfield	*Rot. litt. pat.*, p. 154
	1	Clifton	*Curia Regis Rolls*, vol. 13, no. 805
	7	Crakemarsh	*Book of Fees*, p. 141
	2	Chartley	*HKF*, p. 49
	2	Elford	*HKF*, p. 272
	1	Newcastle	*Rot. litt. pat.*, p. 137
	1	Unidentified	*Pipe Roll 14 Henry III*, pp. 234, 236
Warwick	1	Hartshill, Ansley	GB, PRO, *Close Rolls Henry III*, p. 142
	1	Kingsbury	*Pipe Roll 8 John*, p. 8
	3	Nantwich Barony	*Chs in the PRs*, p. 217n.
Yorks	2	Bingley	*Cal. Ch. Rolls*, 1:115

II. Fees held of the honor of Chester, 1232–42/3.

County	Number	Place	Source
Berks	2	Buscot	*Book of Fees*, p. 847
	¹⁄₁₀	Drayton	*Book of Fees*, p. 858
Bucks	2	Great Brickhill	*Book of Fees*, p. 896
	2	Mentemore	*Book of Fees*, p. 877
	1	Woughton on the Green	*Book of Fees*, p. 872
Derby	¼	Bretby	*Book of Fees*, p. 983
	1½	Newton	*HKF*, p. 41
	2	Rosliston	*Book of Fees*, p. 530
	½	Smisby	*Book of Fees*, p. 530
	½	Stanton by Bridge	*Book of Fees*, p. 995
	2	Walton upon Trent	*Book of Fees*, p. 530

II. Fees held of the honor of Chester, 1232–42/3.—*Continued*

County	Number	Place	Source
Glos	3	Bisley	*Book of Fees*, p. 440
Hunts	1	Upton	*HKF*, p. 26
Lancs	½	Makersfield	*VCH Lancashire*, 1:371
Leics	½	Brooksby	*Book of Fees*, p. 517
	½	Childcote	*Book of Fees*, p. 530
	1	Cossington	*Book of Fees*, p. 520
	1	Diseworth	*Book of Fees*, p. 516
	1/20	Frisby	*Book of Fees*, p. 517
	1	Hoton	*Book of Fees*, p. 517
	½	Houghton on the Hill	*Book of Fees*, p. 520
	¾	Kegworth	*HKF*, p. 79 (shows the fee in the honor for unspecified service *temp.* Ranulf III)
	1¼	Loughborough	*Book of Fees*, p. 517
	1	Nayleston	*Book of Fees*, p. 516
	1¼	Norton next Twycross	*HKF*, p. 57
	½	Prestwald	*Book of Fees*, p. 517
	⅖	Quorndon (Loughborough)	*Book of Fees*, p. 517
	¼	Reresby	*Book of Fees*, p. 517
	½	Rotherby	*Book of Fees*, p. 517
	⅓	Woodthorpe	*Book of Fees*, p. 517
Lincs	1/10	Alkborough	*Book of Fees*, p. 1083
	⅜	Ashby by Partby	*Book of Fees*, p. 1057
	1	Brocklesby	*Book of Fees*, pp. 1014, 1077, 1477
	6	Calceby	*Book of Fees*, p. 1002
	2	Cockerinton, Saltfleetby	*Book of Fees*, p. 1077
	13/20	Elsham	*Book of Fees*, pp. 1012, 1077
	1¾	Friskney, Wainfleet, Dauby, Drexthorpe	*Book of Fees*, pp. 1055, 1056
	¼	Hallington	*Book of Fees*, p. 1055
	1	Hanby	*Book of Fees*, p. 1058
	⅓	Harrington	*Book of Fees*, p. 1064
	½	Harmston	*Book of Fees*, pp. 1077, 1044
	2	Ketsby	*Book of Fees*, p. 1063
	1	Mablethorpe	*Book of Fees*, p. 1077
	11/40	Ruckland	*Book of Fees*, p. 1055
	1¾	Salmonby	*Book of Fees*, p. 1063
	½	Stain, Theddlethorpe	*Book of Fees*, p. 1077
	⅘	Tathwell	*Book of Fees*, p. 1055
	⅔	Thurlby	*Book of Fees*, p. 1058
	1	Tothill	*Book of Fees*, p. 1077
	⅕	Waddington •	*Book of Fees*, p. 1044
	1	Wainfleet, Friskney, "Schekenessa," Braytoft	*Book of Fees*, p. 164
	1/11	Winceby	*Book of Fees*, p. 1063
	⅔	Willoughby	*Book of Fees*, p. 1077
Northants	⅔	Boddington	*Book of Fees*, p. 942

II. Fees held of the honor of Chester, 1232–42/3.—Continued

County	Number	Place	Source
Northants	1/20	Bugbrooke	*Book of Fees*, p. 935
	1	Byfield	*Book of Fees*, p. 495
	1/12	Chadstone	*HKF*, p. 223
	1/3	Middle Chenduit	*Book of Fees*, p. 941
	1/2	Preston	*Book of Fees*, p. 941
	1	Radstone	*Book of Fees*, p. 495
	1/2	Rodeston	*Book of Fees*, p. 941
	2	Slapton	*Book of Fees*, p. 941
	1	Yelvertoft	*Book of Fees*, p. 495
Notts	1	Bunington	*Book of Fees*, p. 533
	1	Sutton upon Soar	*Book of Fees*, p. 533
	1/3	Thorpe in the Glebe	*Book of Fees*, p. 533
Oxon	2	Churchill	*Book of Fees*, p. 839
	3 + 17/60	Unidentified	*Book of Fees*, p. 456
	3 + 3/10	Unidentified	*Book of Fees*, p. 453
	2	S. Weston	*Book of Fees*, p. 447
	1	Tackley	*Book of Fees*, p. 447
	2	W. Shirburn	*Book of Fees*, p. 829
Stafford	1	Drayton Basset	*Book of Fees*, p. 271
	1	Longsdon, Ruston	*Book of Fees*, p. 970
	1	Pattingham	*Book of Fees*, p. 544
	3 1/4	Unidentified	*Book of Fees*, pp. 546, 970
	1/10	Quickhill	*Book of Fees*, p. 970
Sf	3	Framsden, Petthaugh	*Book of Fees*, p. 915
	1	Halesworth	*Book of Fees*, p. 916
	2	Kessingland, Carleton	*Book of Fees*, p. 915
	1	Sotterly	*Book of Fees*, p. 916
Warwick	1	Allesley	*Book of Fees*, p. 510
	1/4	Alspath	*Book of Fees*, p. 510
	1/2	Ansty	*Book of Fees*, p. 510
	3 + 19/24	Coventry	*Book of Fees*, p. 510
	1/2	Exhall	*Book of Fees*, p. 510
	1/4	Wyken	*Book of Fees*, p. 510

III. *Servitia debita* of the honor of Chester previously not noted and falling to the period after 1243.

County	Number	Place	Source
Bucks	1	Great Shenley	*FA*, 1: 82
	1/4	Emton	GB, PRO, *Close Rolls Henry III*, 2:116
Glos	1/4	Weston, Skipton	*FA*, 2:224
Leics	1	Barrow upon Soar	*HKF*, p. 56
	1 1/8	Burton on the Wolds	*HKF*, p. 76
	1/3	Cotes, Heynton	*Close Rolls Henry III*, 2:117
	2	Donnington	*FA*, 3:101; *HKF*, pp. 65–66

III. *Servitia debita* of the honor of Chester previously not noted and falling to the period after 1243.—*Continued*

County	Number	Place	Source
Lincs	½	Brocklesby	*Book of Fees*, p. 1477
	3	Scartho	GB, RC, *Rotuli hundredorum*, p. 290
	23/24	Wolrigby	*Book of Fees*, p. 143
	½	Wrangel	GB, RC, *Rotuli hundredorum*, p. 348
Nf	1/6	Briningham	*FA*, 3:402
	1	Hedenham	*FA*, 3:432
	1	Kirby Bedon	GB, RC, *Placita de quo warranto*, p. 498
	1	Little Framingham	*HKF*, p. 235
	1	Waburn	GB, PRO, *Calendar of Inquisitions post Mortem*, 2:742
Northants	2	Bugbrooke	GB, PRO, *Calendar of Inquisitions post Mortem*, 3:78
	2	Marston St. Lawrence	*FA*, 4:4
Sf	½	Mells	*FA*, 5:58
	¾	Metingham	*HKF*, p. 231
	1/5	Pakefield	*FA*, 5:67
Yorks	1/8	Burton	*FA*, 6:47
	2⅖	Boketon, Newsham in Kirby Ravensworth, Bempton	*FA*, 5:29
	1/16	The same	*FA*, 6:229
	2	Catton	*FA*, 6:47
	5/9	Flaynburgh	*FA*, 6:29
	¼	Full Sutton	*FA*, 6:47
	1/10	Sywardby, Marton	*FA*, 6:29

IV. *Servitia debita* of the honor of Bolingbroke, acquired by Ranulf III in 1198.[3]

The Bolingbroke lands lay in Lincolnshire, and identification of them as belonging to the honor was determined by their attribution in the Great Cowchers, volume 2, folios 249ff.[4] These are the 68¾ fees for which Ranulf frequently accounted at the exchequer during the reign of John and the early years of that of Henry III. Since virtually all the sources are in the *Book of Fees*, it seems redundant to repeat the citation; hence all the page numbers in the right-hand column refer to the *Book of Fees* unless otherwise cited.

APPENDIX

Number	Place	Source
1/8	Allesby	1020
3/5	Asserby	161
1/4	Bassingthorpe	1048
10	Benniworth fees in Halton, Steeping, Kingthorpe	GC, vol. 2, f. 286d.
3/4	Burreth	169
3	Cabourne	155
6 1/6 + 1/46	Calceworth	160–61
3	Claxby, Normanby	1018
3/4	Croxeby	1018
3/4	Elkinton	1054
1/2	Farlsthorpe	1059
1 2/3	Hameringham	1063
2	Harington, etc.	168
1/3	Horsington, Hemingby	1061
3	Horsington	169
3/4	Hotoft	1058
1	Houton	1018
1	Ireby	1020
1/3	Kilingholm	1064
1 2/3	Langton	167, 1063, 1064
2	Little Grimsby	155
1	Little Limberg	1467
4 1/2	Normanby	190, 1018; *HKF*, pp. 186, 188
1	Otteby	197
10	Fee of Hawise de Quency	1002
3	Raithby, Hallington, Tathwell	174
3	Raithby, Hallington	GB, PRO, *Calendar of Inquisitions post Mortem*, 3:317
3/40, 1/12, 1/14	Sausthorpe	1063
1/4	Sausthorpe, Langton	1063
1	Scamblesby	1061
1/2	Stenwith	1035
1/2	Tatinton	1060
1/4	Tefford	168
3/4, 2/15	Theddlethorpe	160, 1058
1/4	Thoriswey	1018
1 1/4	Thurgramby	1088
3/8	Trusthorpe, Fulsthorpe	1087
1/6	Ubethorpe	1051
3/16	Ulceby, Claythorpe	1088

Total: $67 2/3 + 1/14 + 7/16 + 1/46$

V. Miscellaneous matters of military interest.

In Normandy, the fee of the earl of Chester owed 10 knights to the duke, but had enfeoffed 51⅞.[5] The inquests of Philip Augustus following the French conquest of Normandy (1204) show only 23 $^{13}/_{16}$ + 1/10 fees of the earl;[6] I take it that these are part of the 52-odd knights enfeoffed in 1172. I also take it that the 10 fees owed in 1172 had risen to 14 by 1200, since they are described as held for the *vicomte* of the Bessin rather than (as previously) of the *caput* of the Bessin.[7] In addition to these fees, Ranulf also held the castles of S.-Jacques de Beuvron, Avranches, Vire and Barfleur, held as well by his grandfather Ranulf II.[8] The land once held in the west of Guernsey by the earls of Chester was no longer in their holdings by the time of Ranulf III, as it had been lost around 1142 when Geoffrey Plantagenet seized the Channel Islands.[9]

Following is a list of castles held by Ranulf III; it omits those seized and held only briefly, and those for which he was custodian for a short time. Where his tenure of them has been noticed by others (implicitly or directly), I have indicated the secondary rather than the primary source: R. Allen Brown, "A List of Castles, 1154–1216"; the page numbers are indicated in parentheses.

Castle	*County*
Bolingbroke, from 1198 on (262)	Lincs
Bowes (263)	Yorks
Chartley (265; held by Beauchamp of Lammarsh)	Stafford
Chester (265)	Chester
Degannwy (266)	Caernarvonshire
Dunham Massey (267; held by Masseys)	Chs
Hawarden (269; held by Montalts)	Flint
Holywell (269; raised by Ranulf)	Flint
? Hoseley (269)	Flint
Mold (273)	Chs
Oversleyford (Ullerwood) (275; held by the Masseys)	Chs
Pulford (275; held by the barons of Pulford)	Chs
? Wrexham (280)	Denbighshire

The following are unnoticed by Brown, since they fall outside the chronological limitations of his study.

APPENDIX 115

Beeston, begun by Ranulf in 1225 (*Ann. Cestrienses*, p. 54)
Cheylesmore (*VCH Warwick*, 2:290)
Shotwick (H. M. Colvin, ed., *The History of the King's Works*, vol. 1: *The Middle Ages*, ed. R. Allen Brown et al., p. 111)

In addition, Ranulf had custody of the following castles by royal grant.

Richmond, Yorks (1188–99; 1205–18; 1227–29; C. T. Clay, ed., *Early Yorkshire Charters*, vol. 4, pt. 1, p. 93; ibid., 5:319; *Rot. litt. pat.*, p. 51A; GB, PRO, *Patent Rolls*, Henry III, 1225–32, p. 124)
Similly, Normandy (*Rot. litt. pat.*, pp. 1, 7; Stapleton, *Magni rotuli scaccarii Normanniae*, 2:lxxxii. This was held by the earl for most of the period 1199–1204/5; other ancestral Norman castles re-granted by King John are unnoticed here.)
Newcastle-under-Lyme, Stafford (1215–23; *Rot. litt. pat.*, p. 137)
Castle Peak, Derby (1216; although the king ordered Ranulf seised with this fortress, his command was not followed. *Rot. litt. pat.*, p. 153. See Sidney Painter, *The Reign of King John*, p. 356, and J. C. Holt, *The Northerners*, p. 122, n. 1.)
Moulton, Lincs (1216; *Rot. litt. pat.*, p. 164)
Lancaster, Lancs (1216–23; *Rot. litt. pat.*, pp. 164, 176; GB, PRO, *Patent Rolls*, Henry III, 1216–25, p. 84)
Bridgenorth (Stafford), Shrewsbury (Salop) (1216–23; *Rot. litt. pat.*, p. 175)

NOTES

I. THE YOUNG EARL

1. Foote Gower, *A Sketch of the Materials for a New and Compleat History of Cheshire*, p. 16.
2. William Dugdale, *The Baronage of England*, 1:41.
3. Thomas B. Costain, *The Magnificent Century*, p. 15.
4. See my article "Ranulf III of Chester: An Outlaw of Legend?"
5. A simple genealogical chart is in William Farrer, ed., *Early Yorkshire Charters*, vol 2. See also G[eorge] E[dward] C[okayne], *The Complete Peerage*, vol. 3, s.v. "Chester," although with caution, and I. J. Sanders, *English Baronies*, s.v. "Chester," "Bolingbroke," "Huntingdon," "Lincoln."
6. *Ann. Cestrienses*, p. 24.
7. B. E. Harris, "Ranulf III, Earl of Chester," p. 101.
8. Ranulf's gifts of lands *in maritagium*: *Book of Fees*, pp. 122, 163, 168, 83, 166. See *HKF*, 2:83.
9. The marriage portions: *Book of Fees*, p. 170; GB, RC, *Placita de quo warranto temporibus Edw. I. II. & III.*, p. 433. For the date, see C[okayne], *Complete Peerage*, 4:196. Matthew Paris, *Chronica majora*, 4:645.
10. Ranulf's grants *in maritagium*: *Book of Fees*, pp. 154, 163.
11. For the earlier date, Sidney Painter, *Feudalism and Liberty*, p. 238; a date later than 1202 is unlikely, since Philip of Orby, who became justiciar of Chester in that year, here attests without the title. The marriage portions: GB, PRO, *Thirty-fifth Annual Report of the Deputy Keeper of the Public Records*, app., p. 8; GB, PRO, *Lists and Indexes, Supplementary Series*, vol. 5, pt. 3, no. 142.

12. Thomas Stapleton, ed., *Magni rotuli scaccarii Normanniae*, 1:ccxliii; GB, PRO, *Calendar of Documents Preserved in France*, vol. 1, no. 786 (too broadly dated, 1188–1214); Pierre-Hyacinthe Morice, ed., *Mémoires pour servir de preuves a l'histoire ecclésiastique et civile de Bretagne*, vol. 1, col. 707; Gui Alexis Lobineau, *Histoire de Bretagne*, 2:320; *Chester Chartulary*, p. 74; *Cal. Ch. Rolls*, 2:310–11. Both charters fall to the period 1190–94, on the grounds that Roger the Constable, who attested both, did not become constable until 1190, yet he attests without the surname de Lacy, which he adopted in 1194. The apparent reference to Earl Roger of Chester in the *Pipe Roll 5 Richard I*, p. 36, must be a scribal error rather than a reference to Roger the earl's brother; not only was Ranulf earl in 1193, but what appears to be the correct entry in the roll for 1195 reads Earl Hugh (*Pipe Roll 7 Richard I*, p. 165) in an otherwise identically worded entry. Perhaps the Roger is an incorrect extension for Ranulf, as well. Aaron the Jew of Lincoln, to whom both Roger and Hugh were said to owe money, died in 1185. Since Ranulf was then a minor, he cannot have contracted debts to Aaron.
13. For the record of a resounding controversy concerning her legitimacy, see William Beamont, ed., *Tracts Written in the Controversy Respecting the Legitimacy of Amicia, Daughter of Hugh Cyveliok, Earl of Chester*.
14. Innocent III, *The Letters of Pope Innocent III (1198–1216) concerning England and Wales*, no. 600 (1205); cf. John E. Lloyd, *A History of Wales from the Earliest Times to the Edwardian Conquest*, 2:617, n. 29. It is possible that this citation refers to the then-widowed Amicia, but there is no independent evidence that such a marriage ever was even contemplated, although such a union might well have been beneficial to the interests both of Llewelyn and of Ranulf of Chester.
15. W. F. Irvine, *Cheshire Sheaf* 44 (1919): 1134.
16. The Cheshire accounts are in *Chs in the PRs*, pp. 6–24, and singly in the pipe rolls 27 through 33 Henry II, s.v. "Cheshire" in its various Latin forms. These accounts are not well organized. See also GB, Exchequer, *Receipt Roll of the Exchequer for Michaelmas 1185* (31 Henry II).

17. Harris, "Ranulf III, Earl of Chester," p. 101; Ronald Stewart-Brown, *Serjeants of the Peace in Medieval England and Wales*, p. 4.
18. *Ann. Cestrienses*, p. 40.
19. Ibid.; C. T. Clay, ed., *Early Yorkshire Charters*, vol. 4, pt. 1, *Honour of Richmond*, p. 93. Sources reflect great confusion concerning the date of the marriage, but since Henry was in England in February of 1187 and 1188, 1189 must be the correct year.
20. "Annals of Dieulacres Abbey," p. 21.
21. Roger of Howden [Hoveden], *Chronica*, 3:237–38; Walter of Coventry, *Memoriale*, 2:52. Cf. Lionel Landon, ed., *The Itinerary of Richard I*, pp. 85–86.
22. Roger of Howden, *Chronica*, 3:240–43.
23. Ibid., 3:247–49; Walter of Coventry, *Memoriale*, 2:59; Landon, *Itinerary of Richard I*, p. 88. Matthew Paris (*Historia Anglorum*, 2:7) errs in writing that Ranulf bore the crown at Richard's coronation in 1189; Matthew is a late source for events of 1189, and his statement is nowhere corroborated. See, e.g., Landon, *Itinerary of Richard I*, pp. 3–4. On the sword, Edith M. R. Ditmas, "The Curtana or Sword of Mercy."
24. *Red Book*, pp. 755–56; see also Leopold G. Wickham Legg, *English Coronation Records*, pp. 87–88.
25. The earl of Chester bore Curtana in 1308: Thomas Rymer, ed., *Foedera*, vol. 2, pt. 1, p. 33. Legg, *English Coronation Records*, pp. 85, 180, 248.
26. J. H. Round, *The King's Serjeants and Officers of State*, pp. 384, 338–39.
27. See Chap. 4, inf., and notes.
28. Gervase of Canterbury, *Historical Works*, 1:256, cited as well by Round, *King's Serjeants*, p. 339.
29. *Pipe Roll 6 Richard I*, pp. 119, 210, 258. Some time before he left he was present when royal fines were laid: GB, RC, *Fines, sive pedes finium*, 1.lxiii.
30. F. A. Cazel, Jr., "Norman and Wessex Charters of the Roumare Family," p. 77 and nn. The members of the honor are analyzed in appendix 4.
31. On the circumstances of Richard's death, see now John Gil-

lingham, "The Unromantic Death of Richard I," pp. 18–41, and *Richard the Lionheart*, pp. 9–10, 276–77.
32. In Walter of Coventry, *Memoriale*, 2:xxvii.
33. Pierre-Hyacinthe Morice, *Histoire ecclésiastique et civile de Bretagne*, 1:124.
34. Sidney Painter, *William Marshal*, p. 121.
35. J. C. Holt, *The Northerners*, p. 4. If Holt were correct, this Ranulf's territorial ambitions would mirror those of Ranulf II.
36. Frank Barlow, *The Feudal Kingdom of England, 1042–1216*, p. 411.
37. Sidney Painter, *The Reign of King John*, p. 25.
38. "Ranulf III of Chester," p. 104.
39. On these men, see Painter, *William Marshal*; Charles R. Young, *Hubert Walter, Lord of Canterbury and Lord of England*; and Christopher R. Cheney, *Hubert Walter*.
40. Roger of Howden, *Chronica*, 4:88; Walter of Coventry, *Memoriale*, 2:145; Roger of Wendover, *Flores historiarum*, 1:285.
41. *The Making of Magna Carta*, p. 12.
42. Roger of Howden, *Chronica*, 4:89–90; Walter of Coventry, *Memoriale*, 2:146.
43. Rymer, *Foedera*, 1:75–76; for comment, Painter, *Reign of King John*, pp. 94–95.
44. Painter, *Reign of King John*, p. 24: the barons considered "truly dangerous were to be weakened by every possible means. The more moderate dissidents were to be appeased as cheaply as possible. Then the power of the barons considered reliable was to be built up and their fidelity reinforced by gratitude." None of the above policies appears to comprehend the earl of Chester.
45. Costain, *Magnificent Century*, p. 15. Actually, Costain is wrong on both counts: William Marshal was the leading peer (although Ranulf held the most knights' fees), and there were no survivors by 1199 of the aristocracy of the Conquest. If the novelist meant surviving families, he was still wrong.
46. For the following assessment of Ranulf's policies early in the reign of John, see Painter, *Reign of King John*, pp. 13, 20, 25–26.

47. The best edition of this instrument is in H. A. Cronne and R. H. C. Davis, eds., *Regesta regum Anglo-Normannorum 1066–1154*, vol. 3, no. 180.
48. "Ranulf III of Chester," p. 104.
49. "Charters of the Roumare Family," p. 78.
50. See Painter, *Reign of King John*; C. Warren Hollister, "King John and the Historians"; and J. C. Holt, *King John*.
51. Painter, *Reign of King John*, p. 25.
52. *Making of Magna Carta*, p. 12.
53. *Reign of King John*, p. 25.
54. "Ranulf III of Chester," p. 105.
55. For example, Holt, *Making of Magna Carta*, pp. 12–13.
56. Ibid.
57. Ed. Joseph Stevenson, in Radulphus de Coggeshall, *Chronicon Anglicanum*.
58. The actual revolt is discussed by Painter, *Reign of King John*, 48ff.
59. *Red Book*, 2:626. For the later figures, *RHF*, 23:611, 612, 620ff., 633, 636; and Louis-Amédée Léchaudé-d'Anisy, ed., *Grands rôles des échiquiers de Normandie*, 15: 177, 185, 187. It remains true that Ranulf's "scattered fiefs in Normandy deserve elaborate study," as F. M. Powicke observed more than six decades ago (*The Loss of Normandy*, p. 336).
60. Cronne and Davis, *Regesta regum Anglo-Normannorum*, vol. 3, no. 180; to the list of printed editions cited by the editors of the *Regesta*, add Léopold Delisle and Elie Berger, eds., *Recueil des actes de Henri II*, 2:56–57. See also Stapleton, *Magni Rotuli scaccarii Normanniae*, 1: xciv, ccxliv, ccxlv. Although the earls of Chester had held land in Fief le Conte, western Guernsey, they lost it as a result of Ranulf II's opposing the Plantagenets in the civil war of Stephen's reign. Duke Geoffrey of Anjou captured the island in 1142 and divided the fee (John H. le Patourel, *The Medieval Administration of the Channel Islands*, pp. 26, 107). Most of the exchequer accounts for Ranulf's Norman lands before 1204 contribute nothing of interest to Ranulf's biography; they may be found in Léchaudé-d'Anisy, *Grands rôles*, 1: 40, 81, 113, and 2: 113, 37, 92, 94; Stapleton,

Magni rotuli scaccarii Normanniae, 1:40 and 2:497, 383, 531ff., 536–37; Sidney Packard, ed., *Miscellaneous Records of the Norman Exchequer, 1199–1204*, pp. 37–38.
61. *Ann. Cestrienses*, p. 40.
62. Lloyd, *History of Wales*, 1:570; also John Beeler, *Warfare in England, 1066–1189*, p. 262.
63. Sanders, *English Baronies*, pp. 140–41. For Richmond, see C[okayne], *Complete Peerage*, s.v. "Richmond"; Thomas Durham Whitaker, *History of Richmondshire*, and the relevant volumes of *VCH Yorkshire*. The charters of the honor are printed in Clay, *Early Yorkshire Charters*, vols. 4 and 5. Slightly differing versions of the *Genealogia comitum Richmundiae post conquestam Angliae* may be found in *RHF*, 12:569 and in *Monasticon*, 5:574–75.
64. Clay, *Early Yorkshire Charters*, 4:73–74.
65. Morice, *Histoire ecclésiastique*, 1:119. The identical words are found in the earlier work of Lobineau, *Histoire de Bretagne*, 1:172.
66. *Chronicon Briocense*, in Morice, *Mémoires*, vol. 1, col. 40; A. de la Borderie, *Histoire de Bretagne*, 3:286.
67. Kate Norgate, *England under the Angevin Kings*, 2:370.
68. De la Borderie, *Histoire de Bretagne*, p. 272.
69. Walter of Coventry, *Memoriale*, 2:98; Roger of Howden, *Chronica*, 4:7–8. Roger is the source for the rather apoplectic narrative of Morice, *Histoire ecclésiastique*, 1:120–21.
70. C[okayne], *Complete Peerage*, 10:795; Clay, *Early Yorkshire Charters*, 4:93. Both parties were great-grandchildren of Henry I. *Monasticon*, 5:574; *RHF*, 12:569.
71. John Leland, *Collectanea*, vol. 1, pt. 2, pp. 534–35.
72. *Ann. Cestrienses*, p. 46; Ranulf Higden, *Polychronicon*, 8:76; F. M. Powicke, *King Henry III and the Lord Edward*, p. 177, n. 1.
73. *Ann. monastici*, 1:338 (Higden, *Polychronicon*, 8:176).
74. Painter, *Reign of King John*, p. 26; W. L. Warren, *King John*, p. 109.
75. For Fougères, see A. de la Borderie, *Essai sur la géographie féodale de la Bretagne*, pp. 10, 86–88.
76. The composition is best edited in Lewis C. Lloyd and Doris M.

Stenton, eds., *Sir Christopher Hatton's Book of Seals*, no. 236. See also George Ormerod, *The History of the County Palatine and the City of Chester*, 1:39; GB, PRO, *Lists and Indexes, Supplementary Series*, vol. 5, pt. 2, *Duchy of Lancaster . . . Royal Charters*, vol. 1, no. 268; GB, RC, *Rotuli de oblatis et finibus in turri Londinensi asservati tempore regis Johannis*, p. 43. John's confirmation: *Rot. chart.*, p. 104 (Rouen, 1203).

77. GB, RC, *Rotuli de oblatis*, p. 43; *Pipe Roll 4 John*, p. 231, is the first appearance of the balance of seventy-five marks; it was still carried on GB, PRO, Pipe Roll 66 (1222; E.372/66, m.14). Since William du Hommet chose to follow the king of France when Normandy was lost, there was no practical reason why he should have honored his obligation.
78. *Ann. monastici*, 1:338 (Higden, *Polychronicon*, 8:176); Leland, *Collectanea*, vol. 1, pt. 2, p. 534.
79. Landon, *Itinerary of Richard I*, p. 118; Pierre Chaplais, ed., *Diplomatic Documents Preserved in the Public Record Office*, 1:18–20 and source there cited, to which add Rigord, *Gesta Philippi Augusti*.
80. GB, PRO, *Calendar of Documents France*, no. 1363; *Rot. chart.*, 1:30; Rymer, *Foedera*, 1:77.
81. *Rot. litt. pat.*, 1:1; Stapleton, *Magni rotuli scaccarii Normanniae*, 2:lxxxii.
82. Stapleton, *Magni rotuli scaccarii Normanniae*, 2:ccxliii.
83. GB, RC, *Rotuli Normanniae in Turri Londinensi asservati*, 1:39; Léchaudé-d'Anisy, *Grands rôles*, 1:103; Stapleton, *Magni rotuli scaccarii Normanniae*, 2:ccxliii. Stapleton also shows that fifty pounds of the proffer remained unpaid in 1203.
84. Stapleton, *Magni rotuli scaccarii Normanniae*, 2:cxlv; Léchaudé-d'Anisy, *Grands rôles*, 1:104.
85. Harris, "Ranulf III of Chester," p. 105.
86. The story is pieced together from the following sources: GB, RC, *Rotuli Normanniae*, pp. 96–97; Léchaudé-d'Anisy, *Grands rôles*, 1:122–23; *Rot. litt. pat.*, 1:28–29. For comment, see Painter, *Reign of King John*, pp. 26–27; Harris, "Ranulf III of Chester," p. 105. Warren, *King John*, p. 109, found that Ranulf "behaved with dignity and tact" after being made "a butt for the king's bad temper."

87. *Reign of King John*, pp. 26–27.
88. *Rot. litt. pat.*, 1:30.
89. GB, PRO, *Calendar of Liberate Rolls*, 1:103.
90. Powicke, *Loss of Normandy*, p. 258. For the impact of the loss of Normandy on English affairs, see also Holt, *Northerners*, chap. 9.

II. LOYALIST BARON

1. I follow, in general, the interpretations of the reign set forth in Painter, *Reign of King John* and *William Marshal*, augmented by J. C. Holt, *Northerners* and *Magna Carta*. Discussions of the historiography of the reign are most conveniently found in Hollister, "King John and the Historians," and Holt, *King John*, particularly valuable for criticism of the narrative sources.
2. *Reign of King John*, pp. 54–55.
3. *Rot. litt. claus.*, 1:1.
4. Ibid., 1:10. The pipe-roll entries for 1204 contribute nothing to a biography of Ranulf: he was quit of scutage payments in three counties (*Pipe Roll 6 John*, pp. 16, 152, 172).
5. *Rot. litt. claus.*, 1:16. Similar distraint fell upon Roger de Montbegon.
6. *Angevin Kingship*, p. 119.
7. *Rot. litt. pat.*, 1:48b. Jolliffe points out that the king's action in ordering the seizure of Ranulf's and Roger's lands and chattels constituted "distraint without judgment" (*Angevin Kingship*, p. 119).
8. *Reign of King John*, p. 29.
9. Holt, *Making of Magna Carta*, pp. 12–13.
10. One of these, the castellany of S.-Jacques de Beuvron, passed to Guy de Thouars, Constance's third husband, thence to Simon de Dammartin (Philip Augustus, *Recueil des actes de Philippe Auguste*, vol. 2, no. 939; Léopold Delisle, *Cartulaire normand* no. 141), and finally to the rambunctious Peter of Dreux, duke of Brittany, in 1226. For Peter, who will appear again in Ranulf's history, see Sidney Painter, *The Scourge of*

the Clergy: Peter of Dreux, Duke of Brittany, esp. p. 37 for the date.
11. Ann. monastici, 4:393 (Worcester).
12. Clay, Early Yorkshire Charters, vol. 5, pt. 1 (Honor of Richmond), p. 79; the grant excluded the castles of Richmond and Bowes, as well as 9¾ fees retained by the king. Cf. Rot. litt. pat., p. 34b.
13. Rot. litt. pat., p. 51; Clay, Early Yorkshire Charters, vol. 5, pt. 1 (Honor of Richmond), p. 79.
14. Sanders, English Baronies, pp. 140–41.
15. Reign of King John, pp. 27–28.
16. Making of Magna Carta, p. 13. Painter, Reign of King John, p. 29, also stated that John tried "to buy [Ranulf's] loyalty."
17. The point is made by Holt, Northerners, p. 225.
18. Rot. litt. claus., 1:30.
19. Ibid., 1:30, 46.
20. Pipe Roll 7 John, pp. 9, 33 (cf. p. xxv), 62, 64, 65, 218. Pipe Roll 8 John, p. 4.
21. Rot. litt. pat., 1:56; GB, PRO, Calendar of Documents Relating to Scotland, vol. 1, no. 371; GB, RC, Rotuli selecti ad res Anglicas et Hibernicas, p. 1.
22. GB, PRO, Calendar of Documents Scotland, vol. 1, no. 450; Rot. litt. pat., 1:91.
23. Rot. litt. claus., 1:18, 74, 74b. Robert's heirs were still in Ranulf's custody in 1208 (Pipe Roll 17 John, p. 25).
24. Rot. litt. claus., 1:107. The March 1208 grant of all manors of the bishop of Coventry in Cheshire is probably related to John's policies in reaction to the interdict; the order did not follow on the death of Bishop Geoffrey de Muskham, who died in October of 1208 (Rot. litt. claus., 1:107).
25. Rot. litt. pat., vol. 1, no. 1, p. 62 (GB, RC, Rotuli selecti, p. 27).
26. Rot. litt. claus., 1: 66b, 147. Royñg appears in the index volume of the Book of Fees and elsewhere only as an Essex place-name; since there is no evidence that Ranulf held in Essex, I have assumed that the park was not in that county. A further small grant (Rot. litt. claus., 1:122) of provisions falls to August 1212.
27. Rot. litt. claus., 1:122 (GB, PRO, Calendar of Documents Re-

lating to Ireland, vol. 1, no. 439) and 163. The average price of the king's wine varied from less than a pound per tun to somewhat more than two pounds in the later years of John's reign (*Pipe Roll 8 John*, pp. xii, xiii, 144, 217; *Pipe Roll 12 John*, p. xxxvii).

28. *Pipe Roll 10 John*, p. 57; *Praestita Roll 14 John*, in *Pipe Roll 17 John*, p. 89.
29. The best introduction to English-Welsh relations to 1282 remains Lloyd, *History of Wales*, vol. 2.
30. Austin Lane Poole, *From Domesday Book to Magna Carta*, p. 299.
31. *Rot. litt. pat.*, vol. 1, pt. 1, p. 88.
32. *Ann. monastici*, 4:397 (Waverley).
33. *Ann. monastici*, 3:32 (Dunstable); Gervase of Canterbury, *Historical Works*, 2:106. *Pipe Roll 12 John*, p. xxxiii, noting the campaign, describes the justiciar, the bishop, and Ranulf as "the guardians of the kingdom during the king's absence"; the footnotes do not substantiate this designation for the earl of Chester.
34. Dugdale, *Baronage of England*, 1:42; *Brut y Twysogion*; three castles are mentioned by the Dunstable annalist (*Ann. monastici*).
35. *Historical Works*, 2:106.
36. The narrative appears in the following sources: *Cheshire Sheaf* 40 (1945), no. 8626; W. T. Lancaster and W. Paley Baildon, eds., *The Coucher Book of the Cistercian Abbey of Kirkstall*, 8:241–42; *Monasticon*, vol. 6, pt. 1, pp. 315–16; *Journal of the Chester Archaeological and Historical Society*, n.s. 3 (1890): 254 (which errs in assigning the date to 1212, since Roger the constable of Chester died in 1211). John's charter is in Ormerod, *History of Chester*, 1:36.
37. *Reign of King John*, p. 266. Some indication of the massive preparations are to be found in *Pipe Roll 14 John*, pp. xxxij.
38. Notices concerning Ranulf and the proposed Welsh campaign are in the Mise Roll 14 John (GB, RC, *Documents Illustrative of English History*, pp. 266, 253, 247, 238, 249); *Rot. litt. claus.*, 1:121.

39. *Rot. litt. pat.*, 1:100.
40. On him, see two excellent biographies: Young, *Hubert Walter*; and Cheney, *Hubert Walter*.
41. On Stephen, see F. M. Powicke, *Stephen Langton*; and John W. Baldwin, *Masters, Merchants, and Princes: The Social Views of Peter the Chanter and His Circle*, esp. 1:25–31.
42. Innocent III, *Letters of Innocent III*, nos. 941 and 962, and sources there cited.
43. Innocent III, *Letters*, no. 935, and sources. GB, PRO, *The Calendar of Entries in the Papal Registers Relating to Great Britain and Ireland*, 1:39 directs the charge to relations between the king and the *Anglican* [sic] church.
44. *Rot. litt. pat.*, 1: 98–99, 114.
45. C. W. Foster, ed., *The Registrum Antiquissimum of the Cathedral Church of Lincoln*, vol. 1.
46. GB, RCHM. *Fifth Report*, pt. 1, app., pp. 430–31, 454 (more fully).
47. *Rot. chart.*, 1:208b–9; Innocent III, *Letters*, no. 976, and sources there cited.
48. For a discussion of the rather tricky history of this aspect of the Langton controversy, see Painter, *Reign of King John*, pp. 194–202.
49. F. M. Powicke and C. R. Cheney, *Councils and Synods, with Other Documents Relating to the English Church*, vol. 2, pt. 1 (1205–65), pp. 40–41; *Rot. chart.*, 1:202. Reissue: *Foedera*, 1:126–27; *Monasticon*, 2:605–6; Matthew Paris, *Chronica majora*, 2:608–10. Innocent III, *Letters*, no. 1004, and sources there cited.
50. For the 1214 campaigns, see Painter, *Reign of King John*, pp. 226–28, 278–81; Poole, *Domesday Book to Magna Carta*, pp. 458–68.
51. Rymer, *Foedera*, 1:105; Guillelmus Armoricus, *Gesta Philippi Augusti*, in *RHF*, 17: 87–88, 90–91; Rymer, *Foedera*, 1:125; *Rot. chart.*, pp. 197b–98.
52. Guillelmus Armoricus, in *RHF*, 17:103–4 (Guillaume le Breton [Guillelmus Armoricus], *Oeuvres*, p. 298. *Chronico Alberici Trium-Fontium*, in *RHF*, 18:783; *Les gestes de Philippe-*

Auguste, in *RHF*, 17:415; *Rot. litt. pat.*, p. 140 (Rymer, *Foedera*, 1:124). The truce: France, Ministère d'état, *Layettes de Trésor des Chartes*, vol. 1, nos. 1082, 1083.
53. William Stubbs, *The Constitutional History of England*, 2:47.
54. *Northerners*, p. 228.
55. Margaret Wade Labarge, *Simon de Montfort*, pp. 28–29.
56. Painter, *Reign of King John*, pp. 250, 304–5.
57. *Northerners*, pp. 44–46.
58. Holt indicates that the earl's tenants in Richmondshire were in rebellion both against him and against the king.
59. The best treatments of these complicated matters are found in Painter, *Reign of King John*, and *William Marshal*, pp. 170–227; and Holt, *Northerners*. Holt's *Magna Carta*, while not specifically a study of the history of the revolt and civil war, has much of value for the topic.
60. A survey of the literature is Hollister, "King John and the Historians."
61. Poole, *Domesday Book to Magna Carta*, p. 470.
62. Chaplais, *Diplomatic Documents*, vol. 1, no. 19; Walter of Coventry, *Memoriale*, 2:225.
63. Frank Scott Haydon, ed., *Eulogium . . . a monacho quodam Malmesburiensi exaratum*, 3:8 (Leland, *Collectanea*, 2:397). Yet, despite their lack of practical application, manuscripts of the Confessor's laws were still being "copied as late as the fifteenth century": H. G. Richardson, "The English Coronation Oath."
64. Henry Knighton, *Chronicon*, 1:85–86.
65. Harris, "Ranulf III of Chester," p. 112.
66. Gervase of Canterbury, *Historical Works*, 2:109.
67. Below, pp. 77–80.
68. *Rot. litt. pat.*, vol. 1, pt. 1, p. 137. *Rot. chart.*, vol. 1, pt. 1, p. 216. While the original grant specified that the castle was to be held as long as the king wished, the confirmation grants it as long as the earl had heirs of the body to hold it; failing heirs, it was to revert to the king or to his descendants. Ranulf is last noticed as custodian of Newcastle-under-Lyme in 1223; GB, PRO, *Pipe Roll 7 Henry III* (E.372/67), m. 1d.
69. Holt, *Magna Carta*, p. 269.

70. See below, pp. 63–64.
71. Roger of Wendover, *Flores historiarum*, 2:117; Matthew Paris, *Chronica majora*, 2:587–88.
72. *Reign of King John*, pp. 337–38.
73. *Rot. litt. pat.*, vol. 1, pt. 1, p. 150; L. W. Vernon Harcourt, *His Grace the Steward and Trial of Peers*, pp. 104, 196–98. Charles Bémont, *Simon de Montfort, Earl of Leicester*, p. 3, errs in saying that Ranulf received the honor "in full ownership, with all its dependent rights and emoluments." Labarge, *Simon de Montfort*, p. 20, has the terms of the grant correct. For Leicester, see Levi Fox, "The Honor and Earldom of Leicester: Origin and Descent, 1066–1399." *Cal. Patent Rolls*, 1225–32, p. 127.
74. *Rot. litt. pat.*, vol. 1, pt. 1, p. 150; GB, PRO, *Calendar of Documents Ireland*, vol. 1, no. 624.
75. *Rot. litt. pat.*, vol. 1, pt. 1, p. 153.
76. *Reign of King John*, p. 356.
77. *Northerners*, p. 122 and p. 140, n. 1.
78. Rymer, *Foedera*, 1:137. The sheriffs of eight counties were informed that John had returned to the king's allegiance on January 3: *Rot. litt. claus.*, vol. 1, pt. 1, p. 244.
79. Painter, *Reign of King John*, p. 369; *Rot. litt. pat.*, vol. 1, pt. 1, p. 163. Ruald fitzAlan, hereditary constable of the castle, made his peace with the king on the ninth: *Rot. litt. claus.*, vol. 1, pt. 1, p. 245.
80. *Rot. chart.*, p. 221b; William Farrer, ed., *The Lancashire Pipe Rolls and Early Lancashire Charters*, p. 258; GB, RC, *Rotuli de oblatis*, pp. 570–71; Rymer, *Foedera*, 1:136.
81. *Rot. litt. pat.*, vol. 1, pt. 1, pp. 164–64b, 176. He was also named sheriff in Lancashire: ibid., and *Pipe Roll 2 Henry III*, p. xvi, where he replaced Gilbert fitz Renfrew.
82. For what here follows, see, inter alia, H. A. Cronne, "Ranulf de Gernons, Earl of Chester, 1129–1153," and "The Honour of Lancaster in Stephen's Reign"; J. H. Round, "King Stephen and the Earl of Chester."
83. *Regesta regum Anglo-Normannorum*, vol. 3, no. 178.
84. *Rot. litt. pat.*, vol. 1, pt. 1, p. 164.
85. Ibid., 167.
86. Ibid., 175; p. 193 adds the grant of Shrewsbury. R. W. Eyton,

Antiquities of Shropshire, 1:273. He yielded the shrievalties for a year to John Lestrange but was reinstated in 1217: *Pipe Roll 2 Henry III*, p. xvj.
87. *Pipe Roll 17 John*, p. 5; *Pipe Roll 2 Henry III*, pp. xvj, 2, 5.
88. *Reign of King John*, p. 357.
89. While the most important grants to Ranulf attendant upon the rebellion are discussed in the text, there are in addition numerous less grand marks of royal favor from King John: the right to take scutage in the fees which he held in chief in Yorkshire (*Scutage Roll 16 John*, in *Pipe Roll 17 John*, p. 108); grants of small parcels of land (*Rot. litt. claus.*, vol. 1, pt. 1, pp. 194b, 286); custody of lands temporarily in the king's hands (*Rot. litt. claus.*, 1: 313b, 314b, 347; Doris M. Stenton, ed., *Rolls of the Justices in Eyre . . . for Yorkshire in 3 Henry III*, no. 34); custody of some rebels and their heirs (*Rot. litt. claus.*, 1: 167, 192b; *Rot. litt. pat.*, vol. 1, pt. 1, pp. 110, 143, 164, 174b, 193); licenses for Ranulf's men to trade (*Rot. litt. pat.*, vol. 1, pt. 1, pp. 164, 176, 177); a gift of wine (*Rot. litt. claus.*, 2:283). Ranulf was in addition given custody of all lands of the king's enemies which were held of him (*Rot. litt. claus.*, 1: 233, 241); as Doris M. Stenton suggested, this grant "represents John's policy of giving a loyal tenant-in-chief possession of his rebellious tenants' lands. In this way the earl of Chester must have obtained temporary possession of extensive territories" (*Rolls of the Justices in Eyre . . . for Lincolnshire 1218–19 and Worcestershire 1221*, p. lviii and notes).
90. For the French invasion and its aftermath, see Painter, *Reign of King John*, pp. 375ff.
91. *Rot. litt. pat.*, vol. 1, pt. 1, p. 186; Rymer, *Foedera*, 1:141. For other examples of John's ordering castles to be razed, see Holt, *Northerners*, p. 138.
92. Painter, *Reign of King John*, p. 375, and *William Marshal*, pp. 187–88, and sources there cited, to which add Annals of Tewkesbury, in *Ann. monastici*, 1:62.
93. *Cal. Ch. Rolls*, 1:154–55; Reginald R. Darlington, ed., *The Cartulary of Worcester Cathedral Priory*, no. 328.
94. Rymer, *Foedera*, 1:144; translation in Warren, *King John*, p. 255.

95. *Northerners*, p. 252.
96. *King John*, p. 231.

III. A PINCHPENNY PATRON

1. I acknowledge with gratitude the permission of Father M. Basil Pennington of Spencer Abbey to use much of the material relating to Ranulf's patronage of the Cistercian order, as well as the title of this chapter, in this biography: see James W. Alexander, "A Pinchpenny Patron: Ranulf III of Chester."
2. Bennett Hill, *English Cistercian Monasteries and Their Patrons in the Twelfth Century*, p. 64.
3. David Knowles, *The Religious Orders in England*, 1:5.
4. H. M. Colvin, *The White Canons in England*, p. 38.
5. Susan Wood, *English Monasteries and Their Patrons in the Thirteenth Century*, p. 1.
6. Bennett Hill, *Cistercian Monasteries*, p. 51.
7. J. P. Earwaker, *East Cheshire*, 2:432; George Sitwell, *The Barons of Pulford*, pp. 70–71. Earwaker prints the fuller abstract of the charter, Sitwell the fuller witness list.
8. GB, PRO, *Calendar of Documents France*, vol. 1, no. 858; Delisle and Berger, *Recueil des actes*, p. 423, n. 4. For the order of Savigny, merged with the Cistercians since 1148, see Bennett Hill, *Cistercian Monasteries*, pp. 80–116 and notes, and "The Counts of Mortain and the Origins of the Norman Congregation of Savigny," pp. 237–54; Léon Guilloreau, "Les fondations anglaises de l'abbaye de Savigny," pp. 290–335.
9. *Cheshire Sheaf* 52 (1957): 17–27.
10. The dream: *Monasticon*, 5:627–28; *Cheshire Sheaf* 52 (1957): 17–27 contains all the narrative material cited from the foundation history in the *Monasticon*—the editor points out Dugdale's error in ascribing this annal to Henry of Huntingdon. See Alexander, "Pinchpenny Patron," p. 26, n. 14, for a discussion of Wrottesley's amusing suggestion that the foundation of Dieulacres was somehow connected with a (nonexistent) papal dispensation from Ranulf's marriage to Constance of Brittany

(George Wrottesley, ed., *Chartulary of Dieulacres Abbey*, p. 294). For the completion of the precincts, see additionally Higden, *Polychronicon*, 8:198 (Knighton, *Chronicon*, 1:210). The completion of the Dieulacres buildings, associated with the raising of Chartley and Beeston castles, is commemorated in a to-be-forgotten poem found in John W. Hale and F. J. Furnivall, eds., *Bishop Percy's Folio Manuscript*, 1:281–90, the relevant portion (p. 281) of which reads, after bringing Ranulf home from crusade,

>instantlye on his returne
>resoluing now to live in peace
>the great strong castel of Beeston
>he built, with the abbey of Delacreese
>& Chortley castle: — in two yeeres
>those 2 great castles finished were
>in 1220ty
>they were finished perfectlye.

Weep, Muse.
11. *Monasticon*, 5:628.
12. *Monasticon*, 5:629; *Cal. Ch. Rolls*, 4:153; GB, PRO, *Close Rolls Henry III*, 1231–34, pp. 122 (royal confirmation at Ranulf's request), 221. See also GB, RC, *Calendarium rotulorum chartarum et inquisitionum ad quod damnum*, p. 305. For the "perhaps unintentional" grant, with the manor of Leek, of an advowson, see Wood, *English Monasteries*, p. 21. The charter is the springboard for my article ("New Evidence on the Palatinate of Chester") attacking the palatine status of Cheshire in and before Ranulf's time.
13. "Annals of Dieulacres Abbey," p. 24.
14. William Farrer, ed., *Final Concords of the County of Lancaster*, 1:55n; *Rot. litt. claus.*, 1:284. GB, PRO, *Close Rolls Henry III*, 1227–31, pp. 35, 62–63 (1228) (Wrottesley, *Chartulary of Dieulacres Abbey*, p. 341).
15. GB, PRO, Fine Roll 12 Henry III, m. 3.
16. GB, PRO, *Calendar of Charter Rolls Preserved in the Public Record Office*, 4:153–54; *Monasticon*, 5:620; Wrottesley,

Chartulary of Dieulacres Abbey, p. 363. After 1229, since William de Vernon attests as justiciar of Chester, to which office he succeeded in that year.
17. Wrottesley, *Chartulary of Dieulacres Abbey*, p. 315.
18. Ibid., p. 327; GB, PRO, *Calendar of Charter Rolls*, 4:155.
19. For Leek, see Wrottesley, *Chartulary of Dieulacres Abbey*, p. 311 (pp. 311–12 for confirmations); GB, PRO, *Calendar of Charter Rolls*, 4:153; Stephen Langton, *Acta Stephani Langton, 1207–1228*, no. 60 (confirmation). For Sandbach, see GB, PRO, *Calendar of Charter Rolls*, 4:153; Francis Gastrell, ed., *Notitia Cestriensis*, Chetham Society, OS 8, 1:253.
20. *Chester Chartulary*, no. 384, where the attribution to Ranulf III is based upon very puzzling conjecture.
21. Ibid., no. 52.
22. Ibid., no. 147.
23. William Farrer, ed., *Lancashire Inquests, Extents, and Feudal Aids*, 1:230; *VCH Lancashire*, 3:332.
24. Henry III's general confirmation of gifts to this abbey, *Monasticon*, 3:523.
25. *Cheshire Sheaf*, 3d ser., 11 (1914): 88 (no. 2663). If the donor is indeed Ranulf III, the editor's dating is wrong here (1185), since the earl did not come into his majority until 1188/89.
26. GB, PRO, *Calendar of Documents France*, no. 786; Morice, *Mémoires*, vol. 1, col. 707; Lobineau, *Histoire de Bretagne*, 2:320; Stapleton, *Magni rotuli scaccarii Normanniae*, 1:ccxliii. This charter is one of two issued by Ranulf III that are attested by Roger the earl's brother, of whose life there is no other record.
27. *Book of Fees*, p. 155.
28. The most important citations are: *Cal. Ch. Rolls*, 1:204; Doris M. Stenton, *Rolls of the Justices in Eyre . . . for Gloucestershire, Warwickshire, and Staffordshire, 1221, 1222*, nos. 1055, 1363; *Curia Regis Rolls* 11, nos. 290, 743; George Wrottesley, ed., *The Stone Chartulary*, Staffordshire Record Society, vol. 7 (1885), p. 5; *VCH Staffordshire*, 8:77.
29. Thomas Sharp, *Illustrative Papers on the History and Antiquities of the City of Coventry*, p. 197; *VCH Warwick*, 2:103, 8:18.

The grant lies after the autumn of 1224, when the first Franciscans arrived in England, and probably toward the end of the earl's life.
30. *Book of Fees*, p. 174.
31. *Chester Chartulary*, nos. 315 and 53; ibid., no. 598, and *Cal. Ch. Rolls*, 2:310.
32. *Cal. Ch. Rolls*, 5:102; William Dugdale, *The Antiquities of Warwickshire*, p. 102; H. E. Savage, ed., *The Great Register of Lichfield Cathedral, Known as Magnum Registrum Album*, no. 500 (July 1192).
33. Delisle, *Cartulaire normand*, p. 97; 1188–1204.
34. Stapleton, *Magni rotuli scaccarii Normanniae*, 2:ciii n.d.; GB, PRO, *Calendar of Liberate Rolls*, 1:209; GB, PRO, *Close Rolls Henry III*, 1231–34, p. 210.
35. *Rot. chart.*, 1:47b–48; *Cal. Ch. Rolls.*, 4:163.
36. William A. Hulton, ed., *The Coucher Book or Chartulary of Whalley Abbey*, 1:12–13.
37. GB, PRO, *Close Rolls Henry III*, 1231–34, p. 334.
38. W. Rich Jones, ed., *The Register of St. Osmund*, RS, 78, 1:265; *Cheshire Sheaf*, 3d ser., 12 (1915):62 (no. 2900) attributes the grant to Ranulf Gernons.
39. Geoffrey Barraclough, ed., *Facsimiles of Early Cheshire Charters*, p. 27; *Monasticon*, 6:756; Ronald Stewart-Brown, "The Hospital of St. John at Chester," pp. 66–67; Ormerod, *History of Chester*, 1:351.
40. GB, PRO, *Calendar of Liberate Rolls*, 1: 405 and 451.
41. *Chester Chartulary*, p. 96; Gastrell, *Notitia Cestriensis*, 1:117.
42. GB, Exchequer, *Documents Illustrative of English History in the Thirteenth and Fourteenth Centuries*, pp. 169, 215. For general information about medieval English lepers and leprosy, see Stanley Rubin, *Medieval English Medicine*, chap. 6, and Edward J. Kealey, *Medieval Medicus: A Social History of Anglo-Norman Medicine*.
43. See (inter alia) GB, PRO, *Calendar of Liberate Rolls*, 2: 49 and 70, 4:144; GB, PRO, *Close Rolls Henry III*, 1275, p. 209; *Chs in the PRs*, p. 129, Wimark's last appearance in the financial records.

44. *Cheshire Sheaf*, 3d ser., 35 (1940), no. 7837g; Wrottesley, *Chartulary of Dieulacres Abbey*, p. 328.
45. Wrottesley, *Chartulary of Dieulacres Abbey*, pp. 310–11.
46. *Monasticon*, 5:332.
47. *Cistercian Monasteries*, pp. 75ff.
48. Sitwell, *Barons of Pulford*, pp. 70–71; Earwaker, *East Cheshire*, p. 432.
49. *Monasticon*, 1:632.
50. *Cal. Ch. Rolls*, 1:310.
51. Like the previous grant, late in the 1190s; *Cal. Ch. Rolls*, 4:163; *Rot. chart.*, 1:47b–48.
52. Ephraim Lipson, *The Economic History of England*, 1:282–83; a discussion of the topic of immunity from tolls and its ramifications is on pp. 279–87.
53. GB, PRO, *Calendar of Documents France*, no. 538; but this immunity may have applied to English lands as well, since Aunay held lands in Northhamptonshire and Lincolnshire: Donald Matthew, *The Norman Monasteries and Their English Possessions*, p. 118.
54. 1189–1217; *Cal. Ch. Rolls*, 2:290 (cf. GB, RC, *Placita de Quo Warranto*, p. 155).
55. 1207–15; Lloyd and Stenton, *Hatton's Book of Seals*, no. 116.
56. 1230; *Cal. Ch. Rolls*, 4:208–9; *Monasticon*, 5:325.
57. 1217–26; *Cal. Ch. Rolls*, 4:154; Wrottesley, *Chartulary of Dieulacres Abbey*, p. 353.
58. Hulton, *Coucher of Whalley*, pp. 10–11 (early thirteenth century); like the previous charter, this specifically mentions salt as well as all other things which the monks shall buy or sell for their own use.
59. Barraclough, *Early Cheshire Charters*, p. 43, no. 14; *Chester Chartulary*, p. 251, no. 395.
60. *Cal. Ch. Rolls*, 1:427–28; *Monasticon*, 5:324; probably shortly after Ranulf's accession to comital power.
61. Wrottesley, *Chartulary of Dieulacres Abbey*, p. 331; *Cal. Ch. Rolls*, 4:156; William Ayrton, "Records Relating to the River Dee and Its Fisheries," p. 237. For a brief account of the importance of the Cheshire fisheries, see H. J. Hewitt, *Mediaeval*

Cheshire: An Economic and Social History of Cheshire in the Reigns of the Three Edwards, app. F.
62. Hulton, Coucher of Whalley, p. 392; Barraclough, Early Cheshire Charters, p. 25, shows the instrument falling to the period 1199–1203.
63. Cal. Ch. Rolls, 4:154 (no. 11).
64. Ibid., no. 12.
65. Ibid., pp. 154–55 (no. 13).
66. Ibid., p. 155 (no. 14); Wrottesley, Chartulary of Dieulacres Abbey, p. 327.
67. Geoffrey Barraclough, "Some Charters of the Earls of Chester," p. 43, no. 14; abstract in Chester Chartulary, p. 251 (no. 395).
68. Monasticon, 5:325; Cal. Ch. Rolls, 4:208–9; GB, PRO, Twenty-eighth Annual Report of the Deputy Keeper of the Public Records, p. 27.
69. Frank M. Stenton, ed., Documents Illustrative of the Social and Economic History of the Danelaw, 5:cviii, n. 1 (1216–32). VCH Lincoln, 2:155, notes that the house "has very little history."
70. GB, PRO, A Descriptive Catalogue of Ancient Deeds, vol. 1, no. A203.
71. Cal. Ch. Rolls, 1:292.
72. Sidney Painter, Studies in the History of the English Feudal Barony, p. 105.
73. Ibid., p. 116.
74. Ibid., p. 91.
75. See, among many possible sources, ibid., pp. 102–4; Frank M. Stenton, The First Century of English Feudalism, 1066–1166, pp. 104–6; Naomi Hurnard, "The Anglo-Norman Franchises," p. 437.
76. Wood, English Monasteries, pp. 159–60.
77. Clay, Early Yorkshire Charters, vol. 4, pt. 1, pp. 77–78 and plate xv; Monasticon, 6:1114.
78. GB, PRO, Calendar of Documents France, no. 858; cf. Delisle and Berger, Recueil des actes, 4:423, n. 4.
79. Hugh of Welles, Rotuli Hugonis de Welles, episcopi Lincolniensis, 3:151; Monasticon, 4:430.
80. Chester Chartulary, p. 72. The history of the house as outlined

by Tait has not been challenged, let alone superseded, by the superbly incompetent work of R. V. H. Burne, *The Monks of Chester: The History of St. Werburgh's Abbey*. The *Victoria County History of Cheshire* is now being prepared under the editorship of Brian Harris; it should adhere to the high standards of historical scholarship which characterize the more recent volumes of the Victoria histories.
81. William Urry, *Canterbury under the Angevin Kings*, p. 29.
82. *Ann. Cestrienses*, p. 44; Ranulf's pressure is also noted by Urry, *Canterbury*, p. 29. Burne, *Monks of Chester*, p. 13, finds Ranulf muscling into the quarrel "on his return from the Holy Land in 1194"; Ranulf did not leave for crusade until 1218, returning in 1220. The error typifies the reliability of this book. See also M. V. Taylor, ed., *Obits of St. Werburgh's*, in Lucianus, *Liber Luciani de laude Cestrie*.
83. Wrottesley, *Chartulary of Dieulacres Abbey*, pp. 354–55; *Monasticon*, 5:628; *Cal. Ch. Rolls*, 3:154.
84. See Cazel, "Charters of the Roumare Family," p. 77.
85. The case is briefly alluded to by Wood, *English Monasteries*, p. 144; a full discussion, with the emended text of the dispute *ex parte* Croyland, is printed in Doris M. Stenton, *English Justice between the Norman Conquest and the Great Charter, 1066–1215*, pp. 148–211.
86. Wood, *English Monasteries*, p. 144; her citation is to the edition of the case printed by Fulman, now superseded by Doris M. Stenton's edition, wherein the incident referred to is found on p. 198.
87. *English Justice*, p. 149.
88. The dispute is referred to by Wood, *English Monasteries*, p. 62.
89. Hugh of Welles, *Rotuli Hugonis de Welles*, 3:185–86.
90. GB, PRO, The Great Cowcher Books of the Duchy of Lancaster, DL 42/2, ff. 263d, 264, 264d; the document is transcribed and discussed by Jane K. Laurent, "An Edition of Charters from the Coucher Books of the Duchy of Lancaster," pp. 188–205; *Monasticon*, 3:220.
91. *Monasticon*, 3:221. Other settlements between the houses are noted by Wood, *English Monasteries*, p. 62.

IV. FEUDAL LORD AND EARL OF CHESTER

1. By Brian E. Harris, who has kindly provided me with a typescript of his chapter. We are in substantial agreement on the interpretation of the limited data. See as well Tait's introduction to the *Chester Chartulary*.
2. Alexander, "New Evidence," pp. 727–28. Some of the material in this article is also discussed in the present chapter.
3. For a discussion of his borough charters, see Mary Bateson, "The Laws of Breteuil, IV: Burghal Colonization," pp. 96–101; the author attributes to the earl two boroughs which he did not found: Manchester and Stockport.
4. *Cal. Ch. Rolls*, 5:318; Ormerod, *History of Chester*, 2:46; Gastrell, *Notitia Cestriensis*, 1:331 (where the borough is wrongly called Brodsham); comment in James Tait, *Mediaeval Manchester and the Beginnings of Lancashire*, pp. 74, 88n.
5. For the date, C. Stella Davies, *A History of Macclesfield*, p. 7; Ronald Stewart-Brown, ed., *Calendar of County Court, City Court, and Eyre Rolls of Chester, 1259–1297*, p. 243; Gastrell, *Notitia Cestriensis*, 1:290. Ranulf's foundation is implicitly denied by M. W. Beresford and H. P. R. Finberg, *English Medieval Boroughs: A Hand-List*, p. 74.
6. GB, PRO, *Twenty-seventh Annual Report of the Deputy Keeper of the Public Records*, p. 103.
7. John Harland, ed., *Mamecestre*, 1:200–202; discussed in Tait, *Mediaeval Manchester*, pp. 46–47, 62ff.; William E. A. Axon, ed., *The Annals of Manchester*, pp. 11–12.
8. Alphonsus Ballard and James Tait, eds., *British Borough Charters, 1042–1307*, 1: xc, xliv–xlv, and xlv–xlvi.
9. GB, *Eighth Report*, app. 1:356.
10. William Cunningham, *The Growth of English Industry and Commerce during the Early and Middle Ages*, 1:616. This instrument specifically mentions both free burgage and a borough court competent to deal with all but specified crimes.
11. GB, HMC, *Eighth Report*, app. 1:356; *Cal. Ch. Rolls*, 1:247 and 2:487; Harland, *Mamecestre*, 1:189; Rupert H. Morris, *Chester in the Plantagenet and Tudor Periods*, pp. 480–81.
12. See, in order, *Rot. chart.*, 1:183b (Wrottesley, *Chartulary of*

Dieulacres Abbey, p. 310); *Rot. litt. claus.*, 1: 351, 361 (*Cal. Ch. Rolls*, 1:340), 463b, 518, 626, and 2:286.
13. Lipson, *Economic History of England*, 1:226–27.
14. Ibid., 1:228–29; Poole, *Domesday Book to Magna Carta*, p. 77.
15. See, for example, *Rot. chart.*, vol. 1, pt. 1, p. 96; GB, PRO, *Patent Rolls Preserved in the Public Record Office*, Henry III, vol. 1 (1216–25), pp. 447–48, 553; GB, PRO, *Calendar of Patent Rolls*, Henry III, vol. 2 (1225–32), p. 66; *Rot. litt. claus.*, 2:21–22; GB, PRO, *Calendar of Documents Ireland*, nos. 1801, 1930.
16. Painter, *Feudal Barony*, p. 166. Classifications of grants made by Ranulf III of forest rights and related matters: disafforestation, 2; exemption from forest pleas and other jurisdictional quittances, 8; quittance of pannage, 8; land, 1; common, 3; warren, 2; quittance of puture, 10; license to assart, 2; right to take wood, 5; estover, 2; general grant of forest rights to the barons of Cheshire (Cheshire Magna Carta), 1.
17. *Chester Chartulary*, p. 236, no. 353; GB, PRO, *Register of Edward the Black Prince*, 3:34.
18. *Cal. Ch. Rolls*, 2:310–11; *Chester Chartulary*, p. 338, no. 598; GB, PRO, *Register of the Black Prince*, 3:286.
19. Hulton, *Coucher of Whalley*, p. 11; Ronald Stewart-Brown, ed., *Accounts of the Chamberlains and Other Officers of the County of Chester, 1301–1360*, p. 201.
20. Hulton, *Coucher of Whalley*, pp. 11–12; Ormerod, *History of Chester*, 1:38. On the word and function of the sacrabar in this charter, see J. M. Kaye, "The Sacrabar."
21. Hulton, *Coucher of Whalley*, pp. 470–71.
22. *Cal. Ch. Rolls*, 5:103, no. 14; no. 15 is Ranulf III's confirmation.
23. Ibid., nos. 16, 17, 18 (no. 16 = *Monasticon*, 3:179).
24. Stewart-Brown, *Serjeants of the Peace*, p. 116, no. 7.
25. GB, PRO, *Calendar of Patent Rolls*, Edward I, 1:193–94.
26. Wrottesley, *Chartulary of Dieulacres Abbey*, p. 354; *Cal. Ch. Rolls*, 4:154; Stewart-Brown, *Calendar of Rolls Chester*, p. 239.
27. Isaac H. Jeayes, *Descriptive Catalogue of Derbyshire Charters*, no. 1954.
28. *Monasticon*, 5:456, no. v.
29. Stewart-Brown, *Calendar of Rolls Chester*, pp. 229–30, 213.

30. GB, PRO, *Register of the Black Prince*, 3:25.
31. Ibid., 3:26; Stewart-Brown, *Serjeants of the Peace*, pp. 118–19, no. 12, GB, PRO, *Calendar of Patent Rolls*, Edward I, 3:525.
32. *Cheshire Sheaf*, 3d ser., vol. 30 (May 1935), no. 6603.
33. Stewart-Brown, *Serjeants of the Peace*, p. 116, no. 8; *Cheshire Sheaf* 51 (July 1956): 27–28, no. 10136; J. P. Earwaker, "The Ancient Charters and Deeds at High Legh, Cheshire," p. 25.
34. Ormerod, *History of Chester*, 2:339; GB, PRO, *Twenty-seventh Annual Report*, p. 115.
35. GB, PRO, *Calendar of Patent Rolls*, Edward I, 3:499; *Chester Chartulary*, p. 104.
36. The most useful general works on the topic are as follows: Charles Young, *The Royal Forests of Medieval England*; G. J. Turner, ed., *Select Pleas of the Forest*; M. L. Bazeley, "The Extent of the English Forest in the Thirteenth Century"; Nellie Neilson, "The Forests"; Elizabeth Cox Wright, "Common Law in the Thirteenth Century English Forest"; Charles R. Young, "English Royal Forests under the Angevin Kings," and "The Forest Eyre in England during the Thirteenth Century."
37. Turner, *Pleas of the Forest*, p. ix.
38. M. M. Postan, *The Cambridge Economic History of Europe*, vol. 1, *The Agrarian Life of the Middle Ages*, p. 551.
39. Turner, *Pleas of the Forest*, esp. pp. ix and cviii–cviv; Bazeley, "English Forest," pp. 140–45.
40. Turner, *Pleas of the Forest*, pp. xv–xx.
41. Painter, *Feudal Barony*, p. 152.
42. Turner, *Pleas of the Forest*, pp. x–xiii.
43. Painter, *Feudal Barony*, p. 91.
44. Alexander, "New Evidence," pp. 727–28. See also Noël Denholm-Young, *Seignorial Administration in England*, p. 90, on the divergence between theory and practice in the thirteenth century.
45. I owe this suggestion to Charles Young of Duke University.
46. Alexander, "Palatinate of Chester"; this article also reviews the literature, both theoretical and practical, on palatine jurisdiction in England. See as well my "The Alleged Palatinates of Norman England," and "The English Palatinates and Edward I."

47. To the citations in my article "Palatinate of Chester," add Henry Hawes Harrod, "A Defense of the Liberties of Chester, 1450," pp. 28–30. For the palatine duchy of Lancaster, erected in 1351 in the full light of records, see Robert C. Somerville, "The Duchy and County Palatine of Lancaster," and the same author's *History of the Duchy of Lancaster*, vol. 1, 1265–1603. For Durham, Gaillard Thomas Lapsley, *The County Palatine of Durham*. In my article on the origin and original nature of medieval English palatinates ("English Palatinates") I conclude that they emerged as defined entities not before the reign of Edward I. Andrew W. Lewis, "The Capetian Apanages and the Nature of the French Kingdom."
48. Gaines Post, *Studies in Medieval Legal Thought*, p. 280.
49. Geoffrey Ellis, *Earldoms in Fee: A Study in Peerage Law and Family*, pp. 105–6. But there was not a failure of heirs in 1237; see Kenneth Bruce McFarlane, "Had Edward I a 'Policy' towards the Earls?" p. 250. The earldom was seized by Henry III; it did not revert to the Crown through escheat. Another recent author writes of palatinates, ignoring the work of the last twenty-five years on the topic in her conclusions and suggesting that the king had granted to the lords of Chester, Durham, and Lancaster "the full powers he himself had" (Helen M. Jewell, *English Local Administration in the Middle Ages*, pp. 70–72; the quotation is from p. 70).
50. *Chs in the PRs*, p. 30.
51. Harris, "Ranulf III of Chester," p. 110; the exceptions were the king's administration of the county during the earl's minority and his intervention in matters relating to the see of Coventry/Lichfield. In his draft typescript for the first section of the administrative history chapter for the forthcoming *VCH Cheshire*, vol. 2, Harris, however, stresses the bases for Cheshire's "extraordinary status among English counties"; he makes the strongest recent statement arguing for Cheshire's uniqueness in the time of Ranulf III.
52. Harris, "Ranulf III of Chester," pp. 10–12.
53. See my article "English Palatinates."
54. F. A. Cazel, Jr., "The Fifteenth of 1225," p. 71. See also Helen Cam, *Liberties and Communities in Medieval England*, p. 209,

and, for Cheshire, Geoffrey Barraclough, *The Earldom and County Palatine of Chester*, pp. 17–20.
55. Lucianus, *Liber de laude*, p. 65; Barraclough, *Early Cheshire Charters*, p. 12, states that Lucian composed his work in "about 1195."
56. GB, PRO, *Calendar of Patent Rolls*, 1345–48, p. 84 (George Wrottesley, ed., *Extracts from the Coram Rege Rolls of Edward III and Richard II, 1327–1383*, pp. 65–66); abbot of Dieulacres defends a claim to Rudyard (Stafford), GB, RC, *Rotuli hundredorum*, p. 339; abbot of Newstead-on-Ancholm claims a moiety of the vill of Alkborough (Lincs). GB, PRO, *Register of the Black Prince*, 3:92; an inquest into the tenurial history of the lordship of Macclesfield (Chs) is ordered.
57. J. C. Holt is preparing an edition of this document: *Magna Carta and English Charters of Liberties 1100–1225*. Pending publication of this work, see *Chester Chartulary*, pp. 101–9, and GB, PRO, *Calendar of Patent Rolls*, 1292–1300, pp. 499–500. Fragment in Hulton, *Coucher of Whalley*, 1:12n. The document was first called "Magna Carta" by Ranulf's successor, John the Scot; GB, RCHM, *Eighth Report*, app. 1:357. Both Ranulf's and John's charters were confirmed in 1265 and 1300.
58. *Chester Chartulary*, p. 108; here the Cheshire and royal charters are compared, as well. There is little similarity between the two, nor is there between the Cheshire Magna Carta and the great charter of liberties issued by Bishop Antony Bek in the franchise of Durham in 1303 (for this, see Gaillard Thomas Lapsley, *County Palatinate of Durham*, pp. 131–34).
59. Holt, *Magna Carta*, p. 270; but in n. 5 he more cautiously points out that caps. 56 and 60 of the royal charter "imply that no exceptions [from its authority] were intended."
60. Cf. Tait in *Chester Chartulary*, p. 108.
61. Noted as well by C. Warren Hollister, *The Military Organization of Norman England*, pp. 134–35, and I. J. Sanders, *Feudal Military Service in England*, p. 55.
62. Stewart-Brown, *Calendar of Rolls Chester*, pp. xvii–xxvi. See also Barraclough, *Early Cheshire Charters*, p. 48. A brief discussion of Cheshire justice from the standpoint of whether the country was a palatinate is in my "New Evidence," pp. 725–27 and nn.

NOTES TO CHAPTER IV

63. Ronald Stewart-Brown, "The 'Domesday' Roll of Chester," p. 497 and *Calendar of Rolls Chester*, p. xviii, citing GB, Exchequer, *Placitorum abbreviatio temporibus Ric. I, Johann., Henr. III, Edw. I, Edw. II*, pp. 268–69.
64. G. O. Sayles, ed., *Select Cases in the Court of King's Bench under Edward I*, 1:43.
65. Doris M. Stenton, ed., *Pleas before the King or His Justices*, 1: 160 and case no. 2362.
66. *Cheshire Sheaf*, 3d ser., vol. 20 (1923), no. 4711.
67. Elsa de Haas and G. D. G. Hall, eds., *Early Registers of Writs*, pp. xcii–xciii (where it is specifically noted that this is probably not Ranulf's register), and xcv. The register (GB, PRO, Chester 38/13:*Registrum brevium*) is described in N. R. Ker, *Medieval Manuscripts in British Libraries*, vol. 1, London, p. 182.
68. See n. 65; Barraclough, *Earldom of Chester*, pp. 31–33, and *Early Cheshire Charters*, p. 48.
69. C. T. Flower, ed., *Introduction to the Curia Regis Rolls, 1199–1230*, p. 94.
70. D. Stenton, *Pleas before the King*, p. 160.
71. See n. 65 for *mort d'ancestor* and n. 63 for *darrein presentment*. A final concord before the earl and Philip of Orby is in Barraclough, *Early Cheshire Charters*, no. 21 (May 31, 1222); another, Barraclough, *Earldom of Chester*, pp. 31–33, August 27, 1228.
72. M. T. Clanchy, "The Franchise of Return of Writs," pp. 59–82.
73. Theodore F. T. Plucknett, *The Legislation of Edward I*, p. 38; Jean Scammell, "The Origin and Limitations of the Liberty of Durham," p. 457.
74. *De legibus et consuetudinibus Angliae*, 2:346. Cf. Glanvill, *Tractatus de legibus et consuetudinibus regni Angliae*, p. 3 (1.2).
75. Despite Julius Goebel, *Felony and Misdemeanor*, pp. 377–78. See F. Stenton, *English Feudalism*, p. 104.
76. F. Stenton, *English Feudalism*, p. 104.
77. Naomi Hurnard, *The King's Pardon for Homicide before A.D. 1307*, p. 214; she states that this was before 1237 but provides no documentation for Chester. Painter, *Feudal Barony*, p. 112 and n. 78.

78. For an introduction to Cheshire pleas of the sword, see my "New Evidence," pp. 725–26.
79. Barraclough, "Charters of Chester," pp. 41–42 (for Peter the Clerk; 1208–13); *Cheshire Sheaf*, 3d ser., vol. 30 (May 1935), no. 6603 (for John Ardern; 1210–17); Stewart-Brown, *Calendar of Rolls Chester*, pp. 229–30 (for William de Vernon); GB, PRO, *Calendar of Patent Rolls*, 1292–1300, p. 399; *Chester Chartulary*, pp. 102–3; Hulton, *Coucher of Whalley*, 1:12n (fragment; the "Cheshire Magna Carta"; March 1215–October 1216); Rupert H. Morris, *Chester in the Plantagenet and Tudor Periods*, pp. 558–59 (for Peter the Clerk). *Cal. Ch. Rolls*, 1389, p. 318; comment, Tait, *Medieval Manchester*, p. 74 (1209–28; borough of Frodsham).
80. GB, PRO, *Register of the Black Prince*, 3:112; GB, PRO, *Twenty-seventh Annual Report*, p. 115; 1189–1217.
81. GB, PRO, *Twenty-eighth Annual Report*, p. 24; *Cheshire Sheaf*, 3d ser., 10 (1913): 118–19 (no. 2419); ca. 1200.
82. Barraclough, "Charters of Chester" (1208–13), pp. 41–42.
83. *Cheshire Sheaf*, 3d ser., vol. 30 (May 1935), no. 6603.
84. GB, PRO, *Calendar of Patent Rolls*, 1292–1300, p. 499; *Chester Chartulary*, pp. 102–4. See Kaye, "The Sacrabar."
85. Earwaker, "Charters at High Legh," p. 25 (facsimile); ca. 1215.
86. *Cheshire Sheaf* 51 (October 1956): 42, no. 10168; GB, PRO, *Twenty-eighth Annual Report*, p. 62. Richard had been appointed forester by Ranulf's father, Hugh II: *Cheshire Sheaf* 49 (September 1954): 40.
87. Denholm-Young, *Seignorial Administration*, p. 90; cf. F. Stenton, *English Feudalism*, pp. 104–6.
88. GB, RC, *Placita de quo warranto*, p. 714. For comment on this case, see Alexander, "New Evidence," pp. 726–29.
89. *Early Cheshire Charters*, p. 48, and *Earldom of Chester*, passim.

V. "GREATEST BARON OF THE REALM"

1. Ed. Paul Meyer, ll: 15229–54, 15288, 15375–400. Painter, *William Marshal*, p. 193. See also Harris, "Ranulf III of Chester," p. 109.

2. Matthew Paris, *Historia Anglorum*, 2:195, and *Chronica majora*, 3:1; Roger of Wendover, *Flores historiarum*, 2:197; *Annals of Burton*, in *Ann. monastici*, 1:224; *Annals of Waverley*, in *Ann. monastici*, 2:286.
3. Painter, *William Marshal*, p. 195.
4. Ibid., p. 194.
5. F. M. Powicke, *The Thirteenth Century, 1216–1307*, p. 2, and *King Henry III*, 1:4.
6. G. J. Turner, "The Minority of Henry III," pt. 2, p. 217.
7. Bertie Wilkinson, *The Later Middle Ages in England, 1216–1485*, p. 50.
8. G. Ellis, *Earldoms in Fee*, p. 28. He was, however, a member of the royal council in 1222 (*Rot. litt. claus.*, 1: 496, 497) and an exchequer baron in 1223 (*Curia Regis Rolls*, vol. 11, no. 1107).
9. Powicke, *King Henry III*, p. 51.
10. "William de Forz, Count of Aumâle: An Early Thirteenth-Century English Baron," p. 232.
11. Painter, *William Marshal*, pp. 270–74. Painter tartly defended his subject: "The fact that William drew some profit from his occupancy of the high office of regent does not prove that he was not a disinterested ruler. The strict moralist may, if he chooses, point to a blemish in William's record—it can easily bear it."
12. Painter, *William Marshal*, pp. 193–95.
13. Painter, *William Marshal*, p. 195. I have quoted Painter's translation of the address from the *Histoire de Guillaume le Maréchal*.
14. Powicke, *Thirteenth Century*, p. 3.
15. GB, RC, *Statutes of the Realm*, 1:14–16; France, Ministère d'état, *Layettes*, vol. 1, no. 1194.
16. Holt, *Magna Carta*, p. 269; pp. 269–72 contain a splendid introduction to the 1216 reissue of the charter, an introduction which assumes a knowledge of the original Runnymede charter.
17. Powicke, *King Henry III*, p. 50.
18. Holt, *Northerners*, p. 242 and n. 4; D. Stenton, *Rolls Yorkshire*, no. 1145.
19. GB, PRO, Pipe Roll 67 (E. 372/67), mm. 12d, 10, 1d.; *Rott. litt.*

claus., vol. 1, pt. 1, p. 340b; GB, PRO, *Calendar of Documents Scotland*, nos. 687, 712; *Pipe Roll 2 Henry III*, pp. 1–3, 5, 17; Walford D. Selby, ed., *Lancashire and Cheshire Records Preserved in the Public Record Office*, 1:145; Dugdale, *Baronage of England*, 1:44, the probable source for Ormerod, *History of Chester*, 1:34.

20. *Rot. litt. claus.*, vol. 1, pt. 1, p. 308b; GB, PRO, *Calendar of Documents Scotland*, no. 1202; Ormerod, *History of Chester*, 1:38. The earl also is indicated as advising safe-conducts for Hugh de Lacy and Robert Marmion on November 18: GB, PRO, *Patent Rolls*, 1216–25, p. 4; Rymer, *Foedera*, 1:145. He had custody of three royal hostages late in 1217: GB, PRO, *Patent Rolls, Henry III*, 1216–25, pp. 6, 19. Ranulf was informed of the return of several rebels to the king's allegiance: *Rot. litt. claus.*, 1: 330, 333, 338, 373b, 374b, 376. He is mentioned as advising the king: GB, PRO, *Patent Rolls, Henry III*, 1216–25, pp. 28, 172. The pipe roll for 1218 shows numerous quittances by the king's order for the earl: *Pipe Roll 2 Henry III*, pp. 5, 65, 2, 30. Peter de Maulay, constable of Castle Corfe, was directed to release William of Lancaster, son of the rebel Gilbert fitz Renfrew, at the urging of the earl, whose loyalty is highly praised: *Rot. litt. claus.*, 1:335b; Rymer, *Foedera*, 1:146.

21. The best brief discussion of the hereditary claims of Ranulf III on the earldom of Lincoln is James W. F. Hill, *Medieval Lincoln*, pp. 93–96; see also C[okayne], *Complete Peerage*, 7:675 and note g.

22. See below, pp. 75–76.

23. GB, PRO, E.372/76, m. 10.

24. GB, PRO, *Calendar of Inquisitions post Mortem*, vol. 2, no. 777, where it is erroneously stated that Ranulf had held the honor of John.

25. *Rot. litt. claus.*, 1:310; pp. 351 and 355 augment the grant. *Pipe Roll 2 Henry III*, p. 93, enrolls the account. For grants similar to the above, addressed to the sheriffs of sixteen counties: *Rot. litt. claus.*, 1:296.

26. GB, PRO, *Patent Rolls, Henry III*, 1216–25, p. 84; the accounts for the honor are in *Pipe Roll 2 Henry III*, pp. 17–18.

27. Painter, *Scourge of the Clergy*, p. 15.

28. *Rot. litt. claus.*, 1: 340, 350; GB, PRO, *Patent Rolls, Henry III, 1216–25*, p. 120.
29. *Rot. litt. claus.*, 1:361b; GB, PRO, *Patent Rolls, Henry III, 1216–25*, p. 158.
30. *Rot. litt. claus.*, 1:385b; Painter, *Scourge of the Clergy*, pp. 16–17.
31. *Rot. litt. claus.*, 1: 326b, 339; Harcourt, *His Grace the Steward*, p. 104, incorrectly transcribed the name of the manor as "Saudon," rather than the correct Sandon, as found in the close roll. This is Sandon in Berkshire, not that in Essex, which was of the honor of Hatfield Peverel (see *FA*, 6:575, and the *Book of Fees*, p. 1465). Stephen de Segrave and William de Cantilupe, men closely associated with Ranulf, also received lands of the honor of Leicester in the midsummer of 1218: GB, PRO, Fine Roll 2 Henry III, mm. 3 and 4. The close roll (p. 319) also records the gift of Gatehampton, an Oxfordshire manor, in August of 1217.
32. Powicke, *King Henry III*, p. 28.
33. GB, PRO, *Patent Rolls, Henry III, 1216–25*, p. 22; W. W. Shirley, ed., *Royal and Other Historical Letters Illustrative of the Reign of Henry III*, 1:3. January 14, 1217. Powicke, *King Henry III*, p. 28.
34. GB, PRO, *Patent Rolls, Henry III, 1216–25*, pp. 108–9.
35. For what follows, see Matthew Paris, *Chronica majora*, 3:15–17, and *Historia Anglorum*, 2:206–8; Roger of Wendover, *Flores historiarum*, 2:208–11; Walter of Coventry, *Memoriale*, 2:236–38; *Annals of Burton*, in *Ann. monastici*, vol. 1, p. 224; *Annals of Dunstable* in *Ann. monastici*, vol. 3, pp. 49–50; Walter of Guisborough, *The Chronicle of Walter of Guisborough, Previously Edited as the Chronicle of Walter of Hemingford or Hemingburgh*, p. 153; see also George Wrottesley, ed., *An Abstract of the Contents of the Burton Chartulary*, pp. 10–11.
36. Painter, *Feudalism and Liberty*, p. 130.
37. "The Taking of Lincoln," in *The Political Songs of England*, ed. Thomas Wright, p. 24.
38. For what here follows on the battle of Lincoln, see: Painter, *William Marshal*, pp. 213–19; Powicke, *King Henry III*, pp. 11–

13 and 736–39; J. Hill, *Medieval Lincoln*, pp. 201–6; and sources cited in these studies. Tactics are discussed in these works, although the topic is irrelevant for this biography. Meyer, *Guillaume le Maréchal*, ll:16203–24.
39. Michael Lewis, *Ancestors*, p. 85.
40. Clay, *Early Yorkshire Charters*, 6:35; Powicke, *King Henry III*, p. 25; *Rot. litt. claus.*, 2:87–87B. A court case arising from the earl's capture of Maurice and his subsequent imprisonment was taken in 1219; D. Stenton, *Rolls Yorkshire*, cases 315, 1133; and cf. *Cal. Ch. Rolls, Henry III*, vol. 1 (1226–57), p. 115, where Bingley, one of the two settlements in dispute in 1219, is recorded as having been conveyed by Ranulf to William de Cantilupe.
41. GB, PRO, *Patent Rolls, Henry III, 1216–25*, p. 64.
42. *Annals of Burton*, in *Ann. monastici*, 1:224; Walter of Coventry, *Memoriale*, 2:238; *Annals of Dunstable*, in *Ann. monastici*, 3:50; Walter of Guisborough, *Chronicles*, p. 153.
43. G. J. Turner, "The Minority of Henry III," pt. 2, p. 217.
44. Shirley, *Royal Letters*, 1:532. There is no evidence to support Shirley's suggestion that Gualo "seems to have attempted to undermine the power of the regent, by giving him the earl of Chester, one of the most factious and unprincipled nobles of the day, as a colleague" (1:19). Not only do I disagree with Shirley's characterization of Ranulf, but—more important—so, obviously, did the Earl Marshal, whose respect for the earl of Chester was exhibited sufficiently in the discussions concerning the regency following the death of King John.
45. Rymer, *Foedera*, 1:148; Guillelmus Armoricus, *De gestis Philippi Augusti* (*RHF*, 17:111–12). A letter following upon the settlement, from Henry III to Ranulf, is in GB, PRO, *Patent Rolls, Henry III, 1216–25*, p. 91.
46. *History of Wales*, p. 654.
47. *Ann. Cestrienses*, p. 50 (Knighton, *Chronicon*, 1:206). Other notices of Ranulf's role in Welsh affairs, all minor, are to be found in Rymer, *Foedera*, 1:150 (*Rot. litt. claus.*, 1: 378–79, 151).
48. *Ann. Cestrienses*, p. 50.
49. The best narrative of this crusade is Thomas C. Van Cleve, "The Fifth Crusade." For Ranulf's part in the enterprise, see

the following sources, on which my narrative is based: Walter of Coventry, *Memoriale*, pp. 241–42; Roger of Wendover, *Flores historiarum*, 2: 235ff., 262–63; Mathew Paris, *Chronica majora*, 3: 40–41, 67–68; *L'Estoire de Eracles Empereur*, in *Recueil des historiens des Croisades*, vol. 2; *Monasticon*, 5:628; Higden, *Polychronicon*, 8:198; *Ann. monastici*, 1:64 (Tewkesbury), 2:83 (Winchester), 2:289 (Waverley), 4:411 (Worcester), 3:54ff. (Dunstable); *Chron. Alberici Trium-Fontium*, in *RHF*, 18:789; *Chronicon Rotomagensi*, in *RHF*, 18:361. Oliver Scholasticus, *Historia Damiatina*, 202: 159–282, esp. pp. 207–8. See, additionally, Steven Runciman, *A History of the Crusades*, vol. 3, *The Kingdom of Acre*, pp. 132–70. René Grousset's great history of the Crusades is less satisfactory for the Fifth Crusade.
50. "Fifth Crusade," p. 384.
51. A recent addition to the voluminous literature confessing inability to discover medieval people's motivations is a challenging article by Donald E. Queller and Gerald W. Day, "Some Arguments in Defense of the Venetians on the Fourth Crusade."
52. Van Cleve, "Fifth Crusade," p. 410.
53. Ibid., p. 417.
54. *Monasticon*, 5:628 (*Fundationis historia* of Dieulacres).
55. *Ann. Cestrienses*, p. 50; Walter of Coventry, *Memoriale*, 2:246; Higden, *Polychronicon*, 8:198, which wrongly has him erecting Dieulacres Abbey at this point.
56. Shirley, *Royal Letters*, 1:244–46 (Chaplais, *Diplomatic Documents*, vol. 1, no. 140). Powicke, *King Henry III*, p. 158. Ranulf also seems to "have avoided the taxation of 1220 by simply refusing to pay it" (Painter, *Feudal Barony*, p. 79).
57. In general, see Painter, *Scourge of the Clergy*, pp. 17–18; Sanders, *English Baronies*, pp. 140–41.
58. *Rot. litt. claus.*, 1:340; GB, PRO, *Patent Rolls, Henry III, 1216–25*, p. 120; *Rot. litt. claus.*, 1:350 (361b orders a survey of the fees and services of the Richmond lands north of the Humber).
59. GB, PRO, *Patent Rolls, Henry III, 1216–25*, p. 158.
60. D. Stenton, *Rolls Yorkshire*, no. 1145. Stenton queried whether Ranulf was too powerful or too useful to be afforced in this matter; perhaps in the earl's absence, the Earl Marshal felt that

NOTES TO CHAPTER V

confrontation with Ranulf was a risk not worth taking. Other notices of Ranulf's continued interest in the honor are found in the *Book of Fees*, p. 287; D. Stenton, *Rolls Yorkshire*, no. 34; *Pipe Roll 3 Henry III*, p. 131; GB, PRO, *Pipe Roll 4 Henry III* (E.372/64), m. 7d; *Rot. litt. claus.*, 1:451b; GB, PRO, Fine Roll 5 Henry III, pp. 72–73.

61. The complicated history of the honor is traced by Fox, "Honor and Earldom of Leicester," and sources there cited. To Fox's references here add GB, PRO, Fine Roll 2 Henry III, mm. 3, 4.
62. GB, PRO, *Patent Rolls, Henry III*, 1216–25, pp. 163, 254; ibid., 1225–32, p. 124; *Rot. litt. claus.*, 1:446b; Harcourt, *His Grace the Steward*, 1:107. See as well *Rot. litt. claus.*, 1: 445, 495b. The initial grant followed less than two months upon Ranulf's return from crusade.
63. GB, PRO, *Patent Rolls, Henry III*, 1216–25, p. 281.
64. *Rot. litt. claus.*, 1: 443b, 445; GB, PRO, *Calendar of Documents Scotland*, nos. 786, 800; GB, PRO, Pipe Roll 65 (5 Henry III; E.372/65), m. 12; GB, PRO, *Calendar of Documents Scotland*, nos. 790, 791, 797, 819, 820, 843, 844, 866, 870, 892, 894, 926, 927, 951, 1047; Rymer, *Foedera*, 1:165; GB, PRO, *Patent Rolls, Henry III*, 1216–25, p. 285; Turner, "Minority of Henry III," pt. 2, p. 246; *Curia Regis Rolls* 11, nos. 1143 and 1486, and 12, no. 459; GB, PRO, Pipe Roll 66 (6 Henry III; E.372/66), mm. 2, 6; GB, PRO, Pipe Roll 67 (7 Henry III; E.372/67), m. 14d; GB, PRO, Pipe Roll 68 (8 Henry III; E.372/68), mm. 5, 8; GB, PRO, Pipe Roll 69 (9 Henry III; E.372/69), m. 1; GB, PRO, Pipe Roll 70 (10 Henry III; E.372/70), m. 3; Hugh of Welles, *Rotuli*, 3:303. His custody ended in 1227: *Rot. litt. claus.*, 2:183; GB, PRO, *Calendar of Documents Scotland*, no. 1046; C[okayne], *Complete Peerage*, s.v. "Huntington," p. 169.
65. GB, PRO, Fine Roll 2 Henry III (C.60/8), m. 5; *Pipe Roll 2 Henry III*; GB, PRO, *Patent Rolls, Henry III*, 1216–25, p. 319; GB, RC, *Excerpta è rotulis finium in turri Londinensi asservatis, Henrico tertio rege*, pp. 84–85; Stapleton, *Magni rotuli scaccarii Normanniae*, 2:ciii, n. 6; GB, PRO, *Pipe Roll 7 Henry III* (E.372/67), m. 8d.
66. *Pipe Roll 2 Henry III*, p. 2 (a palfrey), p. 5 (seventy marks); *Rot. litt. claus.*, 1:430b (grant of twenty pounds in Lincs); *Pipe Roll*

2 *Henry III*, p. 79 (grant of sixty pounds in Northants); *Rot. litt. claus.*, 1:487b (GB, PRO, Fine Roll 6 Henry III [C.60/12], m. 7) (loan of one hundred pounds); *Rot. litt. claus.*, 1:492 (gift of forty deer); *Rot. litt. claus.*, 1: 500b, 531 (custody of the lands and heirs of William de Somery); *Book of Fees*, pp. 230, 376, 384; *Cal. Patent Rolls*, 1338, p. 34; GB, PRO, Pipe Roll 68 (8 Henry III; E.372/68), m. 2d.; GB, PRO, *Close Rolls Henry III*, 1227–31, pp. 190, 531 (gift of sixty bucks and does for the earl's park at Barrow on Soar), 548b (loan of twenty pounds), 561 (gift of beams). This conclusion supports those of the important and original work of Thomas K. Keefe, *Feudal Assessments and the Political Community under Henry II and His Sons*, soon to be published by the University of California Press.
67. Above, n. 55.
68. For what here follows, see Lloyd, *History of Wales*, pp. 655–63.
69. Ibid., p. 657.
70. *Ann. Cestrienses*, pp. 50–52; Beamont, *Tracts*, p. 507.
71. Rymer, *Foedera*, 1:167–68; *Rot. litt. claus.*, 1:520b.
72. *Ann. monastici* 3:82 (Dunstable), where Ranulf is referred to as Llewelyn's *familiaris et amicus*.
73. GB, PRO, *Patent Rolls, Henry III*, 1216–25, pp. 378–79. As Kate Norgate suggested (*The Minority of Henry III*, p. 194), this ploy was part of the "effort to detach the Welsh of Deheubarth and Powys from obedience to their North-Welsh lord."
74. *Rot. litt. claus.*, 1:564–65; see also Rymer, *Foedera*, 1:170 (attested by Ranulf). I query whether the peace made among Llewelyn, the young Marshal, and Ranulf, placed by the Dunstable annalist in the year 1226, might not in fact pertain to 1223, since no record exists of difficulties with the Welsh in 1226.
75. Painter, *William Marshal*, p. 278.
76. *VCH Lancashire*, 2:193.
77. R. Turner, "William de Forz," p. 242.
78. Powicke, *King Henry III*, p. 50; pp. 68–70 are a concise evaluation of Hubert's character.
79. *King Henry III*, p. 50. For the narrative of events concerning the resumption of the castles, I have relied upon Powicke, *King Henry III*, pp. 48–60, and *Thirteenth Century*, pp. 22–26, and

on R. Turner, "William de Forz," pp. 236–43, except where I have otherwise indicated.
80. Powicke, *Thirteenth Century*, p. 20.
81. R. Turner, "William de Forz," p. 242; Turner wrote that "such men as Fawkes de Breauté, Ranulf of Chester, and William de Forz may have thought in terms of territorial lordships based on their own landholdings and royal offices." Certainly Ranulf's custody of the shrievalties of Shropshire, Staffordshire, and Lancashire, all adjoining his home county of Cheshire, might argue for such an ambition on his part. Surely one traditional contemporaneous view is in error, that which viewed the bipolarity in the question of resumption of the castles as being between those who wished to follow the law and such "feudal anarchists" as Ranulf and William de Forz (G. J. Turner, "Minority of Henry III," pt. 2, pp. 210–11). By no means can the earl of Chester be viewed as an anarchist; rather, as events were to show, the interests of the Crown (although not necessarily of administrative interpretations of these interests) were paramount in Ranulf's policy. Attempts to influence government actions and to overawe the justiciar can hardly be equated with disloyalty or anarchy. I think "anarchists" a bad choice of terminology; what is really meant is whether the king's and the Crown's interests were best served by centralized control of castles and offices by officials directly responsible to the central administration, or by men of independent power whose loyalty to king and crown was beyond impeachment. The actions of such an occasional madcap as William de Forz should not be permitted to taint such of his associates as the earl of Chester, who never, no matter how hard-pressed, allowed his own interest to overcome his strong adherence to the young king; his steadfast devotion to his lord exemplifies the best of knightly (if you would, chivalrous) loyalty.
82. Powicke, *King Henry III*, pp. 49, 55.
83. R. Turner, "William de Forz," pp. 240ff. As Turner notes, the Barnwell canon alleged that Ranulf supported the count of Aumâle until he attacked Fotheringay Castle; yet, his attempts at mediation of the dispute failing, Ranulf had, before learning of the attack on Fotheringay, participated in the ceremony in which

William had been excommunicated (*Ann. monastici*, 3:63–64; Walter of Coventry, *Memoriale*, 2:248). The assault on Fotheringay constituted a direct act of revolt against the monarch; so far Ranulf was unprepared to proceed. See further Matthew Paris, *Chronica majora*, 3:60–61; Roger of Wendover, *Flores historiarum*, 2:255–56. Roger, I think, errs in naming Ranulf as castellan of Fotheringay—his statement, lacking corroborative evidence, is to be rejected.

84. GB, PRO, *Patent Rolls, Henry III, 1216–25*, p. 335.
85. Dating roughly from the time of the intensification of the problems with William de Forz is a letter from Ranulf, Faulkes de Breauté, and others to the pope, informing him of their view of domestic troubles; Rymer, *Foedera*, 1:171.
86. *Ann. monastici*, 3:57.
87. Powicke, *King Henry III*, p. 53.
88. GB, PRO, *Calendar of Papal Registers*, 1:81; Rymer, *Foedera*, 1:167.
89. Powicke, *King Henry III*, p. 56; see also Norgate, *Minority of Henry III*, pp. 181–82.
90. Norgate, *Minority of Henry III*, pp. 181–82; see also Powicke, *King Henry III*, pp. 56–57.
91. Powicke, *King Henry III*, p. 57; Roger of Wendover, *Flores historiarum*, 2:273; Shirley, *Royal Letters*, 1:539; see further Bertie Wilkinson, *The Constitutional History of England 1216–1399*, 1:68–86.
92. Shirley, *Royal Letters*, 1:539; Matthew Paris, *Chronica majora*, 6:69–70.
93. GB, PRO, *Patent Rolls, Henry III, 1216–25*, pp. 481–82.
94. For the events of late November and early December, see *Ann. monastici*, 3:83–84 (Dunstable); Walter of Coventry, *Memoriale*, 2:61–62 (a portion of the *Querimonia* of Faulkes de Breauté). Before the end of the month the flare point of the crisis over repossession had passed into history, but for the quixotic revolt of Faulkes de Breauté in the following year.
95. R. Turner, "William de Forz," p. 242.
96. G. Turner, "Minority of Henry III," pt. 2, pp. 216; Powicke, *Thirteenth Century*, p. 20.
97. For the events of late December, see Walter of Coventry,

Memoriale, 2:262; Roger of Wendover, *Flores historiarum*, 2:276–77 (Matthew Paris, *Chronica majora*, 3:82–83); Matthew of Westminster, *Flores historiarum*, 2:179–80; John of Oxnede, *Chronica*, p. 135; *Ann. monastici*, 3:84 (Dunstable).

98. For a discussion of Langton's policy of excommunicating for obstinacy about castles, see Powicke, *Stephen Langton*, pp. 154–56.

99. Specifically mentioned by Roger of Wendover as companions of Ranulf in surrendering their castles and custodies were the count of Aumâle, John the constable of Chester, Faulkes de Breauté, Robert de Vieuxpont, Brian de Lisle, Peter de Maulay, Philip Marc, and others less significant. Faulkes de Breauté adds that the conservative party had demanded that the justiciar and other officials likewise surrender their castles; Hubert de Burgh surrendered the Tower of London as well as Dover.

100. GB, PRO, *Patent Rolls, Henry III, 1216–25*, pp. 417–18 (Shirley, *Royal Letters*, p. 509); Eyton, *Antiquities of Shropshire*, 1: 250, 275.

101. Powicke, *Thirteenth Century*, p. 25.

102. For what follows on the rebellion of Faulkes, the principal sources are *Ann. monastici*, 3:86–90 (Dunstable); Shirley, *Royal Letters*, 1: 224–26, 233–35 (John Goronwy Edwards, *Calendar of Ancient Correspondence concerning Wales*, p. 14); GB, PRO, *Calendar of Papal Registers*, 1:112; Walter of Coventry, *Memoriale*, 2:259–72, esp. pp. 264–67. Good secondary accounts are by Powicke (*Thirteenth Century*, pp. 25–27, and *King Henry III*, pp. 61–66). See also Norgate, *Minority of Henry III*, pp. 231–49.

103. The exclusion is noted by James F. Baldwin, *The King's Council in England during the Middle Ages*, p. 21.

104. Shirley, *Royal Letters*, pp. 233–35; Norgate described this letter as "a model of quiet dignity" (*Minority of Henry III*, p. 241).

105. *Ann. monastici*, 3:89–90 (Dunstable).

106. Reginald Francis Treharne, *Essays on Thirteenth Century England*, p. 20.

VI. PRUD'HOMME

1. Among others, against the prior of Kenilworth: *Curia Regis Rolls*, vol. 11, nos. 290, 743; *VCH Staffordshire*, 3:241, 8:77; GB, RC, *Calendarium rotulorum chartarum*, p. 51; *Cal. Ch. Rolls*, 1:204; D. Stenton, *Rolls Gloucestershire*, nos. 1055, 1363; Wrottesley, *Stone Chartulary*, p. 5. Against the abbot of Grestain, *Rot. litt. claus.*, 1:515b. Against the abbey of Basingwerk: R. Stewart-Brown, *Calendar of Rolls Chester*, pp. 59–60.
2. For example, Henry de Bracton, *Bracton's Note Book*, no. 944; *Curia Regis Rolls*, vol. 2, nos. 1092 and 1102, and vol. 12, nos. 242, 459, 1222, 1812, 2142, 2217, 2655; GB, PRO, *Lists and Indexes*, vol. 15, *List of Ancient Correspondence of the Chancery and Exchequer*, vol. 1., no. 100; John Parker, ed., *Feet of Fines for the County of York, 1218–1231*, no. 379; *Curia Regis Rolls*, vol. 13, nos. 418, 1526, 2676, 2769; GB, PRO, *Close Rolls Henry III, 1227–31*, p. 394 (*Curia Regis Rolls*, vol 14, no. 2478), and p. 570; *Rot. litt. claus.*, 1:596b; *Curia Regis Rolls*, vol. 11, nos. 2270 and 2403, vol. 12, no. 2052 (see GB, PRO, Great Cowcher Books of the Duchy of Lancaster, vol. 2, ff. 283d–84; *Rot. litt. claus.*, 2:148; GB, PRO, *Lists and Indexes, Supplementary Series*, vol. 5, pt. 3, *Duchy of Lancaster . . . Cartae Miscellaneae*, no. 155); GB, PRO, *Lists and Indexes*, vol. 13, nos. 674, 826 and 1103, and vol. 14, no. 2478 (GB, PRO, *Close Rolls Henry III, 1227–31*, p. 394). See also *Rot. litt. claus.*, 2:165 (noticed by Hurnard, *King's Pardon*, p. 197, n. 5) for an interesting case involving accidental homicide perpetrated by one of the earl's serjeants.
3. John P. Yeatman et al., *Feudal History of the County of Derby*, vol. 1, pt. 1, p. 191; GB, PRO, Fine Roll 8 Henry III, m. 1; GB, PRO, *Calendar of Documents Ireland*, vol. 1, nos. 1372, 1373; GB, PRO, Pipe Roll 68, m. 12d, and 71, m. 2.
4. GB, PRO, Pipe Roll 68, m. 2d (William de Camville); GB, PRO, *Close Rolls Henry III, 1227–31*, p. 63 (lands of Roger de Heyford); GB, PRO, Pipe Roll 73 (1229; E.372/73), m.15d (Robert, son of William de Berkeley), and m. 8d (Richard, son of Robert

de Harecurt); Hugh of Welles, *Rotuli*, 3:194 (Gilbert of Boulogne); *Cal. Patent Rolls, 1227–32*, p. 124 (land and heirs of William Percevall).
5. GB, PRO, *Close Rolls Henry III, 1227–31*, pp. 476, 544; Henry also conceded to the earl hunting rights (*Rot. litt. claus.*, 2:171).
6. The hundred of Willybrook, 1224 (Northants; *Rot. litt. claus.*, 1: 621, 646b); the lands of Colin de Lintot and William de Ovill', 1225 (*Rot. litt. claus.*, 2:10–11); the manor of Navenby, accompanied by the grant of Rossal (Lancs) to the abbot and monks of Dieulacres, 1226 (*Rot. litt. claus.*, 2:160b); the manor of Washingborough (Lincs), 1227 (*Rot. litt. claus.*, 2:200 [the king retained the advowson]: *Cal. Patent Rolls, 1225–32*, p. 271, 1229), a messuage in London formerly in the holdings of Aaron the Jew of Lincoln, 1228 (GB, PRO, *Close Rolls Henry III*, 1227–31, p. 47, and cf. p. 53); custody of a fee in Warwick, 1229 (GB, PRO, *Close Rolls Henry III*, 1227–31, p. 142); the reversion of a third of the barony of Wich Malbank (Chs), 1229 (James Hall, *A History of the Town and Parish of Nantwich*; Ormerod, *History of Chester*, 3:422–23 and note f).
7. GB, PRO, *Close Rolls Henry III, 1227–31*, pp. 158, 176–67. On September 25, 1232, these wapentakes were granted by King Henry to Peter of Dreux: GB, PRO, Fine Roll 16 Henry III, m. 3; *Cal. Patent Rolls, 1225–32*, p. 501.
8. *Cal. Patent Rolls, 1225–32*, p. 124; Harcourt, *His Grace the Steward*, p. 107; Ormerod, *History of Chester*, 1:35; for comment, Painter, *Scourge of the Clergy*, p. 64, and Powicke, *King Henry III*, pp. 178–79. Cf. *Cal. Patent Rolls, 1225–32*, pp. 153–54 (1226).
9. *Cal. Ch. Rolls, 1226–57*, pp. 101–2; GB, PRO, *Close Rolls Henry III*, 1227–31, p. 221; *Pipe Roll 14 Henry III*, p. 330; GB, PRO, Pipe Roll 76, 16 Henry III (E.372/76), m. 13; Farrer, *Final Concords*, 1:112n., and *Lancashire Inquests*, 1:116.
10. *Close Rolls Henry III, 1231–34*, pp. 267, 283.
11. GB, PRO, Great Cowcher, DL.42/1, ff. 79d–80 (the appurtenances of this manor of Bolton are listed); Farrer, *Lancashire Inquests*, 1:29. The purchase fell between October 1229 and May 1230.
12. *Cal. Patent Rolls, 1225–32*, p. 473; issued on May 8, 1232, this

letter postpones a tournament on account of Ranulf's infirmity. Of course, the illness may have been transient, or, contrarily, it may be that he was in steadily declining health unmarked in the sources. Six weeks before his death he was still active in the king's service (ibid., p. 498). Probably the apparent lessening of his activity came from the rise of new blood to national prominence.

13. Foster, *Registrum Antiquissimum*, vol. 1, nos. 220, 221; GB, RC, *Statutes of the Realm*, 1:25–27; Annals of Burton, in *Ann. monastici*, 1:225–36; cf. *Rot. litt. claus.*, 2:78. For the aid, see Cazel, "Fifteenth of 1225"; Sidney Knox Mitchell, *Studies in Taxation under John and Henry III*, pp. 159–69, and *Taxation in Medieval England*, esp. pp. 37–40, 52–53, 74–78, and 139–43.
14. *King Henry III*, p. 37.
15. *Ann. Cestrienses*, pp. 52, 54; Maurice H. Ridgeway and D. J. Cathcart King, "Beeston Castle, Cheshire"; H. M. Colvin, ed., *The History of the King's Works*, vol. 2, *The Middle Ages*, pp. 559–60. The later chroniclers Higden (*Polychronicon*, 8:198) and Knighton (*Chronicon*, p. 210) compress their narratives so as to indicate that immediately upon his return from crusade, Ranulf laid the tax, raised the castles, and erected the abbey. And see Chap. 3, n. 9, above.
16. Brian E. Harris to James W. Alexander.
17. Roger of Wendover, *Flores historiarum*, 2:320–22, Matthew Paris, *Chronica majora*, 3:123–25.
18. Wilkinson, *Later Middle Ages*, p. 55. In the preceding month, the earl had intervened to protect the Jews of Leicester and Coventry (*Rot. litt. claus.*, 2:123a); nothing further is known of this incident or of its context.
19. Mitchell, *Studies in Taxation*, pp. 176–78, and sources there cited, esp. *Ann. monastici*, 2:305 (Waverley), 3:114–15 (Dunstable); Roger of Wendover, *Flores historiarum*, 2:377–78; Matthew Paris, *Chronica majora*, 3:189.
20. William E. Lunt, *Financial Relations of the Papacy with England to 1327*, p. 249.
21. *English Monasteries*, p. 150.
22. C[okayne], *Complete Peerage*, 3:168, anachronistically por-

trays Ranulf as opposing the grant in Parliament, which did not exist as an institution in his lifetime. The tax fell solely upon the clergy, the laity having refused to meet their assessment.

23. Roger of Wendover, *Flores historiarum*, 3:21; Matthew Paris, *Chronica majora*, 3:212. On the aid of 1232, see Mitchell, *Studies in Taxation*, pp. 192–93, 199–206, and *Taxation in Medieval England*, esp. pp. 40–42, 143–45, 151–52, and 200–201.
24. I do not agree with Mitchell (*Taxation in Medieval England*, p. 200) that Ranulf's opposition "indicates individual consent."
25. The history of Anglo-French relations in the thirteenth century is complicated not only by the conflicting aims and ambitions of the kings of the two nations, but also by the consequences of the land hunger of such fractious lords as Peter of Dreux and Hugh of La Marche. The best general accounts of these bewildering matters are: Powicke, *King Henry III*, chaps. 5, 6, and 12, and *Thirteenth Century*, chap. 3; and Painter, *Scourge of the Clergy*.
26. On Poitou and the other French apanages, see Charles T. Wood, *The French Apanages and the Capetian Monarchy*.
27. For the truce, see *Rot. litt. claus.*, 2:212; Rymer, *Foedera*, 1:185–87.
28. GB, PRO, *Close Rolls Henry III*, 1227–31, p. 248. (Shirley, *Royal Letters*, pp. 356–57); see also Sanders, *Feudal Military Service*, p. 121, "A Muster Roll from 1229." It is not clear why Ranulf was directed to come with twenty knights only.
29. *Calendar of Documents Scotland*, vol. 1, no. 1046; GB, PRO, *Close Rolls Henry III*, 1227–31, p. 252.
30. Roger of Wendover, *Flores historiarum*, 2:379; Matthew Paris, *Chronica majora*, 3:191.
31. Chaplais, *Diplomatic Documents*, no. 218 (Shirley, *Royal Letters*, pp. 362–63); GB, PRO, *Close Rolls Henry III*, 1227–31, p. 360; *Curia Regis Rolls*, vol. 14, nos. 28 and 32.
32. Shirley, *Royal Letters*, pp. 377–78 (Chaplais, *Diplomatic Documents*, no. 221; cf. as well no. 219).
33. Roger of Wendover, *Flores historiarum*, 3:6; Matthew Paris, *Chronica majora*, 3:198. The two chroniclers err both in iden-

tifying the count of Brittany as Henry and in their assertion that the castle had been held *jure uxoris* by the earl.
34. GB, PRO, *Close Rolls Henry III, 1227–31*, pp. 410–11; Roger of Wendover, *Flores historiarum*, 3:6. The two letters, one to Ranulf, bear the dates May 21 and 22. See above, p. 73.
35. Painter, *Scourge of the Clergy*, pp. 16–17.
36. *Cal. Patent Rolls, 1225–32*, p. 325; Ormerod, *History of Chester*, 1:41; Bémont, *Simon de Montfort*, pp. 4–5, 333; Labarge, *Simon de Montfort*, p. 29. Harcourt, *His Grace the Steward*, pp. 78–81, alleged Ranulf to have been "insincere" in surrendering the half of the honor to the king and thought that the royal letters placing Simon in possession were not complied with: "One cannot help suspecting that [Ranulf] was the chief source of the difficulty." Yet Simon did homage to the king for these lands on August 13, 1231 (Shirley, *Royal Letters*, 1:401–2; GB, PRO, *Close Rolls Henry III, 1227–31*, p. 543); the date indicated that Ranulf moved quickly to divest himself of the Montfort share of Leicester, since he returned from France in late July and joined the king at Painscastle, where the letters close are attested.
37. *Scourge of the Clergy*, p. 71.
38. There were too few troops—the Chester annalist notes that Henry left his commanders *cum paucis*—for effective operations. *Ann. Cestrienses*, p. 56 (Walter of Guisborough, p. 176); *Ann. monastici*, 1:76–77 (Tewkesbury); Roger of Wendover, *Flores historiarum*, 3:7 (Matthew Paris, *Chronica majora*, 3:199); Shirley, *Royal Letters*, 1:385. See also GB, PRO, *Patent Rolls, Henry III, 1225–32*, p. 401; Rymer, *Foedera*, 1:198.
39. *Scourge of the Clergy*, p. 71.
40. Roger of Wendover, *Flores historiarum*, 3:8; Matthew Paris, *Chronica majora*, 3:200; Morice, *Histoire ecclésiastique*, 1:163 (ex Paris); John of Oxnede, *Chronica*, p. 145.
41. *Scourge of the Clergy*, p. 73; Roger of Wendover, *Flores historiarum*, 3:15; Matthew Paris, *Chronica majora*, 3:204.
42. *RHF*, 21:220; *Ann. monastici*, 3:127 (Dunstable); Morice, *Histoire ecclésiastique*, 1:164; Matthew of Westminster, *Flores historiarum*, 2:201; France, Ministère d'état, *Layettes*, 2: 210,

214; Roger of Wendover, *Flores historiarum*, 3:13; Matthew Paris, *Chronica majora*, 3:204; Morice, *Mémoires*, cols. 875–76.
43. Matthew Paris, *Chronica majora*, 3:204; *Ann. Cestrienses*, p. 56; *Ann. monastici*, 1:79 (Tewkesbury). Cf. GB, PRO, *Close Rolls Henry III*, 1231–34, pp. 132–33.
44. For what here follows, see Powicke, *King Henry III*, pp. 75–83.
45. GB, PRO, *Patent Rolls, Henry III*, 1225–32, p. 498.
46. Roger of Wendover, *Flores historiarum*, 3:35; Matthew Paris, *Chronica majora*, 3:225. *Ann. monastici*, 1:86–87 (Tewkesbury).
47. *Topographer and Genealogist* 2 (1846): 313–14, and Ormerod, *History of Chester*, 1:28; regrant by Henry III, *Cal. Patent Rolls*, 1225–32, p. 508. There is some confusion concerning the date of Ranulf's charter, but it must have been issued after Richard Marshal became earl of Pembroke on August 8, 1231, since he appears on the witness list. But since Ranulf accounted for the third penny of the county at Michaelmas 1232, it seems reasonable to place the grant in October.
48. Lloyd, *History of Wales*, p. 677.
49. *Ann. Cestrienses*, p. 58; Lucianus, *Liber*, p. 101 (obits of Chester Abbey); *Ann. monastici*, 1:87 (Tewkesbury)—as Chester sources, the date of the first two is probably to be preferred to the later dates of Roger of Wendover, Matthew Paris, and Matthew of Westminster. GB, PRO, *Calendar of Liberate Rolls*, 1:210; *Cal. Ch. Rolls*, 1:169, whereby Henry III makes a gift for the soul of Ranulf to Chester Abbey (ibid., p. 172 [December 27], the same sixty-shilling annual grant). Further royal oblations for the repose of the earl are in GB, PRO, *Calendar of Liberate Rolls*, 1: 350, 496, and in GB, RC, *Placita de quo warranto*, p. 705. Ranulf's widow Clemencia survived the earl by twenty years: GB, RC, *Excerpta è rotulis finium*, 2: 139, 173; *Ann. monastici*, 1:305 (Burton). The editor of the *Cal. Ch. Rolls*, 4:218, notes a charter attested by Ranulf as "spurious in form"; it is also chronologically impossible, since Ranulf was dead by 20 Henry III.
50. See, for example, Wood, *English Monasteries*, pp. 130–31, and Philippe Ariès, *The Hour of Our Death*, pp. 261–62.

51. Aemilius Friedberg, *Corpus iuris canonici,* vol. 2, *Decretalium collectiones,* pp. 1272–73. Wood explained that "the patron's choice of a resting-place mattered to the [religious house for reasons of] piety, long-term gain, sentiment, and prestige" (*English Monasteries,* p. 131).
52. Matthew Paris, *Chronica majora,* 3:229–30; "Matthew of Westminster," *Flores historiarum,* 2:206 (ex Paris).
53. *Annals of Dieulacres Abbey,* in *Cheshire Sheaf* 52 (1957): 24.
54. *Monasticon,* 5:627.
55. Ormerod, *History of Chester,* 1:40.
56. *Cal. Patent Rolls,* 1232–47, p. 80.
57. GB, PRO, *Close Rolls Henry III,* 1231–34, p. 181.
58. GB, PRO, *Lists and Indexes, Supplementary Series,* vol. 5, pt. 3, no. 117.
59. For these, see Ronald Stewart-Brown, "The End of the Norman Earldom of Chester"; GB, PRO *Close Rolls Henry III,* 1231–34, pp. 263–64; GB, PRO, *Calendar of Documents Scotland,* no. 1164; GB, PRO, Fine Roll 16 Henry III, m. 1. See also the "Earldom of Chester Case," in Bracton, *Bracton's Note Book,* 3:280–83. The pipe rolls show a large number of obligations owed by the earl on Ranulf's death, but the statements of liabilities are meaningless without a statement of his assets. For the debts: GB, PRO, Pipe Roll 77 (E.372/77), mm. 2, 2d, 5d, 7, 8d, 9d, 10, 10d; Pipe Roll 78 (E.372/78), mm. 3d, 4, 4d, 11, 14; Pipe Roll 79 (E.372/79), mm. 4d, 12, 15, 15d; *Cal. Patent Rolls,* 1232–47, p. 185; Shirley, *Royal Letters,* 2:379.
60. John Harvey, *The Black Prince and His Age,* p. 16.

APPENDIX

1. The feodary (despite variations in the printed versions, and apparent variations of date, the various printed lists are the result of the identical inquest) may be found in the following sources: for comment, see James Tait, "Knight-Service in Cheshire"; R. Stewart-Brown, ed., *Calendar of Rolls Chester,* pp. xlvi–ix and 109–12; *Red Book,* pp. 184–85 (under the year 1252); *Cal. Patent Rolls,* 1338, pp. 33ff., which also includes some other lands

held of the honor outside Cheshire; *Chs in the PRs*, pp. 101ff. and 127–28; for the place names pertaining to this inquest, see the *Cheshire Sheaf*, 3d ser., vol. 1 (1903), no. 777.

2. Tait, "Knight-Service in Cheshire," found 80 knights owing service in Cheshire and 140 from the lands of the honor outside the county, but he based his opinion on Farrer. Farrer himself originally thought that 220 knights was a reasonable estimate of the *servitium debitum* of Chester (*Honors and Knights' Fees*, p. 6), but on second thought raised his enumeration of knights to 250 (p. v). In any case, his confusion of the Bolingbroke fees with those of Chester invalidated his computations and thus justified the present effort, which might perhaps be viewed as well as answering a plaint of over seven hundred years ago: "No rolls of the fiefs which the Earl of Chester held have been found at Chester, with the exception of those in Cheshire" (John LeStrange to Henry III, 1241–45, in J. G. Edwards, ed., *Calendar of Correspondence*, p. 22). For a brief criticism of Farrer's quite understandable confusion, see Sanders, *English Baronies*, s.v. "Bolingbroke" and "Chester," and notes.

3. Cazel, "Charters of the Roumare Family."

4. See Robert Somerville, "The Cowcher Books of the Duchy of Lancaster."

5. *Red Book*, p. 626 (*RHF*, 23:694).

6. The members and their tenants are to be found in *RHF*, 23: 611, 612, 620–21, 633, 636 (Léchaudé-d'Anisy, *Grands rôles*, vol. 15, pt. 1, pp. 177, 185, 187).

7. Stapleton, *Magni rotuli scaccarii Normanniae*, pp. ccxliii–ccxlv.

8. Cronne and Davis, *Regesta regum Anglo-Normannorum*, vol. 3, no. 180.

9. For the holding, see the extract from the Cartulary of Mont St.-Michel, in Robert of Torigny, *Chronicle*, p. 335, no. 18.

BIBLIOGRAPHY

PRIMARY SOURCES

"Annals of Dieulacres Abbey." *Cheshire Sheaf* 52 (1957): 17–27.
Axon, William E. A., ed. *The Annals of Manchester*. London, 1886.
Ayrton, William, ed. "Records Relating to the River Dee and Its Fisheries." *Journal of the Architectural, Archaeological, and Historic Society [of] Chester* 1 (1849–55): 234–50.
Bailey, J. E., ed. "The First Charter of Salford." *Palatine Note-Book*, July 1882, pp. 146–51.
Ballard, Alphonsus, and James Tait, eds. *British Borough Charters, 1042–1307*. 2 vols. Cambridge, 1913.
Barnes, Patricia M., and C. F. Slade, eds. *A Medieval Miscellany for Doris Mary Stenton*. Pipe Roll Society, n.s. 36. London, 1962.
Barraclough, Geoffrey, ed. *Facsimiles of Early Cheshire Charters*. Oxford, 1957.
——. "Some Charters of the Earls of Chester." In *A Medieval Miscellany for Doris Mary Stenton*, edited by Patricia M. Barnes and C. F. Slade. Pipe Roll Society, n.s. 36. London, 1962.
Bateson, Mary, ed. *Records of the Borough of Leicester*. 4 vols. Revised by W. H. Stevenson and J. E. Stocks. London and Cambridge, 1899–1923.
Beamont, William, ed. *Tracts Written in the Controversy Respecting the Legitimacy of Amicia, Daughter of Hugh Cyveliok, Earl of Chester*. Chetham Society, o.s. 78, 1869.
Bémont, Charles, ed. *Chartes des libertés anglaises, 1100–1305*. Paris, 1892.
[Benedict of Peterborough.] *Gesta Regis Henrici Secundi*, vol. 2, edited by William Stubbs. Rolls Series, no. 49. London, 1867.

Bouchart, Alain, ed. *Les Grandes Croniques de Bretagne*. Nantes, 1886.
Boulton, Helen E., ed. *The Sherwood Forest Book*. Thoroton Society Record Series, no. 23, 1965.
Bouquet, Martin, et al., eds. *Recueil des historiens des Gaules et de la France*. New ed., vols. 12–26. Paris, 1876ff.
Bourienne, V., ed. *Antiquus cartularius Ecclesiae Baiocensis [Livre noir]*. 2 vols. Paris and Rouen, 1902–3.
Boyd, W., and W. O. Massingberd, eds. *Lincolnshire Records: Abstracts of Final Concords temp. Richard I, John, and Henry III.* Vol. 1. London, 1896.
Bracton, Henry de. *Bracton's Note Book*. 3 vols. Edited by F. W. Maitland. London, 1887.
———. *De legibus et consuetudinibus Angliae*. Vol. 2. Edited by George E. Woodbine. Revised by Samuel E. Thorne. Cambridge, Mass., 1968.
Brown, R. Allen, ed. *Memoranda Roll 10 John*. Pipe Roll Society, n.s. 31. London, 1957.
Brownbill, John, ed. *The Coucher Book of Furness Abbey*. Vol. 2, pt. 2. Chetham Society, n.s. 76, 1916.
Brut y Twysogion. Edited by John Williams ab Ithel. Rolls Series, no. 17. London, 1860.
Cazel, Fred A., ed. *Foreign Accounts Henry III (1219–1234)*. Pipe Roll Society, n.s. 44. London, 1982.
———. "Norman and Wessex Charters of the Roumare Family." In *A Medieval Miscellany for Doris Mary Stenton*, edited by Patricia M. Barnes and C. F. Slade. Pipe Roll Society, n.s. 36. London, 1962.
Chaplais, Pierre, ed. *Diplomatic Documents Preserved in the Public Record Office*. Vol. 1 (1101–1272). London, 1964.
Christie, Richard C., ed. *Annales Cestrienses: The Chronicle of the Abbey of St. Werburgh at Chester*. Oxford, 1886.
Clay, C. T., ed. *Early Yorkshire Charters*. Vols. 4–6. Yorkshire Archaeological Society, Record Series, Extra Series, 1935–39.
Congregation of St. Maur. *Gallia Christiana in provincias ecclesiasticas distributa*. Vols. 11 and 14. Paris, 1856, 1874.
Cronne, H. A., and R. H. C. Davis, eds. *Regesta regum Anglo-Normannorum 1066–1154*. Vol. 3 (1135–54). Oxford, 1968.

d'Achery, Luc, ed. *Spicilegium*. Paris, 1723.
Darlington, Reginald R., ed. *The Cartulary of Darley Abbey*. Kendal, 1945.
———, ed. *The Cartulary of Worcester Cathedral Priory*. Pipe Roll Society, n.s. 38. London, 1968.
Davies, J. Conway, ed. *Cartae Antiquae, Rolls 11–20*. Pipe Roll Society, n.s. 33. London, 1960.
de Haas, Elsa, and G. D. G. Hall, eds. *Early Registers of Writs*. Selden Society, vol. 87. London, 1970.
de la Borderie, A., ed. *Recueil des actes inédits des ducs et princes de Bretagne*. Rennes, 1888.
Delisle, Léopold, ed. *Cartulaire normand*. Caen, 1952.
———, ed. *Recueil de jugements de l'échiquier de Normandie au XIII siècle (1207–1270)*. Paris, 1864.
——— and Elie Berger. *Recueil des actes de Henri II*. 4 vols. Chartes et diplômes relatifs à l'histoire de France. Paris, 1909–27.
Dilks, Thomas Bruce, ed. *Bridgewater Borough Archives, 1200–1377*. Somerset Record Society, vol. 48, 1933.
Dodwell, Barbara, ed. *The Charters of Norwich Cathedral Priory*. Vol. 1. Pipe Roll Society, n.s. 40. London, 1974 [1965–66].
Dugdale, William, ed. *Monasticon Anglicanum*. New ed. Edited by John Caley, Henry Ellis, and Bulkely Bandinel. 6 vols. London, 1917–30.
Earwaker, J. P., ed. "The Ancient Charters and Deeds at High Legh, Cheshire." *Journal of the Chester Archaeological and Historic Society*, n.s. 1 (1887): 1–29.
Edwards, John Goronwy, ed. *Calendar of Ancient Correspondence concerning Wales*. Board of Celtic Studies, University of Wales, History and Law Series 11. Cardiff, 1935.
———, ed. *Littere Wallie*. Board of Celtic Studies, University of Wales, History and Law Series 5. Cardiff, 1940.
Elvey, G. R., ed. *Luffield Priory Charters*. Vol. 1. Northamptonshire Record Society, 1968.
Eyton, R. W., ed. *Antiquities of Shropshire*. 12 vols. London, 1854–60.
———. *Court, Household, and Itinerary of Henry II*. London, 1878.
Farrer, William, ed. *Early Yorkshire Charters*. Vols. 1–3. Edinburgh, 1914–16.

―――, ed. *Final Concords of the County of Lancaster.* Vol. 1 (1196–1307). Record Society for the Publication of Original Documents Relating to Lancashire and Cheshire, vol. 39, 1899.

―――, ed. *Lancashire Inquests, Extents, and Feudal Aids.* Vol. 1 (1205–1307). Record Society for the Publication of Original Documents Relating to Lancashire and Cheshire, vol. 48, 1903.

―――, ed. *The Lancashire Pipe Rolls and Early Lancashire Charters.* Liverpool, 1902.

Flower, Cyril Thomas, ed. *Introduction to the Curia Regis Rolls, 1199–1230.* Selden Society, vol. 62. London, 1943 (1944).

Foster, C. W., ed. *The Registrum Antiquissimum of the Cathedral Church of Lincoln.* Vol. 1. Publications of the Lincoln Record Society, vol. 27. Lincoln, 1931.

France. Ministère d'état. *Layettes de trésor des chartes.* Vol. 1. Edited by Alexandre Teulet. Paris, 1863.

Friedberg, Aemilius. *Corpus iuris canonici.* Vol. 2, *Decretalium collectiones.* Graz, 1959.

Gastrell, Francis, ed. *Notitia Cestriensis.* Vol. 1. Chetham Society, o.s. 8, 1845.

Gervase of Canterbury. *Historical Works.* Edited by William Stubbs. Rolls Series, no. 73. London, 1880.

Gesta Fulconis filii Warini. Edited by Joseph Stevenson. In *Radulphi de Coggeshall Chronicon Anglicanum.* Rolls Series, no. 66. London, 1875.

[Glanvill.] *Tractatus de legibus et consuetudinibus Anglie qui Glanvilla vocatur.* Edited by G. D. G. Hall. London, 1965.

Goodman, A. W., ed. *Chartulary of Winchester Cathedral.* Winchester, 1927.

Great Britain. Curia Regis. *Curia Regis Rolls Preserved in the Public Record Office.* Vols. 1–14 (1196–1232). London, 1922–61.

―――. *Select Pleas of the Crown.* Edited by F. W. Maitland. Selden Society, vol. 1 (1888).

Great Britain. Exchequer. *The Ancient Kalendars and Inventories of the Treasury of His Majesty's Exchequer.* Vol. 1. Edited by Francis Palgrave. London, 1836.

―――. *Documents Illustrative of English History in the Thirteenth and Fourteenth Centuries.* Edited by Henry Cole. London, 1844.

---. *Liber feodorum: The Book of Fees, Commonly Called the Testa de Nevill.* 3 vols. London, 1920–31.

---. *Placitorum abbreviatio temporibus Ric. I, Johann., Henr. III, Edw. I., Edw. II.* London, 1811.

---. *Receipt Roll of the Exchequer for Michaelmas 1185* [31 Henry II]. London, 1899.

---. *Rotuli de liberate ac de misis et praestitis, regnante Johanne.* Edited by T. D. Hardy. London, 1844.

Great Britain. Parliament. House of Lords. *Reports on the Dignity of a Peer.* Vol. 2. London, 1829.

Great Britain. Public Record Office. *Annual Report of the Deputy Keeper of the Public Records.* 26th, 27th, 28th, and 29th Reports. London, 1865, 1866, 1867, 1874.

---. *Calendar of the Charter Rolls Preserved in the Public Record Office.* 5 vols. (1226–1417). London, 1903–16.

---. *Calendar of Close Rolls Preserved in the Public Record Office, Edward I, 1272–1279.* London, 1900.

---. *Calendar of Documents Preserved in France.* Vol. 1 (918–1206). Edited by John Horace Round. London, 1899.

---. *Calendar of Documents Relating to Ireland.* Vol. 1 (1171–1251). London, 1875.

---. *Calendar of Documents Relating to Scotland.* Vol. 1 (1108–1272). Edinburgh, 1881.

---. *Calendar of Entries in the Papal Registers Relating to Great Britain and Ireland.* Vol. 1 (1198–1304). London, 1893.

---. *Calendar of Inquisitions post Mortem.* Vol. 1, *Henry III*, and vol. 2, *Edward I*. London, 1904, 1906.

---. *Calendar of Liberate Rolls.* Vols. 1–4 (1226–60). London, 1916–1959.

---. *Calendar of Patent Rolls Preserved in the Public Record Office.* 31 vols., Henry III–Edward III (1216–1377). London, 1891–1916.

---. *Close Rolls of the Reign of Henry III Preserved in the Public Record Office.* 3 vols. (1227–51). London, 1902–22.

---. *A Descriptive Catalogue of Ancient Deeds.* Vol. 1. London, 1890.

---. Fine Rolls Henry III. C 60/2–18 Henry III.

———. *The Great Cowcher Books of the Duchy of Lancaster*. DL.41/42.

———. *Inquisitions and Assessments Relating to Feudal Aids*. 6 vols., 1899–1920.

———. *Lists and Indexes*. Vol. 4, *List of Plea Rolls*. New and rev. ed. New York, 1963.

———. *Lists and Indexes*. Vol. 9, *List of Sheriffs for England and Wales*. New York, 1963.

———. *Lists and Indexes*. Vol. 15, *List of Ancient Correspondence of the Chancery and Exchequer*. Rev. ed. London, 1968.

———. *Lists and Indexes*. Vol. 25, *List of Rentals and Surveys*. New York, 1963.

———. *Lists and Indexes, Supplementary Series*. Vol. 5, pt. 2, *Duchy of Lancaster . . . Royal Charters*. Vol. 5, pt. 3, *Duchy of Lancaster . . . Cartae Miscellaneae*. New York, 1964.

———. *Patent Rolls Preserved in the Public Record Office*. Henry III. 2 vols. (1216–1232). London, 1901–3.

———. *Pipe Rolls 4–18 Henry III*. E.372/64–79.

———. *Register of Edward the Black Prince*. 4 vols. London, 1930–39.

Great Britain. Record Commission. *Calendarium rotulorum chartarum et inquisitionum ad quod damnum*. London, 1803.

———. *Calendarium rotulorum patentium in turri Londinensi*. London, 1802.

———. *Documents Illustrative of English History in the Thirteenth and Fourteenth Centuries*. Edited by Henry Cole. London, 1844.

———. *Excerpta è rotulis finium in turri Londinensi asservatis, Henrico tertio rege*. Edited by Charles Roberts. 2 vols. London, 1835–36.

———. *Fines, sive pedes finium*. Edited by Joseph Hunter. London, 1835.

———. *Placita de quo warranto temporibus Edw. I. II. & III.* London, 1818.

———. *Rotuli cancellarii vel antigraphum magni rotuli pipae de tertio anno regni regis Johannis*. London, 1833.

———. *Rotuli chartarum in turri Londinensi asservati (1199–1216)*. London, 1837.

———. *Rotuli curiae regis*. Edited by Francis Palgrave. London, 1835.
———. *Rotuli de oblatis et finibus in turri Londinensi asservati tempore regis Johannis*. Edited by T. D. Hardy. London, 1835.
———. *Rotuli hundredorum temp. Hen. III et Edw. I in turri Lond' et in curia receptae scaccarii West. asservati*. London, 1812.
———. *Rotuli litterarum clausarum in turri Londinensi asservati*. Edited by T. D. Hardy. 2 vols. London, 1833–44.
———. *Rotuli litterarum patentium in turri Londinensi asservati, 1210–1216*. Edited by T. D. Hardy. London, 1835.
———. *Rotuli Normanniae in turri Londinensi asservati*. Vol. 1 (1200–1205). Edited by T. D. Hardy. London, 1835.
———. *Rotuli selecti ad res Anglicas et Hibernicas*. Edited by Joseph Hunter. London, 1834.
———. *Statutes of the Realm*. Vol. 1. London, 1810.
Great Britain. Royal Commission on Historical Manuscripts. *First Report*. London, 1870.
———. *Second Report*. London, 1871.
———. *Fourth Report*. Pt. 1, appendix. London, 1874.
———. *Fifth Report*. London, 1876.
———. *Eighth Report with Appendix*. London, 1881.
———. *Tenth Report*. Appendix, pt. 4 (Westmoreland Manuscripts). London, 1885.
———. *Report on the Manuscripts of the Late Reginald Rawdon Hastings, Esq*. Vol. 1. London, 1928.
Guillaume le Breton [Guillelmus Armoricus]. *Oeuvres*. Edited by Henri François Delaborde. Paris, 1882, 1885.
Hale, John W., and F. J. Furnivall, eds. *Bishop Percy's Folio Manuscript*. London, 1867.
Hall, Hubert, ed. *The Red Book of the Exchequer*. 3 vols. Rolls Series, no. 99. London, 1896.
Halliwell, James O., ed. *Palatine Anthology*. London, 1850.
Hand-List of Charters, Deeds and Similar Documents in the Possession of the John Rylands Library, Manchester. Vol. 1, edited by Robert Fawtier. Vol. 2, edited by Moses Tyson. Vol. 3, edited by Frank Taylor. Manchester, 1925.
Harland, John, ed. *Mamecestre*. Vol. 1. Chetham Society, o.s. 53, 1861.
Harrod, Henry Hawes, ed. "A Defense of the Liberties of Chester,

1450." *Journal of the Architectural, Archaeological, and Historic Society of Chester and North Wales*, n.s. 8 (1908): 18–44.

Haydon, Frank Scott, ed. *Eulogium . . . a monacho quodam Malmesburiensi exaratum*. Rolls Series, no. 9. London, 1863.

Higden, Ranulf. *Polychronicon*. Edited by J. R. Lumby. Vol. 8. Rolls Series, no. 41. London, 1882.

Holt, J. C., ed. *Magna Carta and the English Charters of Liberties 1100–1225*. Oxford, forthcoming.

Hugh of Welles. *Rotuli Hugonis de Welles, Episcopi Lincolniensis*. Edited by W. P. W. Phillimore et al. 3 vols. Canterbury and York Society, vols. 1, 3, and 4, 1907–9.

Hulton, William A., ed. *The Coucher Book or Chartulary of Whalley Abbey*. 4 vols. Chetham Society, o.s. 10, 11, 16, 20, 1847–49.

Innocent III. *The Letters of Pope Innocent III (1198–1216) concerning England and Wales*. Edited by C. R. Cheney and Mary Cheney. Oxford, 1967.

———. *Selected Letters of Pope Innocent III concerning England (1198–1216)*. Edited by C. R. Cheney and W. H. Semple. London, 1953.

Inquisitiones post-mortem, etc., *1327–1366*. Staffordshire Record Society, 3d ser., 1913.

Jeayes, Isaac H. *Descriptive Catalogue of the Charters and Muniments at Berkeley Castle*. Bristol, 1892.

———. *Descriptive Catalogue of Derbyshire Charters*. London, 1906.

John of Oxnede. *Chronica*. Edited by Henry Ellis. Rolls Series, no. 13. London, 1859.

John of Salisbury. *Policraticus*. Vol. 2. Edited by C. C. J. Webb. Oxford, 1909.

Jones, W. Rich, ed. *The Register of St. Osmund*. Rolls Series, no. 78. London, 1883–84.

Knighton, Henry. *Chronicon*. Edited by J. R. Lumby. Rolls Series, no. 92. London, 1889.

Lancaster, W. T., and W. Paley Baildon, eds. *The Coucher Book of the Cistercian Abbey of Kirkstall*. Thoresby Society, vol. 8, 1904.

Landon, Lionel, ed. *Cartae antiquae, Rolls 1–10*. Pipe Roll Society, n.s. 17. London, 1939.

———, ed. *The Itinerary of Richard I*. Pipe Roll Society, n.s. 13. London, 1935.

Léchaudé-d'Anisy, Louis-Amédée, ed. *Grands rôles des échiquiers de Normandie*. Mémoires de la Société des Antiquaires de Normandie, vols. 15 and 16, 1846–52.

Legg, Leopold G. Wickham, ed. *English Coronation Records*. New York, 1901.

Leland, John. *Collectanea*. Vols. 1 and 2, edited by Thomas Hearne. London, 1770.

Lloyd, Lewis, and Doris M. Stenton, eds. *Sir Christopher Hatton's Book of Seals*. Oxford, 1950.

Luard, H. R., ed. *Annales monastici*. 5 vols. Rolls Series, no. 36. London, 1864–69.

[Lucianus.] *Liber Luciani de laude Cestrie*. Edited by M. V. Taylor. Record Society for the Publication of Original Documents Relating to Lancashire and Cheshire, vol. 64, 1912.

Maitland, F. W., ed. *Three Rolls of the King's Court in the Reign of Richard I, A.D. 1194–1195*. Pipe Roll Society, vol. 14. London, 1891.

Maitland, F. W., and William Paley Baildon, eds. *The Court Baron*. Selden Society, vol. 4. London, 1891.

Major, Kathleen, ed. *The Registrum Antiquissimum of the Cathedral Church of Lincoln*. Vol. 6. Publications of the Lincoln Record Society, vols. 41 and 42. Lincoln, 1950.

Matthew Paris. *Chronica majora*. Edited by H. R. Luard. 7 vols. Rolls Series, no. 57. London, 1874–83.

———. *Historia Anglorum*. Edited by Frederic Madden. Rolls Series, no. 44. London, 1866.

[Matthew of Westminster.] *Flores historiarum*. Vol. 2, edited by H. R. Luard. Rolls Series, no. 95. London, 1890.

Meyer, Paul, ed. *L'Histoire de Guillaume le Maréchal*. Paris, 1894–1901.

Michel, Francisque Xavier, ed. *Histoire des ducs de Normandie et des rois d'Angleterre*. Paris, 1840.

Mills, Mabel, and R. Stewart-Brown, eds. *Cheshire in the Pipe Rolls, 1158–1301*. Record Society for the Publication of Original Documents Relating to Lancashire and Cheshire, vol. 92, 1938.

Morice, Pierre-Hyacinthe, ed. *Mémoires pour servir de preuves a l'histoire ecclésiastique et civile de Bretagne*. Vol. 1. Paris, 1742.

Oliver Scholasticus. *Historia Damiatina*. In *Die Schriften des Köl-*

ner Domscholasters usw., edited by H. Hoogeweg. Bibliothek des litterarischen Vereins in Stuttgart, 202:159–282. Tübingen, 1894.

Packard, Sidney, ed. *Miscellaneous Records of the Norman Exchequer, 1199–1204*. Smith College Studies in History, vol. 12. Northampton, Mass., 1927.

Parker, F., ed. *A Chartulary of the Augustinian Priory of Trentham*. William Salt Archaeological Society, vol. 11, 1890.

Parker, John, ed. *Feet of Fines for the County of York, 1218–1231*. Yorkshire Archaeological Society, Record Series, vol. 62, 1921.

Philip Augustus, King of France. *Recueil des actes de Philippe Auguste*. Vol. 1, edited by E. Berger and H. F. Delaborde. Vol. 2, edited by H. F. Delaborde and Ch. Petit-Dutaillis. Vol. 3, edited by M. J. Monicat and M. J. Boussard. Paris, 1916–66.

Pipe Roll Society. *The Great Roll of the Pipe*, 27 Henry II through 3 Henry III. Edited by Doris M. Stenton et al. O.s. 30–38, n.s. 1–42. London: 1909ff.

Powicke, F. M., and C. R. Cheney, eds. *Councils and Synods, with Other Documents Relating to the English Church*. Vol. 2 (1205–1313). 2 pts. Oxford, 1964.

Radulphus de Coggeshall. *Chronicon Anglicanum*. Edited by Joseph Stevenson. Rolls Series, no. 55. London, 1875.

Recueil des historiens des Croisades. Vol. 2, *Historiens occidentaux*. Paris, 1859.

Richardson, H. G. *Memoranda Roll of the King's Remembrancer, 1 John*. Pipe Roll Society, n.s. 21. London, 1943.

Rigord. *Gesta Philippi Augusti*. Edited by H. F. Delaborde. Paris, 1882.

Robert of Torigny. *Chronicle*. In *Chronicles of the Reigns of Stephen, Henry II, and Richard I*, edited by Richard Howlett. Rolls Series, no. 82, vol. 4. London, 1864.

Robinson, Chalfont, ed. *Memoranda Roll 14 Henry III*. Pipe Roll Society, n.s. 31. London, 1933.

Roger of Howden [Hoveden]. *Chronica*. Edited by William Stubbs. Rolls Series, no. 51, vols. 3 and 4. London, 1870, 1871.

Roger of Wendover. *Flores historiarum*. 3 vols. Edited by Henry G. Hewlett. Rolls Series, no. 84. London, 1886–89.

Roper, William O., ed. *Materials for the History of the Church of Lancaster*. Vol. 1. Chetham Society, n.s. 26, 1892.

Rymer, Thomas, ed. *Foedera*. Vols. 1 and 2. New ed. London, 1816.
Savage, H. E., ed. *The Great Register of Lichfield Cathedral, Known as Magnum Registrum Album*. William Salt Archaeological Society, Vol. 48, 1924–25.
Sayles, G. O., ed. *Select Cases in the Court of King's Bench under Edward I*. Vol. 1. Selden Society, vol. 55. London, 1936.
Selby, Walford D., ed. *Lancashire and Cheshire Records Preserved in the Public Record Office*. Record Society for the Publication of Original Documents Relating to Lancashire and Cheshire, vol. 7, 1882.
Shirley, W. W., ed. *Royal and Other Historical Letters Illustrative of the Reign of Henry III*. 2 vols. Rolls Series, no. 27. London, 1862, 1866.
Stanhope, Edward, ed. *Abstracts of the Deeds and Charters Relating to Revesby Abbey, 1142–1539*. Horncastle, 1889.
Stapleton, Thomas, ed. *Magni rotuli scaccarii Normanniae*. 2 vols. London, 1840, 1844.
Stenton, Doris M., ed. *The Chancellor's Roll for the Eighth Year of the Reign of King Richard the First*. Pipe Roll Society, n.s. 7. London, 1830.
———, ed. *The Earliest Lincolnshire Assize Rolls, A.D. 1202–1209*. Publications of the Lincoln Record Society, vol. 22. Lincoln, 1926.
———, ed. *Pleas before the King or His Justices*. 4 vols. Selden Society, vols. 67, 68, 83, 84. London, 1953–67.
———, ed. *Rolls of the Justices in Eyre . . . for Gloucestershire, Warwickshire, and Staffordshire, 1221, 1222*. Selden Society, vol. 59. London, 1940.
———, ed. *Rolls of the Justices in Eyre . . . for Lincolnshire 1218–19 and Worcestershire 1221*. Selden Society, vol. 53. London, 1934.
———, ed. *Rolls of the Justices in Eyre . . . for Yorkshire in 3 Henry III (1218–1219)*. Selden Society, vol. 56. London, 1937.
Stenton, Frank, ed. *Documents Illustrative of the Social and Economic History of the Danelaw*. British Academy, Records of the Social and Economic History of England and Wales, vol. 5. London, 1920.
Stephen Langton. *Acta Stephani Langton, 1207–1228*. Canterbury and York Society, vol. 50, 1950.
Stewart-Brown, Ronald, ed. *Accounts of the Chamberlains and*

Other Officers of the County of Chester, 1301–1360. Record Society for the Publication of Original Documents Relating to Lancashire and Cheshire, vol. 59, 1910.

———, ed. *Calendar of County Court, City Court, and Eyre Rolls of Chester, 1259–1297, with an Inquest of Military Service, 1288.* Chetham Society, n.s. 84, 1925.

Tait, James, ed. *The Chartulary or Register of the Abbey of St. Werburgh Chester.* Chetham Society, n.s. 79 and 82, 1920, 1923.

———. *Domesday Survey of Cheshire.* Chetham Society, n.s. 75, 1916.

Tardif, Ernest-Josef, ed. *Coutumiers de Normandie.* Vol. 1, *Le trés ancien coutumier de Normandie.* Rouen, 1881.

Thomas of Burton. *Chronica monasterii de Melsa.* Edited by Edward A. Bond. Rolls Series, no. 43, vol. 1. London, 1866.

Turner, G. J., ed. *Select Pleas of the Forest.* Selden Society, vol. 13. London, 1901.

Walter of Coventry. *Memoriale.* Edited by William Stubbs. Rolls Series, no. 58. London, 1872–73.

Walter of Guisborough. *The Chronicle of Walter of Guisborough, Previously Edited as the Chronicle of Walter of Hemingford or Hemingburgh.* Edited by Harry Rothwell. Camden Society, 3d ser., vol. 89, 1957.

Warner, G. F., and H. J. Ellis, eds. *Facsimiles of Royal and Other Charters in the British Museum.* Vol. 1. London, 1903.

Wharton, Henry, ed. *Anglia sacra.* Vol. 1. London, 1691.

William of Nangis. *Chronicon.* In *Spicilegium,* edited by Luc d'Achery. Paris, 1723.

Wright, Thomas, ed. *The Political Songs of England.* Camden Society, o.s. 6. London, 1839.

Wrottesley, George. *An Abstract of the Contents of the Burton Chartulary.* Staffordshire Record Society, vol. 5, pt. 1, 1884.

———, ed. *Chartulary of Dieulacres Abbey.* William Salt Archaeological Society, vol. 9, 1906.

———, ed. *Extracts from the Coram Rege Rolls of Edward III and Richard II, 1327–1383.* William Salt Archaeological Society, vol. 14, 1893.

———, ed. *The Stone Chartulary.* Staffordshire Record Society, vol. 7, 1885.

SECONDARY SOURCES

Alexander, James W. "The Alleged Palatinates of Norman England." *Speculum* 56 (1981): 17–27.
———. "The English Palatinates and Edward I," *Journal of British Studies* 22 (Spring 1983): 59–83.
———. "New Evidence on the Palatinate of Chester." *English Historical Review* 85 (1970): 715–29.
———. "A Pinchpenny Patron: Ranulf III of Chester." *Cîteaux* 1 (1971): 23–39.
———. "Ranulf III of Chester: An Outlaw of Legend?" *Neuphilologische Mitteilungen* 83 (February 1982): 152–57.
Ariès, Philippe. *The Hour of Our Death*. New York, 1982.
Ashton, J. W. "Rymes of Randolph, Earl of Chester." *English Literary History* 5 (1938): 195–206.
Ault, W. O. *Private Jurisdiction in England*. New Haven, 1923.
Auvry, Claude. *Histoire de la congrégation de Savigny*. Edited by A. Laveille. 3 vols. Paris and Rouen, 1896–98.
Baldwin, James F. *The King's Council in England during the Middle Ages*. Oxford, 1913.
Baldwin, John W. *Masters, Merchants, and Princes: The Social Views of Peter the Chanter and His Circle*. Princeton, N.J., 1970.
Barlow, Frank. *Durham Jurisdictional Peculiars*. Oxford, 1950.
———. *The Feudal Kingdom of England, 1042–1216*. London, 1961.
Barraclough, Geoffrey. *The Earldom and County Palatine of Chester*. Oxford, 1953.
Bateson, Mary. "The Laws of Breteuil, IV." *English Historical Review* 16 (1901): 92–110.
Bazeley, M. L. "The Extent of the English Forest in the Thirteenth Century." *Transactions of the Royal Historical Society*, 4th ser. (1921) : 140–72.
Beeler, John. *Warfare in England, 1066–1189*. Ithaca, N.Y., 1966.
Bémont, Charles. *Simon de Montfort, Earl of Leicester*. Translated by E. F. Jacob. Oxford, 1930.
Beresford, M. W., and H. P. R. Finberg. *English Medieval Boroughs: A Hand-List*. Newton Abbot, 1973.
Blackstone, Sir William. *Commentaries on the Laws of England*. 4 vols. 1765. Reprint. London, 1966.

Bloch, Marc. *Les caractères originaux de l'histoire rurale française.* New ed. Paris, 1955.

Bouard, Michel de. "La Duché de Normandie." In Vol. 1 of *Histoire des institutions françaises au Moyen Age,* edited by Ferdinand Lot and Robert Fawtier. Paris, 1957.

Boussard, Jacques. *Le gouvernement d'Henri II Plantagenêt.* Paris, 1956.

Brown, R. Allen. "A List of Castles, 1154-1216." *English Historical Review* 74 (1959): 249-80.

Burne, R. V. H. *The Monks of Chester: The History of St. Werburgh's Abbey.* London, 1962.

Cam, Helen. "The Evolution of the Medieval English Franchise." *Speculum* 32 (1957): 427-42.

―――. *Liberties and Communities in Medieval England.* London, 1963.

Cartellieri, Alexander. *Philipp II. August, König von Frankreich.* Vols. 1-4. Leipzig and Paris, 1899-1922.

Cazel, F. A., Jr. "The Fifteenth of 1225." *Bulletin of the Institute of Historical Research* 34 (1961): 67-81.

―――. "Norman and Wessex Charters of the Roumare Family." In *A Medieval Miscellany for Doris Mary Stenton,* edited by Patricia M. Barnes and C. F. Slade. Pipe Roll Society, n.s. 36. London, 1962.

Chaytor, H. J. *Savaric de Mauléon, Baron and Troubadour.* Cambridge, 1939.

Cheney, Christopher Robert. "The Alleged Deposition of King John." In *Studies in Medieval History Presented to Frederick Maurice Powicke,* edited by R. W. Hunt, W. A. Pantin, and R. W. Southern. Oxford, 1948.

―――. *Hubert Walter.* London, 1967.

Chrimes, S. B. *English Constitutional Ideas in the Fifteenth Century.* Cambridge, 1936.

Clanchy, M. T. "The Franchise of Return of Writs." *Transactions of the Royal Historical Society,* 5th ser., 17 (1967): 59-82.

Clapham, J. H. *The Cambridge Economic History.* Vol. 1. Cambridge, 1942.

C[okayne], G[eorge] E[dward]. *The Complete Peerage.* 13 vols. in

14. New ed., revised and enlarged by Vicary Gibbs. London, 1910–59.

Colvin, H. M., ed. *The History of the King's Works*. Vols. 1 and 2, *The Middle Ages*, edited by R. Allen Brown, H. M. Colvin, and A. J. Taylor. London, 1963.

———. *The White Canons in England*. Oxford, 1951.

Cooke, J. H. *Bibliotheca Cestriensis*. Warrington, 1904.

Costain, Thomas B. *The Magnificent Century*. New York, 1951.

Coulton, G. G. *Medieval Village, Manor, and Monastery*. New York, 1961.

Cronne, H. A. "The Honour of Lancaster in Stephen's Reign." *English Historical Review* 50 (1935): 670–80.

———. "Ranulf de Gernons, Earl of Chester 1129–1154." *Transactions of the Royal Historical Society*, 4th ser., 20 (1937): 103–34.

———. "The Royal Forest in the Reign of Henry I." In *Essays in British and Irish History in Honour of J. E. Todd*, edited by H. A. Cronne et al. London, 1949.

Cunningham, William. *Growth of English Industry and Commerce during the Early and Middle Ages*. Vol. 1. Cambridge, 1915.

Davies, C. Stella. *A History of Macclesfield*. Manchester, 1961.

Davis, David Brian. *The Problem of Slavery in Western Culture*. Ithaca, N.Y., 1966.

Davis, G. R. C. *Medieval Cartularies of Great Britain: A Short Catalogue*. London, 1958.

Davis, H. W. C. *England under the Normans and Angevins, 1066–1272*. New York and London, 1928.

de la Borderie, A. *Essai sur la géographie féodale de la Bretagne*. Rennes, 1889.

———. *Histoire de Bretagne*. Vol. 3. Rennes, 1906.

Delisle, Léopold. "Des revenus publics en Normandie." *Bibliothèque de l'Ecole des Chartes* 10 (1848/49): 173–210 and 257–89, and 11 (1849): 400–457.

Denholm-Young, Noël. *Richard of Cornwall*. Oxford, 1947.

———. *Seignorial Administration in England*. Oxford, 1937.

"Descent of the Earldom of Lincoln." In vol. 1 of *Topographer and Geneologist*, edited by John Gough Nichols. London, 1846.

Ditmas, Edith M. R. "The Curtana or Sword of Mercy." *Journal of* the British Archaeological Association, 3d ser., 29 (1966): 122–33.

Douglas, David C. William the Conqueror. Berkeley and Los Angeles, 1964.

Dugdale, Sir William. The Antiquities of Warwickshire. London, 1656.

———. The Baronage of England. Vol. 1. London, 1675.

Duggan, A. P., and M. W. Greenslade. Victoria History of the County of Stafford. Vol. 3. Oxford, 1970.

Earwaker, J. P. East Cheshire. 2 vols. London, 1877, 1880.

Ellis, Clarence. Hubert de Burgh: A Study in Constancy. London, 1952.

Ellis, Geoffrey. Earldoms in Fee: A Study in Peerage Law and Family. London, 1963.

Farrer, William. Honors and Knights' Fees. 3 vols. London, 1923, 1924, and Manchester, 1925.

Flower, Cyril Thomas. Introduction to the Curia Regis Rolls, 1199–1230 A.D. Selden Society, vol. 62. London, 1944.

Fox, Levi. "The Honor and Earldom of Leicester: Origin and Descent, 1066–1399." English Historical Review 54 (1939): 385–402.

Franklin, Alfred. Les Sources d'histoire de France. Paris, 1877.

Fraser, C. M. A History of Antony Bek, Bishop of Durham 1283–1311. Oxford, 1957.

Galbraith, V. H. Roger Wendover and Matthew Paris. Glasgow, 1944.

Gillingham, John. Richard the Lionheart. New York, 1978.

———. "The Unromantic Death of Richard I." Speculum 54 (1979): 18–41.

Gleason, Sarell Everett. An Ecclesiastical Barony of the Middle Ages: The Bishopric of Bayeux, 1066–1204. Cambridge, Mass., 1936.

Goebel, J. Felony and Misdemeanor. New York, 1937.

Gower, Foote. A Sketch of the Materials for a New and Compleat History of Cheshire. 3d ed. London, 1800.

Guilloreau, Léon. "Les Fondations anglaises de l'abbaye de Savigny." Revue Mabillon 5 (1909): 290–335.

Hall, James. A History of the Town and Parish of Nantwich. Nantwich, 1883.

Harcourt, L. W. Vernon. *His Grace the Steward and Trial of Peers*. London, 1907.
Harris, Brian E. "Administrative History." Draft typescript for vol. 2 of *Victoria County History of Cheshire*. Forthcoming.
———. "Ranulf III, Earl of Chester." *Journal of the Chester Archaeological Society* 58 (1975): 99–114.
Harvey, John. *The Black Prince and His Age*. Totowa, N.J., 1976.
Haskins, Charles Homer. *Norman Institutions*. 1918. Reprint. New York, 1960.
Hewitt, Herbert James. *Mediaeval Cheshire: An Economic and Social History of Cheshire in the Reigns of the Three Edwards*. Chetham Society, n.s. 88. Manchester, 1929.
Hibbert, F. A. *Monasticism in Staffordshire*. Stafford, 1909.
Hill, Bennett. "The Counts of Mortain and the Origins of the Norman Congregation of Savigny." In *Order and Innovation in the Middle Ages*, edited by William C. Jordan, Bruce McNab, and Teofilo F. Ruiz. Princeton, N.J., 1976.
———. *English Cistercian Monasteries and Their Patrons in the Twelfth Century*. Urbana, Ill., 1968.
Hill, James W. F. *Medieval Lincoln*. Cambridge, 1965.
Hilton, R. H. *The Decline of Serfdom in Medieval England*. Studies in Economic History, edited by M. W. Flinn. London, 1969.
———. "Freedom and Villeinage in England." *Past and Present* 31 (1965): 3–19.
Holdsworth, William S. *A History of English Law*. Vol. 1. 7th ed. Revised by A. L. Goodhart and H. G. Hanburg with introductory essay and additions by S. B. Chrimes. London, 1956.
Hollister, C. Warren. "King John and the Historians." *Journal of British Studies* 1 (1961): 1–19.
———. *The Military Organization of Norman England*. Oxford, 1965.
Holt, J. C. *King John*. London, 1963.
———. *Magna Carta*. Cambridge, 1965.
———. *The Making of Magna Carta*. Charlottesville, 1965.
———. *The Northerners*. Oxford, 1961.
Homans, George C. *English Villagers of the Thirteenth Century*. Cambridge, 1941.

Hunt, R. W., W. A. Pantin, and R. W. Southern, eds. *Studies in Medieval History Presented to Frederick Maurice Powicke*. Oxford, 1948.

Hurnard, Naomi. "The Anglo-Norman Franchises." *English Historical Review* 64 (1949): 289–327, 433–60.

———. *The King's Pardon for Homicide before A.D. 1307*. Oxford, 1969.

Janauschek, P. Leopold. *Originum Cisterciensium*. Vol. 1. 1877. Reprint Vienna, 1964.

Jenkins, J. G., ed. *The Victoria History of the County of Staffordshire*. Vol. 8. London, 1963.

Jeulin, P. "Un grand 'honneur' anglais: Aperçus sur le 'comté' de Richmond." *Annales de Bretagne* 42 (1935): 265–302.

Jewell, Helen M. *English Local Administration in the Middle Ages*. Newton Abbot and New York, 1972.

Jolliffe, J. E. A. *Angevin Kingship*. 2d ed. London, 1963.

Kaye, J. M. "The Sacrabar." *English Historical Review* 83 (1968): 744–58.

Kealey, Edward J. *Medieval Medicus: A Social History of Anglo-Norman Medicine*. Baltimore, 1981.

Keefe, Thomas K. *Feudal Assessments and the Political Community under Henry II and His Sons*. Berkeley and Los Angeles, forthcoming.

Ker, N. R. *Medieval Manuscripts in British Libraries*. Vol. 1, London. Oxford, 1969.

Knowles, David. *The Religious Orders in England*. Vol. 1. Cambridge, 1956.

Labarge, Margaret Wade. *Simon de Montfort*. London, 1962.

Lapsley, Gaillard Thomas. *The County Palatinate of Durham*. New York, 1900.

———. "The Court, Record and Roll of the County in the Thirteenth Century." *Law Quarterly Review* 51 (1935): 299–325.

———. *Crown, Community and Parliament*. Edited by Helen Cam and G. Barraclough. Oxford, 1951.

Laurent, Jane K. "An Edition of Charters from the Cowcher Books of the Duchy of Lancaster." M.A. thesis, University of Georgia, 1971.

le Patourel, John H. *The Medieval Administration of the Channel Islands.* Oxford, 1937.
Lewis, Andrew W. "The Capetian Apanages and the Nature of the French Kingdom." *Journal of Medieval History* 2 (1976): 119–34.
Lewis, Michael. *Ancestors.* London, 1966.
Lipson, Ephraim. *The Economic History of England.* Vol. 1, *The Middle Ages.* London, 1949.
Lloyd, John E. *A History of Wales from the Earliest Times to the Edwardian Conquest.* 3d ed. 2 vols. London, 1939.
———. "The Welsh Chronicles." *Proceedings of the British Academy* 14 (1928): 369–91.
Lobel, M. D., ed. *Victoria County History of Oxford.* Vols. 6 and 8. London, 1959, 1964.
Lobineau, Gui Alexis. *Histoire de Bretagne.* 2 vols. Paris, 1707.
Lunt, William E. *Financial Relations of the Papacy with England to 1327.* Boston, 1939.
McFarlane, Kenneth Bruce. "Had Edward I a 'Policy' towards the Earls?" In *The Nobility of Later Medieval England.* Oxford, 1973.
Madox, Thomas. *Baronia Anglica.* London, 1741.
———. *The History and Antiquities of the Exchequer of the Kings of England.* 2d ed. 2 vols. London, 1769. Reprint. 1969.
Matthew, Donald. *The Norman Monasteries and Their English Possessions.* Oxford, 1962.
Mitchell, Sydney Knox. *Studies in Taxation under John and Henry III.* New Haven, 1914.
———. *Taxation in Medieval England.* Edited by Sidney Painter. New Haven, Conn., 1951.
Morice, Pierre-Hyacinthe. *Histoire ecclésiastique et civile de Bretagne.* Vol. 1. Paris, 1750.
Morris, Rupert H. *Chester in the Plantagenet and Tudor Periods.* Chester, n.d.
Morris, W. A. *The Constitutional History of England to 1216.* New York, 1930.
———. *The Medieval English Sheriff to 1300.* Manchester, 1927.
Neilson, Nellie. "The Forests." In vol. 1 of *The English Government at Work, 1327–1336*, edited by W. A. Morris. Cambridge, Mass., 1940.

Nichols, John. *The History and Antiquities of the County of Leicester.* Wakefield, 1795.
Norgate, Kate. *England under the Angevin Kings.* 2 vols. London, 1887.
———. *John Lackland.* London, 1902.
———. *The Minority of Henry III.* 1916.
Ormerod, George. *The History of the County Palatine and City of Chester.* 3 vols. 2d ed., revised and enlarged by Thomas Helsby. London, 1882.
———. *Miscellanea Palatina.* London, 1851.
O'Sullivan, Jeremiah F. *Cistercian Settlements in Wales and Monmouthshire 1140–1540.* New York, 1947.
Otway-Ruthven, A. J. "The Constitutional Position of the Great Lordships of South Wales." *Transactions of the Royal Historical Society,* 5th ser., 9 (1958): 1–20.
Page, William, ed. *Victoria County History of Warwickshire.* Vol. 2. 1908.
Painter, Sidney. *Feudalism and Liberty.* Edited by F. A. Cazel. Baltimore, 1961.
———. *The Reign of King John.* Baltimore, 1949.
———. *The Scourge of the Clergy: Peter of Dreux, Duke of Brittany.* Baltimore, 1937.
———. *Studies in the History of the English Feudal Barony.* Baltimore, 1943.
———. *William Marshal.* Baltimore, 1933.
Pape, T. *Medieval Newcastle-under-Lyme.* Manchester, 1928.
Petit-Dutaillis, Ch. *Etude sur la vie et la regne de Louis VIII.* Paris, 1894.
———. *Studies and Notes Supplementary to Stubbs' Constitutional History.* Vol. 2. 1914.
Plucknett, Theodore F. T. *A Concise History of the Common Law.* 5th ed. Boston, 1956.
———. *Legislation of Edward I.* Oxford, 1962.
Pollock, Frederick, and Frederic William Maitland. *The History of English Law.* 2 vols. 2d ed. Cambridge, 1968.
Poole, Austin Lane. *From Domesday Book to Magna Carta.* 2d ed. Oxford, 1955.
———. *Obligations of Society in the Twelfth and Thirteenth Centuries.* Oxford, 1946.

Post, Gaines. *Studies in Medieval Legal Thought.* Princeton, N.J., 1964.
Postan, M. M. *The Cambridge Economic History of Europe.* Vol. 1, *The Agrarian Life of the Middle Ages.* 2d ed. Cambridge, 1966.
Powicke, F. M. "The Compilation of the *Chronica Majora* of Matthew Paris." *Proceedings of the British Academy* 30 (1944): 147–60.
———. *King Henry III and the Lord Edward.* Oxford, 1947.
———. *The Loss of Normandy.* 2d ed. Manchester, 1961.
———. *Stephen Langton.* London, 1965.
———. *The Thirteenth Century, 1216–1307.* Oxford, 1953.
Queller, Donald E., and Gerald W. Day. "Some Arguments in Defense of the Venetians on the Fourth Crusade." *American Historical Review* 77 (1972): 717–37.
Ramsay, James H. *The Angevin Empire.* New York, 1903.
———. *The Dawn of the Constitution.* Oxford, 1908.
Rees, William. *South Wales and the March, 1284–1415.* Oxford, 1924.
Renn, Derek F. *Norman Castles in Britain.* New York, 1968.
Richardson, H. G. "The English Coronation Oath." *Speculum* 24 (1949): 60–61.
———. *The English Jewry under the Angevin Kings.* London, 1960.
Ridgeway, Maurice H., and D. J. Cathcart King. "Beeston Castle, Cheshire." *Journal of the Chester and North Wales Architectural, Archaeological and Historic Society* 46 (1959): 1–24.
Round, J. H. *The King's Serjeants and Officers of State.* London, 1911.
———. "King Stephen and the Earl of Chester." *English Historical Review* 10 (1895): 87–91.
———. *Peerage and Pedigree: Studies in Peerage Law and Family History.* 2 vols. London, 1910.
Rubin, Stanley. *Medieval English Medicine.* Newton Abbot, 1974.
Runciman, Steven. *A History of the Crusades.* Vol. 3, *The Kingdom of Acre.* Cambridge, 1953.
Russell, J. C. "Social Status at the Court of King John." *Speculum* 12 (1937): 319–29.
Saint-Sauveur, E. Durtelle de. *Histoire de Bretagne.* Vol. 1. Rennes, 1957.
Salzman, L. F. *English Industries of the Middle Ages.* Oxford, 1923.

———. *English Trade in the Middle Ages*. Oxford, 1931.
———, ed. *Victoria County History of Warwickshire*. Vols. 5 and 6. London, 1949, 1951.
Sanders, I. J. *English Baronies*. Oxford, 1960.
———. *Feudal Military Service in England*. Oxford, 1956.
Scammell, Geoffrey V. *Hugh du Puiset, Bishop of Durham*. Cambridge, 1956.
Scammell, Jean. "The Origin and Limitations of the Liberty of Durham." *English Historical Review* 81 (1966): 449–73.
Sharp, Thomas. *Illustrative Papers on the History and Antiquities of the City of Coventry*. Birmingham, 1871.
Shaw, Ronald Cunliffe. *The Royal Forest of Lancaster*. Preston, 1956.
Siedschlag, Beatrice N. *English Participation in the Crusades, 1150–1220*. Privately printed, 1939.
Sitwell, George. *The Barons of Pulford*. Scarborough, 1889.
Somerville, Robert. "The Cowcher Books of the Duchy of Lancaster." *English Historical Review* 51 (1936): 598–615.
———. "The Duchy and County Palatine of Lancaster." *Transactions of the Historic Society of Lancashire and Cheshire* 103 (1952): 59–67.
———. *History of the Duchy of Lancaster*. Vol. 1, 1265–1603. London, 1953.
Stein, Henri. *Bibliographie générale des cartulaires français*. Paris, 1907.
Stenton, Doris M. *English Justice between the Norman Conquest and the Great Charter, 1066–1215*. Memoirs of the American Philosophical Society, vol. 60. Philadelphia, 1964.
Stenton, Frank M. *The First Century of English Feudalism, 1066–1166*. 2d ed. Oxford, 1961.
Stewart-Brown, Ronald. "The 'Domesday' Roll of Chester." *English Historical Review* 37 (1922): 481–500.
———. "The End of the Norman Earldom of Chester." *English Historical Review* 35 (1920): 26–54.
———. "The Exchequer of Chester." *English Historical Review* 57 (1942): 289–97.
———. "The Hospital of St. John at Chester." *Transactions of the Historic Society of Lancashire and Cheshire* 78 (n.s. 42, 1926): 66–106.

---. *Serjeants of the Peace in Medieval England and Wales.* Manchester, 1936.

Strayer, Joseph R. "Knight Service in Normandy." In *Anniversary Essays in Medieval History by Students of Charles Homer Haskins,* edited by Charles H. Taylor and John L. Lamonte. Boston and New York, 1929.

Stubbs, William. *The Constitutional History of England.* 3d ed. Vols. 1, 2. Oxford, 1880, 1883.

Sutherland, Donald W. *Quo Warranto Proceedings in the Reign of Edward I, 1278–1294.* Oxford, 1963.

Tait, James. "Knight-Service in Cheshire." *English Historical Review* 57 (1942): 437–59.

---. *Mediaeval Manchester and the Beginnings of Lancashire.* Manchester, 1904.

---. "The Two Earliest Municipal Charters of Coventry." *English Historical Review* 36 (January 1921): 50–53.

Tillman, H. *Die päpstlichen Legaten in England bis zur Beendigung der Legation Gualas (1218).* Bonn, 1926.

Titow, J. Z., *English Rural Society.* New York, 1969.

Topographer and Genealogist. Vol. 2, 1846.

Tout, Margaret. "Comitatus Palacii." *English Historical Review* 35 (1920): 418–19.

Tout, Thomas Frederick. *Chapters in the Administrative History of Mediaeval England.* 6 vols. 1928–37. Reprint. New York, 1967.

---. "The Fair of Lincoln and the 'Histoire de Guillaume le Maréchal.'" In vol. 2 of *The Collected Papers of Thomas Frederick Tout.* Manchester, 1934.

Treharne, Reginald Francis. *Essays on Thirteenth Century England.* London, 1971.

Turner, G. J. "The Minority of Henry III." *Transactions of the Royal Historical Society,* n.s. 18 (1904): 245–95, and 3d ser. (1907): 205–62.

Turner, Ralph V. *The King and His Courts.* Ithaca, N.Y., 1968.

---. "William de Forz, Count of Aumale: An Early Thirteenth-Century English Baron." *Proceedings of the American Philosophical Society,* 115, no. 3 (June 1971): 221–49.

Urry, William. *Canterbury under the Angevin Kings.* London, 1967.

Van Cleve, Thomas C. "The Fifth Crusade." In *A History of the*

Crusades, edited by Kenneth M. Setton, vol. 2, *The Later Crusades*, edited by Robert Lee Wolff and Harry M. Hazard. Madison, Wis., 1969.

Vaughan, Richard. *Matthew Paris*. Cambridge, 1958.

Vinogradoff, Paul. *Villeinage in England*. Oxford, 1927.

Walker, R. F. "Hubert de Burgh and Wales, 1218–1232." *English Historical Review* 244 (1972): 465–94.

Ward, A. W., and A. R. Watter. *Cambridge History of English Literature*. Vol. 2. Cambridge, 1908.

Ward, H. D. D., and J. A. Herbert. *The Catalogue of Romances in the Department of Manuscripts in the British Museum*. London, 1883–1910.

Warren W. L. *Henry II*. Berkeley and Los Angeles, 1973.

——. *King John*. Berkeley and Los Angeles, 1978.

Whitaker, Thomas Durham. *History of Richmondshire*. 2 vols. London, 1823.

Wightman, W. E. *The Lacy Family in England and Normandy, 1066–1194*. Oxford, 1966.

——. "The Palatinate Earldom of William Fitz Osbern in Gloucestershire and Worcestershire (1066–1171)." *English Historical Review* 77 (1962): 6–17.

Wilkinson, Bertie. *The Constitutional History of England 1216–1399*. Vols. 1, 3. York, 1948, 1961.

——. *The Later Middle Ages in England, 1216–1485*. New York, 1969.

Williams, A. H. *An Introduction to the History of Wales*. Vol. 2. Cardiff, 1941.

Wilson, Richard M. *The Lost Literature of Medieval England*. 2d ed. London, 1970.

Wood, Charles T. *The French Apanages and the Capetian Monarchy*. Cambridge, Mass., 1966.

Wood, Susan. *English Monasteries and Their Patrons in the Thirteenth Century*. Oxford, 1955.

Wright, Elizabeth Cox. "Common Law in the Thirteenth Century English Royal Forest." *Speculum* 3 (1928): 166–91.

Yates, Joseph Brooks. "The Rights and Jurisdiction of the County Palatine of Chester, the Earls Palatine . . . " In vol. 2 of *Chetham Miscellanies*. Manchester, 1886.

Yeatman, John P., et al. *Feudal History of the County of Derby.* 5 vols. in 9. 1886–1907.

Young, Charles R. "English Royal Forests under the Angevin Kings." *Journal of British Studies* 12 (1972): 1–14.

———. "The Forest Eyre in England during the Thirteenth Century." *American Journal of Legal History* 18 (1974): 321–31.

———. *Hubert Walter, Lord of Canterbury and Lord of England.* Durham, N.C., 1968.

———. *The Royal Forests of Medieval England.* Philadelphia, 1979.

INDEX

Arthur of Brittany, 3, 7, 8, 11, 14

Bolingbroke, honor of, 7
Brian de Lisle, 33, 75

Canterbury, archbishops of. *See* Hubert Walter, Stephen Langton
Cheshire, county of, 52–69, 93; boroughs and fairs in, 52–55; comital justice in, 64–68; forests in, 55–60; Magna Carta of, 57, 63–68; palatinate of, 60–68
Chester, earldom and honor of, 48, 52–69
Clemencia, countess of Chester, 15, 16, 40
Combermere, Cistercian abbey, 39, 45, 47
Constance of Brittany, 3, 8, 10, 12–14, 49, 97
Cornwall, earl of. *See* Richard

Derby, earl of. *See* William de Ferrers

Dieulacres, Cistercian abbey, 37, 39, 40, 41, 44, 45, 46, 49, 55, 56, 68, 80, 94, 100, 101
Durham, bishop of. *See* Hugh du Puiset

England, kings of. *See* Henry III, John, Richard I
Essex, earl of. *See* Geoffrey fitzPeter
Eustace de Vesci, lord of Alnwick, 21, 29

Faulkes de Breauté, 35, 75, 84, 85, 88–92
France, kings of. *See* Louis VIII, Philip II
Fulk fitzWarin, 12
Fulk Paynel, 15–17

Geoffrey fitzPeter, justiciar, earl of Essex, 8, 22, 26
Gilbert de Clare, earl of Gloucester, 88
Gloucester, earl of. *See* Gilbert de Clare

INDEX

Gualo, papal legate, 69, 71, 72, 75–77

Henry III, king of England, 31, 37, 40, 55, 59, 69, 70, 71, 74, 77, 82, 84, 86–88, 94–99
Hubert de Burgh, justiciar, 27, 70, 71, 72, 77, 82, 83, 85, 88, 89, 93, 96, 99, 100, 102
Hubert Walter, archbishop of Canterbury, 5, 8, 24
Hugh du Puiset, bishop of Durham, 4, 5
Hugh of Welles, bishop of Lincoln, 26, 50

Innocent III, Pope, 18, 24, 25, 26, 30, 78

John, king of England, 4, 5, 7–37 passim, 50, 55, 68, 69, 71, 72, 77, 84, 85, 89, 90, 92, 94
John de Lacy, constable of Chester, 2, 23, 28, 33, 41, 78, 100, 101
John the Scot, earl of Chester, 2, 6, 44, 62, 81, 82, 88

Lancashire, royal demesne in: granted to Ranulf III, 92
Lancaster, honor of, 34, 89
Leicester, honor of, 32–33, 81, 97–98
Lincoln, earldom of, 73, 100
Lincoln, earls of. *See* John de Lacy, Ranulf III
Llewelyn ap Iorwerth, prince of Gwynedd, 3, 19, 22, 23, 77, 82, 83, 90, 99

Louis VIII, king of France, 35, 73–77, 80, 81, 95, 96

Magna Carta, 18, 27, 30, 31, 32, 72, 84, 93

Pandulf, papal legate, 24, 25
Palagius, papal legate, 78–80
Pembroke, earls of. *See* William Marshal, William Marshal the Younger
Peter des Roches, bishop of Winchester, 22, 69, 71, 75, 76, 85, 88, 89, 99
Peter of Dreux, duke of Brittany, 73, 74, 80, 81, 92, 96–98
Peter the Clerk, chancellor of Cheshire, 57, 62, 66, 67
Philip II, king of France, 4, 13, 14, 17, 20, 24, 27, 32

Ranulf II, earl of Chester, 2, 9, 10, 34, 40, 56, 73
Ranulf III, earl of Chester and Lincoln: minority and genealogy, 1–4; relations with Richard I, 4–7; relations with John, 7–11, 16–24, 26–36; and Normandy, 12–17, 96–99; and Wales, 19–20, 22–24, 27, 82–83; patronage of religion, 37–51; governance of Cheshire and of the honor of Chester, 52–69; relations with Henry III, 69–77, 83–100; and Fifth Crusade, 79–80
Richard, earl of Cornwall, 94

INDEX

Richard I, king of England, 2, 4, 5, 6, 13–15, 24, 28, 31, 45

Richmond, honor of, 10, 13, 20, 73–74, 80–81, 92, 97

Robert fitzWalter, lord of Dunmow, 29, 75, 78

Roger de Lacy, constable of Chester, 9, 16, 17, 21, 23, 33, 62

Saher de Quency, earl of Winchester, 2, 31, 75, 78

St. Werburgh Abbey (Chester Abbey), Benedictine, 38, 41, 42, 43, 45, 47, 49, 55, 100

Salisbury, earl of. *See* William Longsword

Simon III de Montfort, 2, 32, 97–98

Spalding, Benedictine abbey, 43, 45, 50, 51

Stanlaw, Cistercian abbey, 43, 46, 56

Stephen Langton, archbishop of Canterbury, 25, 26, 70, 86, 88, 89, 91

Surrey, earl of. *See* William de Warenne

William de Ferrers, earl of Derby, 2, 5, 6, 9, 10, 20, 26, 28, 31, 33, 35, 69, 71, 74–76, 84, 85, 92, 93

William de Forz, count of Aumâle, 32, 35, 75, 85, 88, 90

William de Vernon, justiciar of Cheshire, 56, 62

William de Warenne, earl of Surrey, 20, 28, 32, 35, 77

William Longsword, earl of Salisbury, 5, 23, 26, 32, 75–77

William Marshal, earl of Pembroke, 8, 10, 21, 26, 28, 35, 36, 69, 70–72, 74–77, 83, 85

William Marshal the Younger, earl of Pembroke, 35, 80, 82, 85, 94, 98

Winchester, earl of. *See* Saher de Quency